Veggie OUTLAWS
★ MOST WANTED ★
Vegan Recipes

LINDA PURCELL

Golden Middle
Publishing
Vancouver ● Canada

Copyright © 2022 by Linda Purcell
Published by Golden Middle Publishing

All rights reserved. No part of this publication may be reproduced, stored in a retrieval system, or transmitted, in any form or in any means — by electronic, mechanical, photocopying, recording, or otherwise – without prior written permission. Permissions@Golden-Middle.com

Names: Purcell, Linda, author, photographer. | Smilenova, Venera, illustrator. | Vasileva, Zapryanka, illustrator. | Tohmé, Nour, illustrator.

Title: Veggie outlaws : most wanted vegan recipes / by Linda Purcell.

Description: Vancouver, British Columbia: Golden Middle Publishing, [2022] | Includes index.
Identifiers: ISBN 9781777276331 (paperback) | ISBN 9781777276300 (hardcover) | ISBN 9781777276348 (ebook)

Subjects: LCSH: Vegan cooking. | Cooking (Natural foods) | LCGFT: Cookbooks.
Classification: LCC TX837 .P87 2021 (print) | LCC TX837 (ebook) | DDC 641.5/6362--dc23

Interior design by Paulina Rzeszutek and Linda Purcell
Ebook design by
Cover design by Ronald Cruz, cruzialdesigns.com

The recipes, information, nutritional data, procedures, ideas, and suggestions in this book are provided as helpful information to the reader. However, they are not to be considered professional advice on any matter relating to their health and well-being or on the subjects discussed. The author and publisher are not offering any medical advice or instruction. The information in this book is not intended as a substitute for consulting with your physician. Neither the author nor the publisher shall be liable or responsible for any loss or damage allegedly arising from any information or suggestions in this book. References are provided for informational purposes only and do not constitute an endorsement of any product, website, or other sources. Readers should be aware that the websites and products listed in this book may change.

Dedication

This book is dedicated to my mother, Jeanne Ouston, who first taught me how to cook. My love of cooking comes from hours spent in the kitchen with her making tasty treats. Some of my fondest memories were making pies and other goodies with her when I was little. I fell in love with the magic of transforming soft, malleable pastry into warm pockets of sweet or savoury delight. I can still remember taking that first bite, my mouth filling with warm, gooey brown sugar and cinnamon wrapped in flakey pastry. To this day, I think of my mom whenever I smell the soothing aroma of fresh, crisp apples baking with fragrant spices.

Contents

Hows And Whys To Veggie OUTLAWS Recipes

Introduction	3
Meet the Veggie OUTLAWS	4
The Myths We Are Shooting Down	7
For Everyone — from the Non-Vegan to the Vegan Curious to the Vegan Purist	7
Recipe Tricks and Tips	8
Signposts (aka: Icons) Explained	8
Nutritional Details	12
Breakout Tricks Explained	12
Ingredients Explained	13
Tasty Additions	24

Brunch

On the Sweeter Side	27-33
Breakfast Standards	35-43
Savoury Starts	44-52

Appies

Dips and Spreads	55-64
Mushroom Bites	65-70
Crunchy Appies	71-74

Salads and Dressings

Full-Meal Salads	77-80
Salads with Nuts	81-88
Must-Try Salads	89-92
Easy Salads	93-96

Soups

Creamy Soups	99-104
Lentil Soups	105-108
Other High-Protein Soups	109-112
Comfort Soups	113-116

Sides
Just Veggies	119-126
Protein Powered Side Dishes	127-132
Special Spuds	133-136
Extras	137-142

Pasta and Risotto
Macaroni	145-148
Seasonal Pasta	149-154
Risotto	155-156

Meals
On the Lighter Side	159-163
Meals - Wrap It Up!	164-168
Meals - One-Dish Meals	169-180

Mains
With Rice	183-192
Stir-Fries	193-196
Must Haves	197-200

Holiday Meal
Sides	203-212
Holiday Mains	213-218
Great Additions	219-224

Desserts
With Chocolate	227-230
Cupcakes and Cookies	231-236
Fruity Treats	237-242
Pastries	243-247

Index — 249

Acknowledgements — 257

About the Author — 258

A Note to Parents and Families — 259

HOWS AND WHYS TO VEGGIE OUTLAWS RECIPES

Hows And Whys To Veggie OUTLAWS Recipes

Introduction	3
Meet the Veggie OUTLAWS	4
The Myths We Are Shooting Down	7
For Everyone — from the Non-Vegan to the Vegan Curious to the Vegan Purist	7
Recipe Tricks and Tips	8
Signposts (aka: Icons) Explained	8
Nutritional Details	12
Breakout Tricks Explained	12
Ingredients Explained	13
Tasty Additions	24

Introduction

Howdy partner! Welcome to Veggie OUTLAWS — Most Wanted Vegan Recipes.

This extraordinary recipe book will delight anyone hankering for some down-home cooking made with delicious plant-based foods. Here, you'll find good eats that satisfy both the body and the soul.

The Veggie OUTLAWS are a crew of renegade veggies on an epic culinary adventure to create the most wanted vegan recipes. On their journey, they tear down many misleading plant-based eating myths. The tale is told Veggie OUTLAWS don't carry pistols — never, ever would they bring hurt to anyone. Instead, they shoot seeds of change. Armed with intriguing ideas about the benefits of eating plant-based foods and loaded with flavourful fixings like delicious sauces, spices, and fillings, they've got what a body needs. They're quick on the draw with vegan recipes made with a tasty twist and heaped full of healthy ingredients. These myth-busters follow their own path and take no prisoners. They've been known to say, "If the good sheriff don't like it, he can lock us up. That's if he can find us." (You'll find them hidin' out in the small town of Livewood, but they can be seen kicking up their heels at many a shindig, hanging around having fun, and serving up great food.)

Hop on board and discover just how good vegan food can taste.

Rounded up here are 175 of the most wanted vegan recipes (96 primary and 79 supplementary) to tempt anyone who enjoys making and serving appetizing food. All the primary dishes are listed under the table of contents by category — Brunch, Appies, Salads and Dressings, Soups, Sides, Pasta and Risotto, Meals, Mains, Holiday Meal, and Desserts.

Many of the supplementary recipes (aka: Tasty Additions) are vital, providing that something special. These sauces, dips, dressings, fillings, condiments, etc., can be mixed and matched with many other dishes, especially when you are looking for something truly spectacular. A few of the most wanted Tasty Additions are listed under the table of contents, so you can quickly find just what you are craving. A complete listing of all the supplementary recipes can be found in the Index.

Cooking is very personal. Part of the fun of creating good food is making the dish the way you like it — with or without substitutions and based on what you have in your fridge and cupboard. However, these recipes have been tested many times, and often even a small change can drastically change the end result. For that reason, it is best to make the recipes as written the first time to experience them the way they are intended. After that, feel free to experiment and share your successes at https://veggieoutlaws.com/ and @veggieoutlaws on Facebook, Instagram, and Pinterest.

Meet the Veggie OUTLAWS

The jig is up. We're here to spread the truth about plant-based eating. "We" in this book refers to us, the Veggie OUTLAWS.

Cashew Sue

Daisy day! I'm Cashew Sue, and I'm lookin' forward to havin' some fun with y'all. I grew up in a large family, and I'm used to havin' lots of folks hangin' around, especially the Veggie OUTLAWS. We usually gather at my place for a bit of frolickin', chit chattin' about healthy foods, and of course eatin'. Conversing about everyone's right to live and eat the way they want is what I love best. My mission is to shoot down the divisive idea that if you're not 100% vegan, you're on the "other" side. Openin' people's eyes to the notion of eatin' more plant-based foods pleases me plenty. So the crew and I welcome you here whether you're vegan, cheagan (a vegan who often cheats — like if someone's grandma offers you a cookie, you accept and eat it even if they're made with milk and eggs), vegetarian (a vegan who eats dairy, honey, or eggs), pescatarian, flexitarian, ketotarian, freegan (a vegan who relaxes their veganism if they are given something for free, even if it contains animal products), veggan (a vegan who eats eggs), pegan (a plant-based paleo who eats plenty of veggies along with plant-based proteins and healthy fats), plant-based, whole-foods plant-based, or non-vegan. So if you happen by the town of Livewood, stop in and cozy up for a visit.

Strawberry Sal

Howdy-do! I live by my lonesome outta town in a small, cozy cabin. Golly, but I do love Livewood. Most folks here are just plain friendly, but healthy eating ain't loved by all. The meat-eating sheriff, who thinks he's the biggest toad in the puddle, chased us out. So, now we're livin' outlaw, and nobody can tell us what to eat. The General Store is within two whoops and a holler, and I visit there daily for a look-see. I mosey on by the Carnivores neighbourhood on my way to the market. I just smile and nod whenever someone makes a hullabaloo about their views. The townies mean well, but they've been scooped into believing negative myths about eating vegan foods. Sometimes I hear, "How can your grub be only vegetables? Another time it might be, "Vegan food tastes terrible. How can you exist without cheese?" The worst one is, "Being vegan makes you sick — here, eat this steak before you turn green." Crimany, but I do get tired of hearing there ain't nothin' to eat except low-nutrient carbs or tasteless tofu. Nohow is it hard to be vegan. It's time for me to step up and take action. To pick up my shooter, which is loaded with herbs and spices, and spread the word that "vegan food tastes good!"

Carrot Rick

I am pleased to make your acquaintance. Me, I'm savvy about anything concerning well-being, superfoods, and healthy eating. Dang, but I do love to read. When I'm not wrangling up new recipes, I can be found studying the best ways to use fruits, veggies, and other bounties of the earth to make delicious meals. You can count on me to polish my spectacles with a fancy kerchief and start jawing about how to keep a body healthy with toothsome chow. It may seem like high-falutin' talk — but I know what's essential in feeding an outlaw, whether on the run or relaxing at the homestead. Strawberry Sal and I have been friends for a long time, and she's got me all fired up to bust down the conventional myths against vegan eating. Sal and I are in cahoots, but we don't always see eye-to-eye on the whole kit and caboodle behind the science. ('Cause she skips over the research.) When it comes to healthy eating, everyone's got their own view. Many a night, Sal and my voices ring out across the fire, discussing the latest news on the nutrition front. Last week it was the virtues of the bettermost oil for baking — olive or coconut.

Potato Pat

Hiya! I'm glad you're here. My name's Potato Pat, and I identify as both a root and a vegetable. If you need anythin', just gimme a hollerin' — I'm a helpful tater, and I always have a mind to help anyone who's in need. Carrot Rick and Strawberry Sal make a racket many a night with all their discussin', but they're just passionate. I often amble on over and add my two bits. I like to remind 'em there's more than one way to look at a thing. Sal can get as mad as a March hare if someone's forcin' their views on her. 'Course, no one likes that, and provided I don't get my dander up, she usually gets the long and short of what I'm sayin'. Everyone, including Sal, Rick, and the Townies, have a right to live and eat the way they want. The townies are good folk, and they're always up to bend an elbow with

a mug of beer, a plate of fries, and a chat. For me, any time's a good time for munchin' on a heap of good food. Some say I have a sweet tooth, but I say I just love eatin' healthy morsels that fill my belly. I may live alone in my cozy shack, but if the walls start closin' in, I just head over to Cashew Sue's abode. It's fun hangin' out and drinkin' coffee (with lots of our vegan milk mixture, cane sugar, and a sprinklin' of chocolate).

Saucy Peanut

G'day! My name's Saucy Peanut, but you can call me SP. I'm handy with a lasso and can rope an apple right off the tree, whip it into the air, slice it coming down, and have it land in the pot, ready for stewin'. Ain't nothin' like Saucy Apple Compote served up warm with a couple of Savoury Sweet Potato Pancakes. But I digress. I'm not a big talker, but I am passionate about tasty plant-based meals. You're in the right place if you're yearnin' for some delicious food. Give me a holler if you find yourself feelin' peckish. Just leave a note in the springhouse, and I'll steer you in the right direction. Be seein' ya soon.

Broccoli Bandit

Halloo, over here in the corn stalks. Name's Broccoli Bandit, but I'm hidin' out in the maize, ready to make a quick getaway. No, you can't see my face. I'm layin' low for a while. Ever since the Sheriff and I had that big blowout, I've been on the dodge. The old gruff said that if I'm vegan, I've got an eatin' disorder. When I told him he was cracked, he tried to give me a whippin', but I whomped him right back. Next thing you know, I'm sittin' in jail, with him tryin' to feed me fried eggs. He said it was for my own good. Lucky for me SP was around. She helped me escape out the back. By the way, I wish you well in eating delicious plant-based foods. Shh!! I hear the Sheriff a coming. I've got to get a wiggle on and hightail it outta here.

The Myths We Are Shooting Down

We are the Veggie OUTLAWS, renegades rebelling against the status quo and conventional wisdom that defends the consumption of animal products. We are myth-busters on a ground-breaking journey to spread the truth that vegan food tastes good. Using great-tasting recipes, we shoot down negative myths about eating vegan foods. We turn plant-based ingredients into healthy, delicious recipes that feed both body and soul. Our recipes contain a healthy balance of vitamins, minerals, and essential nutrients. We create flavour explosions by adding herbs and spices and use tantalizing sauces to produce delectable plant-based delights.

These are a few of the myths that we are shooting down:

- Vegan food tastes terrible.
- Vegan food is nothing but tasteless vegetables.
- Vegan food does not contain enough protein.
- Vegan diets lack essential minerals.
- Vegan diets lack absorbable vitamins.
- It is unhealthy to eat only plant-based foods.
- Vegan food is mostly all carbs, which is bad for you.
- You need dairy to get calcium because a vegan diet does not provide enough.
- Vegan diets lack amino acids.
- It's hard to consume enough quality fats on a vegan diet.
- Being vegan makes you sick, weak, or tired.
- It's too difficult to be vegan.
- A vegan diet relies heavily on soy.
- A vegan diet is an extreme diet.
- Vegans eat only salad.
- A person is either vegan or not — there is no middle ground.

For Everyone — from the Non-Vegan to the Vegan Curious to the Vegan Purist

Veggie OUTLAWS — Most Wanted Vegan Recipes was created to share appetizing plant-based foods with everyone. Here you will find answers to the question, "What do vegans eat?" This book aims to make plant-based eating an accepted norm, encouraging anyone and everyone to make, eat, and share delicious meals. Do it for your health, longevity, and increased energy. Do it to show compassion for animals and our planet. Do it for your taste buds, and to enjoy guilt-free delights.

If you are new to plant-based eating, start adding at least one plant-based meal to your menu each week. For example, try instituting a Meatless Monday, a Vegan Taco Tuesday, or a Vegan Wrap It Up Saturday.

Despite where you are on your journey, join our community of fearless trailblazers. Experiment, have fun, and help spread the joy of plant-based eating.

Recipe Tricks and Tips

We've discovered what works and have shared below our secrets for success.

An easy tip to simplify the process is to make up batches of Tasty Additions (page 24) ahead of time and freeze them in serving sizes. That way, they are ready to use whenever you need them. Try it for Farmesan — Fake'n Bacon— Roasted Bulb of Garlic — Garlic Cashew Creme Cheez — Basil Cashew Creme Fraîche, just to name a few.

We've got you covered so you can quickly find recipes that meet your needs. Below is a listing of all the easy-to-follow signposts (aka: icons) that direct you to the dishes that meet your time demands or nutritional requirements.

Great recipes start with a solid base of wholesome goodness. Take a look-see through our carefully selected, preferred ingredients outlined below.

Signposts (aka: Icons) Explained

Each recipe includes signposts (aka: icons) that point you in the right direction. At a glance, you can quickly see pertinent details about each dish, including prep and cooking times, dietary considerations, and relevant nutritional values.

Creating the Recipe

The preparation, cooking, and serving size are shown for each recipe as follows:

Prep time

The prep time includes the time it takes to follow the directions and excludes the cooking time, which is shown separately. The clock begins and ends with the directions. The calculation starts once all the ingredients have been prepared and are laid out ready to go.

For example, if the ingredient list states, "1 cup diced onion," the prep time does not include the time it takes to cut the onion. However, if the ingredient reads as "1 large onion," the prep time calculation includes how long it takes to cut the onion, as specified in the directions.

The stated time is "active" and excludes marinating, soaking, or setting time. When "inactive" time is part of the directions, this is shown separately beside the prep time as "+ time to marinate, soak, or set."

    prep time: 55 minutes + time to marinate

The inactive time is not displayed if the ingredient list states the item needs to be pre-marinated, pre-soaked, or pre-set.

> ⅓ cup raw cashews, soaked in water for at least 4 hours

The prep time for supplementary recipes (aka: Tasty Addition) is not displayed when shown as a single ingredient line item. This item should already be available before you begin preparing the primary recipe.

> 1½ cups Fresh Tomato Salsa (page 51)

When a supplementary recipe preparation is included under the directions, the prep time is added to the total time.

Sometimes the Tasty Addition is optional but is still detailed in full under the directions. In that case, a second prep time is provided for the addition.

For example,

> Creamy, Dreamy Rice Pudding with Steeped Strawberries and Coconut Whipped Creme (page 33).
>
> > Creamy, Dreamy Rice Pudding: prep time: 15 minutes + time to soak rice and raisins
> >
> > Steeped Strawberries: prep time: 5 minutes + time to steep
> >
> > Coconut Whipped Creme: prep time: 10 minutes

Cook time

The total time is "active" cooking time and includes stovetop and oven cooking time but excludes any preheating or post-setting time. The calculation is based on cooking each component independently. When you can save time by cooking several recipe items simultaneously, we will include a Breakout Trick to help you speed up the process.

When supplementary recipes are included under the directions, the cooking time is calculated in the total time. For optional supplementary recipes a second cooking time is provided.

Makes

The serving size varies per recipe and includes both the number of and the size of each serving.

This cookbook contains recipes with varying levels of complexity.

The complexity ranges from effortless to elaborate. The following signposts point to the level of time and effort required:

In a Snap

 These recipes are quick and easy. You can expect an active Prep time of 20 minutes or less and an active Cook time of no more than 30 minutes.

In short order

These recipes can be put together with little effort because they are easy to prepare, and although they often have a longer cooking time, the end result is sure to please. You can often speed up the process with a few nifty tricks. In general, you can expect to have them prepared in under 35 active minutes with an active cooking time of no more than 60 minutes.

A little longer

These recipes take a little longer to prepare and cook, but good taste is worth the effort. You can expect to prepare the recipe between 25 and 55 active minutes with an active cooking time of under 90 minutes.

More Time

These recipes require more time and effort, and you can expect a longer cooking time, but folks will be delighted with every bite. Expect between 45 and 95 active minutes to prepare, with an active cooking time between 90 minutes and 3 hours. It's a good idea to read the whole recipe before you start and break down some of the steps over several days to streamline the process.

The dietary info is noted for each recipe using the following icons:

Not all the possible allergens have been specified, but a few of the more standard ones are noted. Please double-check the ingredient lists on the products you are using to ensure they, too, are certified peanut, nut, soy, gluten, or allergen-free.

This dietary information is provided only as a guideline. It should not be considered professional advice on any matter relating to health and well-being. Please use your own judgment before following the recipes, especially if you or anyone you are cooking for has an allergy.

 represents *Peanut-free recipes*. Note that peanuts are part of the legume family and are not considered tree nuts. All recipes in the book are peanut-free except two recipes. Rainbow Rice Wraps and Peanutty Stir-Fry are NOT peanut-free.

 represents *Nut-free recipes*. These recipes do not contain any tree nuts. Some examples of tree nuts include almonds, Brazil nuts, cashews, hazelnuts, macadamia nuts, pecans, pine nuts (pignolias), pistachio nuts, and walnuts. However, these recipes may contain peanut, coconut, or nutmeg, which have "nut" in their names but are not considered tree nuts.

 represents recipes with a *Nut-free Option* after minor adjustments.

 represents *Soy-free* recipes that do not use any soy products whatsoever.

 represents recipes with a *Soy-free Option* after minor adjustments.

 represents *Gluten-free* recipes. This icon can appear with recipes that use oats, which are not considered wheat, and, as such, do not contain gluten. However, if this is important, you should only use certified gluten-free oats because sometimes oats are packaged in facilities that also package wheat.

 represents recipes with a *Gluten-free Option* after minor adjustments.

 represents *Low-fat* recipes with 3 g or less fat per serving.

 represents recipes with a *Low-fat Option* after minor adjustments.

Nutrient info is noted for each recipe using the following icons:

Daily Requirement	Vitamin A	Vitamin C	Potassium	Iron	Calcium	Dietary Fibre
Over 50%	A	C	K	Fe	Ca	🍃
26–50%	A	C	K	Fe	Ca	🍃
10–25%	A	C	K	Fe	Ca	🍃

Eating the proper nutrients is vital to ensure good health, and you may want to cook specific recipes that provide just what your body craves. The icons above highlight rich sources of minerals, vitamins, and nutrients in each recipe.

The icon is shaded all in grey when a recipe is a very high nutrient source (over 50% of the recommended daily requirement). The icon is shaded grey except in the upper tip when a recipe is a high nutrient source (between 25% and 50% of the daily requirement). The icon is shaded grey in the bottom portion only when the recipe is a lower nutrient source (between 10% and 25% of the daily requirement).

Note: These are listed in each recipe from highest to lowest source and not alphabetically.

Nutritional Details

Each recipe outlines the nutritional details. This information shows the per-serving value for calories, milligrams of sodium, and grams of carbs, total fat, protein, and sugar. These figures, and the data provided by the nutrient icons, dietary icons, and other pertinent details, are estimates. They are provided as a general guideline only.

Please note that the food's nutritional value can vary greatly depending upon the brand, the size and type of food, the way the nutritional value is calculated, and other factors. Use the dietary data at your own discretion. If you require accurate information, you must seek it yourself or consult a professional nutritionist or health care provider.

When a supplementary recipe is optional but detailed in full under the directions, the nutritional details are provided separately.

Breakout Tricks Explained

You'll find Breakout Tricks throughout the book. While developing these delicious recipes, we discovered many lip-smacking secrets that we want to share. Breakout Tricks include clever ways to help you be more efficient. Using these little time-saving tips and helpful tricks, you can break free of the obstacles that may stand in the way of your plant-based enjoyment.

> *Here, you will see how to quickly alter the recipe to meet your nut-free or soy-free alternative needs.*

Some things that you can expect to find:

- Quick notes about how to simplify a task or alter an ingredient.
- Learn about an unusual spice or ingredient, what it is and where to find it.
- Discover fascinating facts about some of the components or tasks involved.

Ingredients Explained

Great recipes start with a solid base of wholesome goodness. Take time to peruse these carefully selected and preferred ingredients. The recipes throughout the cookbook utilize good fixings (aka: pantry staples, sauces, condiments, seasonings, and spices).

Below is a listing of those that work the best and why they are preferred. If you want to try them yourself, mosey on over to the Veggie OUTLAWS General Store for more details on how to source them at https://veggieoutlaws.com/ or click on the QR Code

You might see a page number noted in brackets beside an ingredient when reading a recipe. That page number refers you to this list where you can find more information about the item.

- **Agave Nectar:** Raw blue agave nectar is a liquid sweetener from the blue agave plant. This sweetener has a low glycemic index. When a liquid sweetener is required, either agave nectar or maple syrup makes excellent alternatives.

- **Almond and Almond Meal:** Flour made from ground almonds. Almond flour has the skin removed with a finer consistency. Almond meal contains the skin and is coarser. These two forms are often interchangeable, but almond flour is preferable because it is finer and makes for superior baked goods.

- **Amchur Powder:** Aka: dried mango powder (and sometimes spelled amchoor or aamchur) adds a little zing to your food. This tangy spice made from dried and powdered green mangos is often used in Indian cuisine.

- **American Saffron:** This spice is actually safflower (aka: yellow saffron) and does not taste like pure saffron. It adds a nice mild flavour to dishes. You can use pure saffron instead of American saffron, but much less is required for the same effect. In place of ½ tsp of American Saffron, you only need a few strands of pure saffron, and it is best to add it just before serving. Please note American saffron is related to ragweed and can cause allergic reactions in people sensitive to other plants in this family.

- **Ancho Chili Pepper, ground:** This is the dried form of the poblano pepper. It is a tasty addition to many meals when ground into powder. Due to its smoky and sweet quality with mild to moderate heat level, it increases the flavour profile of Mexican-style dishes. For the best flavour, buy dried poblano peppers and grind them into a powder using a spice or coffee grinder. A simpler option is to buy the McCormick Gourmet brand of Ancho Chili Pepper. Although we recommend ground Ancho chili pepper powder, which is a common pepper used in Mexican and Southwestern cuisine, you can use your favourite blend of ground chili pepper.

- **Apple Cider Vinegar:** Bragg is the preferred brand because it is raw, organic, and contains Mother of Vinegar, which is naturally occurring strands of proteins, enzymes, and beneficial bacteria.

- **Aquafaba:** A fancy way of saying drained chickpea (garbanzo bean) water. Aquafaba is known in the vegan universe as an egg white substitute. All the recipes have been prepared with salt-free aquafaba, and the easiest way to get some is to open a can of salt-free chickpeas. Place a bowl under a colander and drain the chickpeas, reserving the flavourless, odourless liquid. This magic elixir is a slightly thick liquid made of starch and a small amount of protein with binding, thickening, and emulsifying properties. Two tablespoons of aquafaba equal one egg white, and three tablespoons of aquafaba equal one whole egg. There are many uses for the remaining chickpeas, and a good option is to roast them (see Zesty Chickpeas, page 73).

- **Arrowroot Powder:** Made from starch derived from the roots of the arrowroot plant, arrowroot powder and arrowroot starch are the same thing. Like cornstarch and tapioca flour, arrowroot powder can be used as a thickener. However, each of these thickeners has different properties. Each acts differently depending on how they are cooked, and each should be used accordingly. Arrowroot powder can be used with acidic liquids without losing its thickening properties. It stays stable at low temperatures (making it suitable for use in frozen foods) and has a mild flavour. However, arrowroot powder needs to reach a reasonably high temperature to thicken. When used in sauces or desserts, arrowroot powder produces a glossy shine.

- **Baking Powder and Baking Soda:** Both baking powder and baking soda (sodium bicarbonate) help foods rise while baking. These powdered leaveners produce tiny air bubbles (mainly carbon dioxide). Once activated, you must cook the mixture within 20 minutes to ensure its wondrous rising properties work correctly. These leaveners produce the best results when they are fresh. To test baking powder, add ½ teaspoon of baking powder to 2 tablespoons of warm water. To check baking soda, add ½ teaspoon of baking soda to 1 tablespoon of vinegar. If the mixture foams, it is good to use. Otherwise it needs replacing.

- **Balsamic Reduction:** By reducing balsamic vinegar to a glaze, the vinegar's tartness is nicely balanced by the sweetness that develops through the reduction. Store-bought balsamic glazes often have thickeners, sweeteners, stabilizers, emulsifiers, and chemical colourings. Nonna Pia's is an excellent store-bought option because it is only made with balsamic vinegar and cane sugar. However, balsamic reduction is much healthier and less expensive to make at home. Plus, you can make it quickly (in 15–20 minutes) without too much fuss. To make your own: Heat 1 cup of good quality Modena balsamic vinegar in a small pot on medium heat. If you like it a little sweeter, you can add up to 4 tablespoons of brown sugar. Bring to a boil, reduce to medium-low, and let simmer, stirring often. Cook until the vinegar reduces by half and thickens enough to coat the back of a spoon. Remove from heat and let cool. The glaze continues to thicken as it cools.

- **Beans, Dried Versus Canned:** Use dried beans and cook them yourself whenever possible. Getting that great flavour takes a little longer than opening a can, but it is worth it. Dried beans are usually soaked for several hours or overnight before cooking, but using an Instant Pot or pressure cooker can dramatically reduce the time and effort. The Instant Pot makes the cooking quick and easy; simply throw unsoaked dried beans (chickpeas, pinto beans, white beans, or black beans) into the Pot. Then add liquid and a little salt, and turn it on. There are pros and cons to using dried versus canned. Obviously, canned is easier but is also more expensive. On the other hand, cooking dried beans results in better flavour and texture than canned.

- **Bestcestershire Sauce:** Veggie OUTLAWS Most Wanted vegan Worcestershire sauce provides umami and is a staple in these recipes. Although you can use other brands in these recipes, this version will provide the best results. You can find the recipe at https://veggieoutlaws.com/.

- **Black Indian Salt:** Aka: Kala Namak is Indian volcanic rock salt and provides an eggy flavour to foods. Black salt is lower in sodium, has fewer additives, and often contains more minerals than regular table salt.

- **Black Mustard Seeds:** These seeds are typically dry roasted or heated in hot oil to bring out their flavour, which is more pungent than yellow mustard seeds. This spice is often used in Indian cooking.

- **Black Sesame Seeds:** Stronger with a nuttier flavour and a bit more crunch than regular sesame seeds, they are an equally good source of antioxidants and phytonutrients.

- **Bolita Beans:** These pinkish coloured beans are similar to pinto beans, but they are a little sweeter with a creamier texture. It is believed this bean was cultivated and developed by the Spanish, who settled in northern New Mexico.

- **Bragg All Purpose Liquid Soy Seasoning or Tamari:** Either of these liquid seasonings adds flavour and umami to recipes. Bragg soy seasoning is unfermented liquid aminos (concentrated amino acids derived from soybeans) made from certified non-GMO soybeans and purified water with no added table salt. Tamari, in contrast, is made from fermented soybeans and is a little thicker and less salty than soy sauce. Bragg All Purpose Liquid Soy Seasoning is our preferred choice for adding umami and is either referred to as Bragg soy seasoning or Bragg seasoning throughout the book. However, a few recipes work better with tamari. These have been noted with tamari as the first choice (like the Stir-Fries (page 193 and 195), the Crunchy Lettuce Wraps (page 164), and the Rainbow Rice Wraps (page 167). If you want to avoid soy, you can try Bragg Organic Coconut Liquid Aminos All-Purpose Seasoning. Coconut aminos are made from coconut tree nectar.

- **Brown Sugar:** Whenever possible, use demerara brown sugar as it undergoes minimal processing and retains some vitamins and minerals. However, feel free to use regular brown sugar in a pinch, provided it is organic and not processed using bone-char.

- **Butter, Vegan:** When cooking with oil, most of these recipes use olive or grapeseed oil which are less processed and healthier than vegan butter. But sometimes, only the taste of butter will do. When that's the case, try Becel vegan margarine, which has a nice buttery flavour. Earth Balance Soy Free Buttery Spread is also a great choice.

- **Cane Sugar:** Use organic, natural, raw, or unrefined cane sugar whenever possible. We do not recommend refined white sugar because it is generally processed using bone chard derived from animals.

- **Cashew Cremes:** Several recipes use raw, soaked cashews (sometimes mixed with raw, soaked pine nuts) as the base to create a variety of creamed cashew staples, such as different types of cheez, fraîche, aioli, or icing. Soaking the nuts helps give them a smooth and creamy mouth-feel when they are pureed. When soaking cashews, it is a good idea to drain, rinse, and re-soak them several times to ensure the water remains clear. Often, the water can darken between rinses. Each recipe is slightly different. Find full details throughout the cookbook — Cashew Creme (page 155), Cashew Cheez (page 145), Garlic Cashew Creme Cheez (page 216), Cashew Creme Fraîche (page 101), Basil Cashew Creme Fraîche (page 69), Chipotle Aioli (page 135), and Cashew-Date Icing (page 231). Double or triple any one of these recipes and then freeze in ½-cup containers for easy use when needed.

- **Chia Seeds, Ground:** Chia seeds are small, dark, and flat oval seeds typically grown in Latin America. When ground into a powder and combined with water, chia seeds develop a viscid coating that gives them a gel-like texture. This mixture makes a good alternative for eggs in vegan recipes when 1 tablespoon of ground chia seeds is combined with 3 tablespoons of water. Ground chia seeds also act as a binding agent and add structure to recipes, making them an excellent addition to Coconut Whipped Creme (page 33). Place seeds in a spice or coffee grinder and grind to a powder. Store any excess in the freezer for easy use in the future.

- **Chickpeas and Garbanzo Beans:** These names are interchangable, because they both mean thee same thing. Chickpea is the English name, whereas garbanzo bean is the Spanish name. Soaking dried chickpeas is less expensive than using canned ones. However, canned is quicker and is an easy source of aquafaba (see above).

- **Chickpea flour:** Aka: garbanzo flour, gram flour, besan flour, chickpea powder, and cici bean flour. This flour is popular in Middle Eastern and Indian cooking. In some cases, it works well for baking or as an egg substitute. Because it is made from finely milled chickpeas, this flour is a high source of protein, dietary fibre, and iron.

- **Chili-Style Beans, Canned:** Heinz is our preferred choice when the recipe calls for canned chili-style beans. This variety has a lovely flavour and is super easy to use, especially in Let's Flex Tacos (page 183) and Seriously the Best Chili con Veggies (page 175). Please note that chili-style beans are not canned chili.

- **Chili Peppers:** There are many different types of chili peppers — in order from mildest to hottest — banana, Anaheim, poblano, jalapeño, chipotle, Hatch, and serrano. When cooking with chilies, you can take your pick depending on your spice tolerance and heat-seeking desire. Most of the heat in chili peppers can be found in the seeds. If you want to reduce some of the hotness, remove some, if not all, of the seeds. You may see the word "chili" spelled "chile" or "chilli." Though "chili" is most common, at least in North America. In this book, we use the Spanish spelling for the Hatch pepper and go with "chile" because Hatch peppers are grown in New Mexico. Otherwise we use "chili" for all other chili peppers.

- **Chipotle Peppers in Adobo Sauce:** Chipotle peppers are jalapeño peppers that have been ripened before being dried and smoked. Adobo is a tangy and slightly sweet Mexican sauce made with spices, tomatoes, garlic, and vinegar. The Casa Fiesta brand of Chipotle Peppers in Adobo Sauce is a good option.

- **Cocoa and Cacao:** There is cocoa powder and there are cacao nibs — both come from the cacao bean, which like other beans, has many health benefits. Both have no added sugar or fats, can lower blood pressure, lower bad cholesterol, and boost good cholesterol. Cocoa powder is made from cacao beans that have been processed to isolate the cocoa. Cacao nibs are not processed. Instead, they are small pieces of broken cacao beans that are somewhat bitter but add a nice touch to some recipes. Prana brand is a good option for cacao nibs. Anthony's brand is a good option for cocoa powder. Some people prefer cocoa powder that has been processed using the Dutch process because it has a smoother flavour. However, that method removes almost half the phytonutrients.

- **Coconut Oil:** This is the best and easiest fat to use for pastry because it produces a nice flakey shell. One trick for creating great pastry is using coconut oil in a semi-solid state. Coconut oil purchased at the store is typically in a scoopable form, not too solid and not too liquid. However, if your oil is too liquidy, you will need to firm it up. Place the coconut oil in the refrigerator for 30 minutes, remove it, and stir. If it is too firm, let it sit on the counter for up to 30 minutes at room temperature. If the oil is not in a consistent semi-solid state after this, repeat the process.

- **Cornstarch:** This powder comes from corn's endosperm (part of the kernel). Like arrowroot powder and tapioca flour, corn starch can be used as a thickener. However, each of these thickeners has different properties. Each acts differently depending on how they are cooked, and each

should be used accordingly. Cornstarch tends to create a cloudy appearance in finished dishes. However, it doesn't clump up and dry out when exposed to hot air (like tapioca). Once heated, cornstarch absorbs the liquid and expands, becoming an excellent thickening agent for gooey fillings.

- **Creamy Vegan Tomato Soup:** A couple of the recipes call for creamy vegan tomato soup — Cabbage Roll Casserole (see page 191) and Grandma's Macaroni, Creamy Style (see page 147). Imagine is our preferred brand because it is vegan and tastes the best.

- **Dal:** Aka: daal, dhal, or dahl is a pulse. (Pulses are legumes, including dried peas, lentils, beans, and chickpeas.) Dal is a lentil and does not require pre-soaking. There are many types, but toor dal (yellow split lentils) has the best flavour and cooks fairly quickly.

- **Dried Mushroom Powder:** Ground-up dried mushrooms add umami (see below). An easy do-it-yourself alternative is buying dried mushrooms and grinding them into a powder with a spice or coffee grinder. About ¼ cup of dried mushrooms grinds into approximately 2 tablespoons of powder.

- **Eggplant:** Aka: aubergine is typically purple in colour, but you can find up to 8 different varieties. All the recipes use the globe eggplant (aka: American eggplant), the largest and fattest type.

- **Parmesan:** This is the Veggie OUTLAWS version of vegan parmesan cheese (page 89). You can find several vegan parmesans at the store, but we recommend making your own. Most store-bought versions are highly processed and lacking in nutrients.

- **Five-Spice Powder:** This combination of five spices — cinnamon, cloves, fennel, star anise, and Sichuan (or black) peppercorns — stirs up five taste sensations: sweet, sour, bitter, salty, and umami. The blend is often used in Chinese, Vietnamese, and Hawaiian cuisine.

- **Flax Seeds:** Ground flax seeds combined with water creates a thick gelatinous mixture that works well to replace eggs in some recipes. The general ratio of one tablespoon of ground flax seeds to three tablespoons of water equals one egg. Depending on the recipe, the amount of water could be reduced. We have specified the optimal ratio in each recipe.

- **Flour:** Whole-wheat flour is used in the majority of the recipes. The goal is to create super tasty, plant-based recipes made with healthy ingredients. Whole-wheat is quite simply a more nutritious choice over all-purpose flour. Sift the whole-wheat flour and discard any large flakes that do not filter through. Some baking recipes call for whole-wheat pastry flour, which produces lighter and softer baked goods. The pastry flour is more finely ground, has no bran flakes, and has a lower protein content. All-purpose flour trumps whole-wheat in a couple of recipes but for a healthier choice, use unbleached all-purpose flour. Substituting gluten-free flour may affect the final result because not all recipes have not been tested with gluten-free alternatives (unless expressly stated).

- **Golden Berries, Dried:** Aka: Inca berry, Peruvian groundcherry, poha berry, goldenberry, husk cherry, and cape gooseberry have a tart, complex flavour with a touch of sweetness. Dried golden berries are highly nutritious and are an excellent source of antioxidants and phytonutrients with anti-inflammatory benefits.

- **Green Beans:** There are several types of green beans: French, long green beans, and regular. French green beans (aka: Haricots Verts) are slightly longer and skinnier than regular green beans. The long bean (aka: asparagus bean, yardlong bean, long-podded cowpea, snake bean, or Chinese long bean) is not as sweet as green beans but shares a similar taste. Unless noted in the recipe, use regular green beans.

- **Hemp Hearts:** This is a fancy way of saying hulled hemp seeds. Hemp hearts are healthy, do not contain any cannabidiol (CBD or THC), and are a good source of protein, dietary fibre, iron, and potassium.

- **Herbs, Herbs, and More Herbs:** Most recipes call for fresh herbs, such as basil, cilantro, marjoram, mint, oregano, parsley, rosemary, sage, and thyme. Fresh is always best; however, fresh is not always available. Feel free to substitute one teaspoon of the dried herb for one tablespoon of the fresh herb.

- **Lavender:** This herb can add flavour and colour in either fresh or dried form but be sure to use "culinary lavender." If using fresh, double the amount of the dried equivalent. Lavender is often ground into a powder or infused into a liquid before cooking. It tastes great when combined with other herbs like rosemary, oregano, or thyme. One option is to buy it directly from a lavender farm.

- **Lemon & Herb Seasoning:** This spice combines lemon peel, herbs and spices and adds a nice zingy flavour. Try the Club House brand, which has no artificial flavours or colours, is gluten-free, and is certified Halal..

- **Lime Leaf:** Aka: kaffir lime, makrut lime, or Thai lime comes from a citrus fruit found in Southeast Asia and southern China. Lime leaf is often used in Thai cooking. It may be hard to find, but it is worth the effort. Lime leaf freezes well, so freeze any extra fresh leaves for future use.

- **Milk:** Many different kinds of vegan milk have been tested in creating and developing these recipes. After much experimentation, we have found that combining three types together results in the best taste. The winning mixture is oat milk plus cashew milk with a small amount of canned full-fat coconut milk. The recipes in this book taste best made with this prescribed Milk Mixture but feel free to use the milk of your choice (though results cannot be guaranteed). Plus, our Milk Mixture (page 27) is so good it should be outlawed! (It is incredibly delicious in coffee or tea.)

- **Molasses:** A few recipes use molasses, which does double duty as a sweetener and

a unique flavouring. Blackstrap molasses is preferable over fancy molasses because it is lower in sugar, higher in nutrients, and has a more robust flavour.

- **Mushroom Broth:** Using mushroom broth adds both umami (see below) and nutrition. You can make your own Mushroom Broth (page 211) and freeze it in 2 cup servings for easy use. Alternatively, you can buy mushroom broth. Pacific Foods is a good option because it is organic.

- **Mushrooms:** 'Shrooms are a great source of nutrients, taste, texture, and umami (see below). Not only are they good for you, but they also have a meaty texture and a complex savoury flavour. Many different varieties are available, but use either brown or white cremini mushrooms unless otherwise stated in the recipe.

- **Nutmeg:** Fresh nutmeg is preferable, and grating it as needed provides the best flavour. The recipes call for ground nutmeg. You will have the best results when you grate it fresh yourself, but pre-packaged ground nutmeg also works.

- **Nuts and Peanuts:** Plenty of people love nuts, but nuts don't love everyone. For this reason, each recipe will state if it is nut-free or peanut-free. However, you need to use your judgment before following the recipe, especially if you or anyone you are cooking for has an allergy. Despite having "nut" in their names, coconut and nutmeg are not considered tree nuts. Although coconut and nutmeg are fruit seeds, some people allergic to tree nuts can also have a reaction. Consult your allergist before trying coconut or nutmeg in any of our recipes. For more information, check out https://foodallergycanada.ca/allergies/tree-nuts/.

- **Oats:** This grain is naturally gluten-free and is not made from wheat, but oats are often processed, produced, or packaged alongside wheat. If avoiding wheat is important, you should only use certified gluten-free oats. For the best results, use rolled oat flakes, not the quick-cooking variety.

- **Oil Spray:** These recipes were developed with a focus on healthy ingredients while minimizing the amount of added fat. Use a reusable oil dispenser with a spray nozzle that lightly and evenly dispenses small amounts of cooking oil to reduce fat consumption. This is a good option for greasing baking dishes, pan-frying foods, or spraying on salads. Many different dispensers are on the market, but the Evo Oil Sprayer bottle provides the best results.

- **Oils:** Different oils have different smoke points and should be used accordingly. The smoke point, aka: the burning point of oil, is the temperature at which the oil starts to break down, release chemicals, develop a bitter or burnt flavour, and potentially become harmful to the body. Olive oil (see below) has a lower smoke point than grapeseed oil. For this reason, grapeseed oil is preferred when cooking at higher temperatures. Occasionally a recipe calls for coconut oil, which refers to unrefined, cold-pressed, virgin coconut oil. Sometimes toasted sesame oil is required, which is more flavourful than plain sesame oil.

- **Olive Oil:** Many recipes call for olive oil. It is essential to use high-quality olive oil because the flavour of the oil is often an integral component of the final result. Extra-virgin olive oil (EVOO) is a healthier choice. It uses a cold-press process and is made by grinding olives into a paste and extracting the pure oil without heat.

- **Onions, Sautéed:** Our perferred method is to sauté diced onions in ¼ cup of low-sodium vegetable broth rather than 1 or 2 tablespoons of oil. If you substitute oil for vegetable broth, use less oil. The broth is preferred in most cases because it is lower in fat, is healthier, and produces a more robust flavour. However, there are times when sauteeing the onions in oil is needed for the recipe. In this case, it has been included in the details.

- **Organic Versus Conventional:** Buying and using organic fruits and vegetables is preferable. Although the recipes do not specify organic ingredients, use as many organic ingredients as you can get your hands on. They quite simply taste better and are healthier.

- **Pumpkin:** Be sure to use sweet cooking pumpkins and not the jack-o'-lantern type (these are not meant to be cooked). To roast the pumpkin, preheat the oven to 400°F. Cut a fresh sweet cooking pumpkin in half, remove seeds, and place skin side up in a baking dish. If the pumpkin is small, bake it whole, but be sure to poke it with a fork to let steam escape as it cooks. When cooking, add a small amount of water to the bottom of the roasting pan and bake for 35–45 minutes or until a fork easily pierces the skin and sinks into the flesh. Remove from the oven and let cool. When cooled, remove the meat from the skin, discard any remaining seeds, and measure out 2 cups. Purée in a food processor or blender. If you have extra cooked pumpkin, divide it into 2-cup portions, package in individual containers, and freeze. If substituting butternut squash for pumpkin, follow the same baking directions.

- **Quinoa:** This grain is a fantastic substitute for rice. It is high in fibre, is a complete source of protein, and has loads of nutrients, including B vitamins, iron, potassium, calcium, magnesium, phosphorus, and zinc. Quinoa is easy to digest, gluten-free, a great source of antioxidants, and easy to prepare. However, the natural coating on quinoa seeds (saponin) is bitter and hard to digest. For that reason, it is essential to rinse quinoa before cooking. Our favourite brand is Avafina, they produce only organic products, and pre-wash all their quinoa. https://www.avafina.com/

- **Rice:** Rice absorbs ten times more arsenic than other grains while it grows. Arsenic naturally occurs in water, soil, and rocks, but higher levels of arsenic accumulate when pesticides and herbicides are used. However, arsenic levels vary depending on the region. For this reason, Lundberg rice is a good option because they monitor and test the arsenic levels in their rice. We recommend using whole grain rice because it has more fibre, more nutrients, and other health benefits. https://info.lundberg.com/faq/arsenic

- **Salt:** All recipes were created with sea salt unless otherwise stated. Sea salt is used because it is usually derived from evaporating seawater and retains trace minerals like magnesium, potassium, calcium, and other nutrients. Plus, it adds extra flavour and provides more options in texture from coarse to fine.

- **Shichimi Togarashi:** AKA: Japanese 7 Spice Blend combines seven spices, including red chili pepper, Japanese pepper (sansho), orange peel, sesame seeds, nori, and ginger.

- **Spike Gourmet Natural Seasoning:** An all-purpose seasoning is a must-have staple in the kitchen. Spike Natural Gourmet Seasoning from Modern Products (a Gaylord Hauser creation) is used in many of the recipes. This is a delicious and healthy blend of 39 exotic herbs, vegetables, and spices with the perfect amount of sea and earth salt crystals. Old Bay Seasoning is a good alternative. Old Bay is made by McCormick & Co. and is made from 18 spices, including celery, paprika, salt, and red and black pepper.

- **Sprouted Lentils or Mixed Bean Sprouts:** A couple of the recipes call for sprouted lentils or mixed bean sprouts. You can generally find mixed bean sprouts in the produce section of the grocery store. However, it is much less costly and super easy to make your own sprouted lentils at home, but it does take a few days. To make 4 cups of sprouted lentils, rinse and drain ½ cup of dried brown or black lentils (Puy lentils work well) at least three times in cold water. Place rinsed lentils in a clean 4-cup jar, cover with water, and sit overnight. The next day, drain and rinse the lentils. Cover the jar with a mesh lid and place the jar in a bowl with the mesh top facing downwards. Let sit overnight. Daily, rinse the lentils and return the jar to the bowl with the mesh top facing downwards. Do this for 3–4 days or until the lentils sprout. Once sprouted, rinse one final time, remove from the jar, and spread out to dry before refrigerating in an airtight container.

- **Sugar:** When applicable, recipes were created with cane sugar (see above) unless otherwise stated. If the recipe calls for powdered sugar, you can make your own by grinding cane sugar in a spice grinder or food processor until powdery. The cane sugar will double in size when powdered.

- **Tabasco Sauce:** This hot sauce is made from peppers, vinegar, and salt and adds a nice kick to foods. Tabasco sauce is made by McIlhenny Company.

- **Tapioca Flour:** Tapioca flour and tapioca starch are the same. They come from the starchy pulp derived from the root of the cassava plant (note this is not the same thing as cassava flour which uses the whole root). Like cornstarch and arrowroot powder, tapioca flour can be used as a thickener. However, each of these thickeners has different properties. Each acts differently depending on how they are cooked, and each should be used accordingly. Tapioca flour thickens at lower temperatures and is suitable for low-heat applications. Tapioca flour stays stable in cold temperatures and is ideal for frozen foods. Tapioca flour has little flavour and creates a beautiful glossy shine

- **Umami:** This Japanese word basically means "savoury essence of deliciousness." Typically, foods with higher amino acid glutamate levels tend to have umami, and often, plant-based foods lack this nutrient. A simple solution is to add seasoning and flavours that boost umami. Some favourite umami seasonings include Bragg All Purpose Liquid Soy Seasoning (or tamari, a Japanese soy sauce), Spike Gourmet Natural Seasoning (or Old Bay Seasoning), Bestcestershire Sauce (vegan Worcestershire sauce), and dried mushroom powder.
- **Vegetable Broth:** Many of the recipes use vegetable broth (and sometimes mushroom broth) in place of olive oil, especially when sautéing onions. For the best results, use low-sodium vegetable broth. However, if you can't find a low-sodium version, reduce the salt in the recipe (all recipes are based on low-sodium vegetable broth).
- **Water:** Use filtered water in all recipes for the best results.
- **Whole Grains:** Whenever possible, the recipes use whole grains or ingredients made from whole grains, resulting in super tasty, plant-based dishes made with healthy ingredients. Whole grains include the entire grain kernel — all three parts of the grain: the bran, germ, and endosperm. Refined grains have the bran and germ removed, which also removes most of the protein and nutrients. Whole-grain foods fit the bill because they are a great way to sneak more nutrients, minerals, and vitamins into your diet.
- **Za'atar:** This aromatic blend of thyme, oregano (or marjoram), toasted sesame seeds, and lemony sumac is often used in Persian cooking. Its blend of different flavours, textures, and fragrances adds a unique flavour to foods. If you do not have this spice on hand, use ⅛ teaspoon each of dried thyme, oregano, and sesame seeds in place of ¼ teaspoon za'atar. nutrients,

References are provided for informational purposes only and do not constitute an endorsement of any product, website, or other sources. Readers should be aware that the websites and products listed in this book may change.

Tasty Additions

This is a quick listing of a few of the most in-demand tasty additions. Find a full listing in the Index under Tasty Additions: Full Listing.

Basil Cashew Creme Fraîche	69
Cashew Cheez	145
Cashew Creme Fraîche	101
Cashew-Date Icing	231
Chipotle Aioli	135
Chocolate Sauce	227
Cilantro-Lime Dressing	79
Coconut Whipped Creme	33
Easy Guacamole	183
Farmesan	89
Fresh Tomato Salsa	51
Garlic Cashew Creme Cheez	216
Healthier Pastry	216
Mashed Potatoes	172
Milk Mixture	27
Quick and Creamy Mushroom Gravy	172
Roasted Bulb of Garlic	139
Roasted Carrots	213
Snappy Peanut Sauce	193
Steeped Strawberries	33
Sun-Dried Tomato Pesto	197
Tasty Tofu	193
Tender and Crispy Croutons	89
Teriyaki Sauce	195
Veggie OUTLAWS Hoisin Sauce	164

BRUNCH

On the Sweeter Side

Choco-Razzmatazz Muffins	27
Orange, Zucchini, Date, Walnut Spice Muffins	29
Lemon and Hemp Loaf	31
Creamy, Dreamy Rice Pudding with Steeped Strawberries and Coconut Whipped Creme	33

Breakfast Standards

Melt-in-Your-Mouth Pancakes	35
Guiltless French Toast	37
Golden Granola	39
Fancy Un-Omelet with Best Bechamel Sauce	41

Savoury Starts

Chickpea Frittata with Tarragon Sauce	44
Broccoli Fritters	47
Savoury Latke-Style Sweet Potato Cakes with Saucy Apple Compote	49
Mexican-Style Rice and Beans with Fresh Tomato Salsa	51

Choco-Razzmatazz Muffins

prep time: 20 minutes + time to chill pan before baking   cook time: 15 minutes   makes: 6 muffins

Rich in

These muffins are doubly good — not only 'cause they have double chocolate, but they're also doubly healthy. Made with wholesome ingredients and no added sugar, they're sure to hit the spot as an early morning treat on the homestead. They're also great to have on hand anytime you're feeling peckish. Of course, if you have a sweet tooth, you can always add a dab of Cashew-Date Icing (page 231), but for us, they fit the bill just as they are. Potato Pat is wild for them 'cause they're downright amazing, mouth-watering moist, and, well, perfect.

For nut-free, replace cashew milk with vegan nut-free milk of your choice and omit the walnuts or pecans.

INGREDIENTS

¼ cup grapeseed oil + ½–1 tsp for greasing the pan
1 tbsp ground flax seeds
3 tbsp water
1⅓ cups whole-wheat flour
¼ cup cocoa powder
½ tsp baking powder
½ tsp baking soda
¼ tsp salt
Milk Mixture (1 cup)
    ⅔ cup oat milk
    ¼ cup cashew milk
    4 tsp coconut milk
1 tsp vanilla extract
½ cup dark chocolate chips
½ cup fresh or frozen whole raspberries
2 tbsp chopped walnuts or pecans

DIRECTIONS

1. Preheat oven to 375°F. Spray a 6-hole muffin tin with oil or, using a pastry brush, spread a thin layer inside each hole (½ tsp oil). Add paper liners (if using) and spray or oil the bottom of the liners to ensure muffins don't stick (½ tsp oil).
2. In a deep bowl, mix 1 tbsp ground flax seeds with 3 tbsp water and let thicken for at least 5 minutes.
3. In a large bowl, sift 1⅓ cups whole-wheat flour, ¼ cup cocoa powder, ½ tsp each baking powder and baking soda, and ¼ tsp salt. Mix with a fork until well combined.
4. To the thickened flax mixture, add 1 cup Milk Mixture (⅔ cup oat milk, ¼ cup cashew milk, and 4 tsp coconut milk), ¼ cup grapeseed oil, and 1 tsp vanilla extract. Using a hand mixer, beat on high for 2–3 minutes, making sure to create some bubbles. This is an essential step as it helps the muffins rise during cooking.
5. Create a well in the centre of dry ingredients and slowly pour in wet ingredients, stirring until just combined. Do not overmix.
6. Gently fold in ½ cup each dark chocolate chips and whole raspberries and 2 tbsp chopped nuts.
7. Spoon mixture into prepared muffin tin. Fill to just below the top of each muffin hole. Refrigerate for 10–15 minutes before baking. This step lets the gluten relax (important when using whole-wheat flour) and chills the oil, giving the muffins more time to rise.
8. Bake for 15 minutes (check at the 10-minute mark). Muffins are done when tops spring back when touched, a toothpick comes out clean when inserted into the centre of a muffin, and the cooked batter has pulled away from the top edge of the muffin tin.
9. Remove from the oven and let set for 5 minutes before removing muffins from the pan. Eat immediately or cool on a rack.

NUTRITION: PER MUFFIN: Calories 325; Carbs 38g; Fat 20g; Protein 5g; Sodium 306mg; Sugar 12g

Orange, Zucchini, Date, Walnut Spice Muffins

prep time: 25 minutes + time to chill pan before baking   cook time: 25 minutes   makes: 12 muffins

Rich in

The compelling flavour combination of orange, date, and walnut dances in your mouth, creating a rousing whirl of delight. Carrot Rick is the mastermind behind this muffin. He's all atingle 'cause while you're having fun eating them, your body rejoices from the nutritious boost it receives. Rick specifically designed a muffin that incorporates zucchini — a vegetable packed full of vitamins, minerals, and antioxidants but low on calories. Potato Pat convinced him to add a smidgeon of crunchy pleasure for the topping. Pat says it's the bettermost part, but Rick's adamant the zucchini is the boss, and for Strawberry Sal, she loves the dates. The combination really works, and without a doubt, this muffin is above-board one of the best ways to start a busy day.

Zest the orange before cutting and juicing.
For nut-free, replace cashew milk with vegan nut-free milk of your choice and replace the walnuts with raisins.

INGREDIENTS

¼ cup grapeseed or olive oil + ½–1 tsp for greasing the pan
2 tbsp ground flax seeds
⅓ cup water
1 cup all-purpose flour
1 cup whole-wheat pastry flour
2 tsp baking powder
1 tsp baking soda
1 tsp ground cinnamon
1 tsp ground nutmeg
1 tsp ground allspice
½ tsp salt
Milk Mixture (makes ½ cup)
   ⅓ cup oat milk
   2 tbsp cashew milk
   2 tsp coconut milk
½ cup sugar
½ cup orange juice (about 2 oranges)
1 tsp vanilla extract
½ tsp orange extract
1 cup grated zucchini (about 1 large)
1 cup chopped dates, pits removed
½ cup chopped walnuts
2 tbsp orange zest (about 1 orange)

CRUMBLED WALNUT TOPPING

   ¼ cup sugar
   2 tbsp crumbled walnuts
   1 tbsp orange zest (about ½ orange)

DIRECTIONS

1. Preheat oven to 375°F. Spray a 12-hole muffin tin with oil or, using a pastry brush, spread a thin layer inside each hole (½ tsp oil). Add paper liners (if using) and spray or oil bottom of liners to ensure muffins don't stick (½ tsp oil).

2. In a deep bowl, mix 2 tbsp ground flax seeds with ⅓ cup water and let thicken for at least 5 minutes.

3. In a large bowl, sift 1 cup each all-purpose flour and whole-wheat pastry flour, 2 tsp baking powder, 1 tsp each baking soda, ground cinnamon, ground nutmeg, and ground allspice, and ½ tsp salt. Mix with a fork until well combined.

4. To the thickened flax mixture, add ½ cup Milk Mixture (⅓ cup oat milk, 2 tbsp cashew milk, and 2 tsp coconut milk), ½ cup each sugar and orange juice, ¼ cup grapeseed oil, 1 tsp vanilla extract, and ½ tsp orange extract. Using a hand mixer, beat on high for 2–3 minutes, making sure to create some bubbles. This is an essential step as it helps muffins rise during cooking.

5. Create a well in the centre of dry ingredients and slowly pour in wet ingredients, stirring until just combined. Do not overmix.

6. Gently fold in 1 cup each grated zucchini and chopped dates, ½ cup chopped walnuts, and 2 tbsp orange zest.

7. Prepare **Crumbled Walnut Topping**: In a small bowl, mix ¼ cup sugar, 2 tbsp crumbled walnuts, and 1 tbsp orange zest.

8. Spoon muffin mixture into prepared muffin tin. Fill each hole to just below the top rim. Sprinkle each muffin with 1 tsp Crumbled Walnut Topping.

9. Refrigerate for 10–15 minutes before baking. This step lets the gluten relax (important when using whole-wheat flour) and chills the oil, giving the muffins more time to rise.

10. Bake for 20–25 minutes or until muffin tops spring back up when pressed, a toothpick comes out clean when inserted into the centre of a muffin, and the cooked batter has pulled away from the top edge of the muffin tin.

11. Remove from oven and let set for 15 minutes. Then, remove from the pan and let cool on a wire rack.

NUTRITION: PER MUFFIN: *Calories 242; Carbs 39g; Fat 9g; Protein 5g; Sodium 177mg; Sugar 20g*

Lemon and Hemp Loaf

Lemon and Hemp Loaf: prep time: 25 minutes	cook time: 70 minutes	makes: 12 x ¾" slices
Lemon glaze: prep time: 5 minutes	cook time: 1 minute	makes: 12 x 2-tsp

  Rich in

The lemony-sweet taste and crunchy texture of this loaf are addictive. You'll have a hard time stopping at just one piece, and before long, you and your guests will be hungering for more. We love the toasted hemp hearts, which add extra protein, and when paired with the toasted millet and poppy seeds, they create a surprising pop with each bite. Sure as rain, Potato Pat's hand will reach for another slice while chuckling, "The Lemon Glaze is the best part. It truly is the icing on the cake (or rather the topping on the loaf)."

Zest the lemon before cutting and juicing.
Roasting grains and seeds on dry heat with plenty of swirling and stirring helps distribute the heat and encourages even roasting on all sides.
For nut-free, replace cashew milk with vegan nut-free milk of your choice.

INGREDIENTS

½ cup hemp hearts
¼ cup dry millet
1 cup coconut oil + ½ tsp for greasing the pan
3 tbsp ground flax seeds
½ cup water
Milk Mixture (makes 1¼ cups)
    ¾ cup + 4 tsp oat milk
    ¼ cup + 1 tbsp cashew milk
    1 tbsp + 2 tsp coconut milk
2 tbsp lemon juice (about 1 lemon)
1 cup whole-wheat flour
1 cup all-purpose flour
3 tbsp poppy seeds
2 tbsp lemon zest (about 2 lemons)
1 tbsp baking powder
1½ tsp salt
1 tsp baking soda
¾ cup sugar
1 tsp lemon extract

LEMON GLAZE (optional, makes ½ cup)
    1 tsp coconut oil
    1 cup powdered sugar
    1½ tbsp lemon juice (from 1 lemon)

DIRECTIONS

1. Roasted hemp hearts: Place medium pan on medium-high heat. Add ½ cup hemp hearts and swirl pan or stir seeds to keep them moving. Cook for 3–5 minutes or until hemp darkens slightly and a nutty aroma develops. Transfer roasted hearts to a small bowl.

2. Roasted millet: To the same pan on medium-high heat, add ¼ cup dry millet. Swirl pan or stir grains to keep them moving. Cook for 3–5 minutes or until grains darken slightly and a toasty aroma develops. Transfer roasted millet to a small bowl.

3. Preheat oven to 350°F. Use a pastry brush to spread ½ tsp coconut oil in a 5- x 9-inch loaf pan.

4. In a small dish, mix 3 tbsp ground flax seeds with ½ cup water and let thicken for at least 5 minutes.

5. In a deep bowl, add 1¼ cups Milk Mixture (¾ cup + 4 tsp oat milk, ¼ cup + 1 tbsp cashew milk, and 1 tbsp + 2 tsp coconut milk) and 2 tbsp lemon juice. Set aside for at least 5 minutes, as lemon juice will cause milk to thicken slightly.

6. In a large bowl, sift 1 cup each whole-wheat flour and all-purpose flour. Add ½ cup toasted hemp hearts, ¼ cup toasted millet, 3 tbsp poppy seeds, 2 tbsp lemon zest, 1 tbsp baking powder, 1½ tsp salt, and 1 tsp baking soda. Stir until well combined.

7. To thickened Milk Mixture, add thickened flax seed mixture, 1 cup coconut oil, ¾ cup sugar, and 1 tsp lemon extract. Using a hand mixer, beat on high for 2–3 minutes, making sure to create some bubbles. This is an essential step as it helps the loaf rise during cooking.

8. Make a well in dry ingredients and slowly pour in the wet ingredients, stirring until combined. Do not overmix.

9. Pour the mix into the prepared loaf pan and bake for 45–60 minutes or until the top springs back when touched, a toothpick comes out clean when inserted into the centre of the loaf, and the cooked batter has pulled away from the top edge of the pan.

10. Remove from oven and let set for 15 minutes. To remove it from the pan, insert a knife around the edges and remove the loaf to a wire rack. Cool for an additional 30 minutes before icing.

11. Prepare **Lemon Glaze**: In a small pan, melt 1 tsp coconut oil and sift in 1 cup powdered sugar. Slowly pour in 1½ tbsp lemon juice, whisking continuously until smooth. If you feel it is too dry, add more lemon juice, ½ tsp at a time, until you achieve your desired consistency. Glaze should be syrupy.

12. Once the loaf is cooled, spread Lemon Glaze evenly across the top with a spatula or palette knife.

NUTRITION: **LEMON AND HEMP LOAF ONLY** - *PER ¾" SLICE: Calories 354; Carbs 31g; Fat 25g; Protein 6g; Sodium 517mg; Sugar 14g;* **LEMON GLAZE** - *PER 2-TSP SERVING: Calories 46; Carbs 11g; Fat 0g; Protein 0g; Sodium 0mg; Sugar 10g*

Creamy, Dreamy Rice Pudding with Steeped Strawberries and Coconut Whipped Creme

Rice Pudding: prep time: 15 minutes + time to soak rice and raisins   cook time: 60 minutes
Steeped Strawberries: prep time: 5 minutes + time to steep
Coconut Whipped Creme: prep time: 10 minutes

makes: 8 x ½-cup
makes: 8 x 1½-tbsp
makes: 8 x 2-tbsp

Rich in

Potato Pat loves rice pudding, and Carrot Rick loves to use whole ingredients. So, the two of them put their heads together and concocted this healthy and nutritious improvement of classic rice pudding. Soaking the grains first is the key to a soft and creamy treat. If you want a rice pudding experience that no other can hold a candle to, just follow these directions as written. However, if you have a mind for it, you can tinker with the ingredients and still deliver a fantastic taste. For example, you can use any milk you choose. Another option is to try the recipe with or without raisins or fresh berries. You can even use leftover rice. The pudding is excellent hot or cold and is dang good on its own, but Stepped Strawberries and Coconut Whipped Creme send the texture and flavour over the top.

Use Lundberg-brand rice, which contains less arsenic than other brands (page 21).
For the best whipped coconut creme, use brands of coconut milk without added guar gum. The guar gum prevents the coconut milk from separating properly and will not whip up as nicely.
For nut-free, replace cashew milk with vegan nut-free milk of your choice.

INGREDIENTS

- 1 cup raw short-grain brown rice + water for soaking
- 1 tbsp apple cider vinegar
- 1 cup golden raisins + 1 tsp for topping + boiling water for soaking
- 1 cup cashew milk, divided into ¾ cup + ¼ cup
- ¾ cup + 2 tbsp water, divided into ¾ cup + 2 tbsp
- ½ tsp salt
- 1 tbsp ground flax seeds
- 1 cup coconut milk
- ¾ cup oat milk
- 2 tbsp brown sugar
- 1 tbsp maple syrup
- 1 tsp vanilla extract
- ground nutmeg for garnish

STEEPED STRAWBERRIES (for topping — optional, makes ¾ cup)

- 1 cup sliced fresh strawberries
- 1 tsp sugar
- 1 tsp maple syrup
- 1 tsp orange juice or a liqueur of your choice (we like Disaronno or Grand Marnier)

COCONUT WHIPPED CREME (for topping — optional, makes 1 cup)

- 13.5-oz can coconut milk, refrigerated overnight
- ½ tsp ground chia seeds (optional, but helps whipped creme retain its shape and texture)
- 1 tbsp sugar
- 1 tsp vanilla extract

DIRECTIONS

1. The night before you cook the pudding.

   a. Rinse 1 cup raw short-grain brown rice several times before soaking it in water overnight. Rinse and replace water once or twice. At least 4 hours before cooking rice, rinse and replace water, then add 1 tbsp apple cider vinegar.

   b. Prepare *Steeped Strawberries* at least 4 hours ahead of time (we do it the night before). In a small bowl, add 1 cup sliced fresh strawberries and 1 tsp each sugar, maple syrup, and orange juice or liqueur. Stir, cover, and refrigerate. Let steep for at least 4 hours. Strawberries are ready once a lovely syrup has formed.

2. In a small bowl, place 1 cup golden raisins, cover with boiling water, and soak for at least 15 minutes.

3. Separately drain and rinse the soaked rice and raisins. In a medium saucepan, add soaked, drained, and rinsed rice and raisins, ¾ cup each cashew milk and water, and ½ tsp salt. Bring to a boil, then lower heat, cover, and simmer until all liquid is absorbed (about 30 minutes).

4. In a small dish, mix 1 tbsp ground flax seeds with 2 tbsp water and let thicken for at least 5 minutes.

5. To the cooked rice and raisins, add 1 cup coconut milk, ¾ cup oat milk, ¼ cup cashew milk, 2 tbsp brown sugar, 1 tbsp maple syrup, and 1 tsp vanilla extract. Bring to a boil before adding thickened flax seed mixture. Stir well, reduce heat, and simmer for about 20 minutes or until liquid is mostly absorbed, stirring often.

6. Prepare *Coconut Whipped Creme*: (Prepare while pudding simmers.)

   a. Put a deep bowl and the blades of an electric hand mixer in the freezer to cool for at least 10 minutes before whipping.

   b. Open chilled can of coconut milk without shaking, remove hardened coconut cream from the top of the can, and place it in the chilled bowl. Sprinkle ½ tsp ground chia seeds on top of the hardened coconut cream and whip with an electric hand mixer on high for about 3 minutes. As coconut milk thickens, add 1 tbsp sugar and 1 tsp vanilla extract. Continue beating for a few minutes. Cover and refrigerate until the rice pudding is ready. Whipped creme will retain its whipped texture, especially if you use ground chia seeds, which work as a stabilizer.

7. Remove pudding from the stovetop and let set for at least 10 minutes before serving. For each serving, scoop out ½ cup rice pudding, and top with 1½ tbsp Steeped Strawberries, 2 tbsp Coconut Whipped Creme, a sprinkling of ground nutmeg, and finish off with a golden raisin.

NUTRITION: RICE PUDDING ONLY - *PER ½-CUP SERVING: Calories 220; Carbs 38g; Fat 7g; Protein 4g; Sodium 189mg; Sugar 17g;* **STEEPED STRAWBERRIES** - *PER 1½-TBSP SERVING: Calories 13; Carbs 3g; Fat 0g; Protein 0g; Sodium 0mg; Sugar 2g;* **COCONUT WHIPPED CREME** - *PER 2-TBSP SERVING: Calories 96; Carbs 2g; Fat 9g; Protein 1g; Sodium 13mg; Sugar 1g*

BRUNCH - ON THE SWEETER SIDE

Melt-in-Your-Mouth Pancakes

prep time: 15 minutes   cook time: 15 minutes   makes: 10 x 4" pancakes

Rich in

By Jiminy! These little cakes have it all. Not only are they completely vegan, but they have a creamy melt-in-your-mouth texture. Some folks call'em flapjacks due to flipping (aka: flapping) them on the griddle. They're simply delightful with a slap of vegan butter, a splash of maple syrup, and a sprinkling of fresh berries. Also, they go over big when served up with Coconut Whipped Creme (page 33) and syrup. However, if you want to keep it simple, they're delectable when slathered with peanut butter and jam. Cashew Sue often makes these flapjacks for a fun dinner meal and serves them up with savoury veggie breakfast sausages. Best of all, leftover pancakes can be refrigerated and then popped in the toaster to reheat. Presto! A sleight of hand conjures up a lovely pancake meal.

For nut-free, replace cashew milk with vegan nut-free milk of your choice.

INGREDIENTS

Milk Mixture (makes 2 cups)
  1⅓ cups oat milk
  ½ cup cashew milk
  2 tbsp + 2 tsp coconut milk

2 tbsp apple cider vinegar

1¾ cups whole-wheat flour

2 tsp baking powder

1 tsp sugar

½ tsp baking soda

½ tsp salt

¼ cup aquafaba (optional, omit for a denser pancake) (page 14)

3 tbsp + ¼–1 tsp olive oil for greasing the pan

1 tsp vanilla extract

DIRECTIONS

1. In a large bowl, add 2 cups Milk Mixture (1⅓ cups oat milk, ½ cup cashew milk, and 2 tbsp + 2 tsp coconut milk) and 2 tbsp apple cider vinegar. Stir and set aside for at least 5 minutes, as apple cider vinegar will cause milk to thicken slightly.

2. In a medium bowl, sift 1¾ cups whole-wheat flour, 2 tsp baking powder, 1 tsp sugar, and ½ tsp each baking soda and salt. Stir until well combined.

3. Add to thickened milk, ¼ cup aquafaba, 3 tbsp olive oil, and 1 tsp vanilla extract. Using a hand mixer, beat on high for 3–5 minutes or until the mixture becomes foamy. This is an essential step as it helps the pancake form those important bubbles during cooking.

4. Make a well in the centre of dry ingredients and pour in the foamy liquid. Gently stir until just blended. Do not overmix, as this may cause your cakes to become tough.

5. Place griddle (flat grill) or frying pan on medium heat for about 5 minutes without adding oil. Pan is hot when a splash of sprinkled water dances on it. (Using your fingertips, flick a little bit of water on the pan to test.) Spray heated pan with oil or, using a pastry brush, spread a little oil (¼ tsp) on the pan and heat for 30 seconds–1 minute.

6. Use a ⅓-cup measuring cup to create the perfect-sized pancake. Scoop up batter with measuring cup and pour evenly onto the pan using a circular motion. Cook until bubbles form (2–3 minutes). Flip the pancakes and cook the other side for about 3 minutes or until nicely browned. Add more oil to your pan before cooking additional pancakes.

7. Serve immediately. Plan for 2–3 pancakes per serving size, and let your guests add toppings according to taste.

NUTRITION: PER 4" PANCAKE: *Calories 140; Carbs 18g; Fat 7g; Protein 3g; Sodium 623mg; Sugar 1g*

Guiltless French Toast

| prep time: 20 minutes | cook time: 20 minutes | makes: 10 slices |

Rich in

Yippee-ki-yay kiddos, we're having French toast today! Whenever we hear those words, we know it's time to start drooling 'cause we love French toast. Especially this version, which isn't only guiltless, but it's also low in fat and high in yumminess. When dished up with syrup and fruit and perhaps a little Coconut Whipped Creme (page 33), anyone within shouting distance will be racing to the table. Another great idea is to use French toast instead of boring ol' bread to fancy up scrumptious veggie sandwiches. If you're planning to use this toast as a coating for a fried veggie sandwich, just omit the sugar and replace the vanilla extract, cinnamon, and nutmeg with savoury seasonings. If you have any leftovers — which is highly unlikely — refrigerate and then reheat in the toaster. Voilà! Just like new.

INGREDIENTS

¼ cup ground flax seeds

1 cup soy milk, divided into 2 x ½ cup

½ cup soft tofu

¼ cup oat milk

2 tbsp sugar

1 tbsp nutritional yeast

1 tsp vanilla extract

1 tsp finely ground black Indian salt (page 15)

½ tsp ground cinnamon

¼ tsp ground nutmeg

10 slices of slightly stale, whole-grain sourdough bread or bread of your choice

½–1 tsp olive oil for greasing the pan

DIRECTIONS

1. In a small bowl, mix ¼ cup ground flax seeds with ½ cup soy milk and let thicken for at least 5 minutes.

2. In a narrow, flat dish (that 2 slices of bread can fit into nicely), add thickened flax seed mixture, ½ cup each soy milk and soft tofu, ¼ cup oat milk, 2 tbsp sugar, 1 tbsp nutritional yeast, 1 tsp each vanilla extract and finely ground black Indian salt, ½ tsp ground cinnamon, and ¼ tsp ground nutmeg. Whisk until well combined.

3. Heat griddle (flat grill) or frying pan on medium heat for about 5 minutes without adding oil. Pan is hot when a splash of sprinkled water dances on it. (Using your fingertips, flick a little bit of water on the pan to test.) Spray heated pan with oil or, using a pastry brush, spread a little oil (½ tsp) on the pan and heat for 30 seconds–1 minute.

4. Dip 2 slices of bread into the liquid mixture just before placing them on the griddle. Ensure bread soaks up plenty of liquid, but not so much that it becomes soggy. Slightly stale bread works the best.

5. Cook each side for 5–10 minutes or until brown. Repeat with remaining bread. Add more oil to your pan before cooking additional slices.

6. Serve immediately. Dish 2–3 slices per person and let your friends and family add their own toppings.

NUTRITION: *PER SLICE (without toppings):* Calories 153; Carbs 29g; Fat 2g; Protein 6g; Sodium 230mg; Sugar 6g

Golden Granola

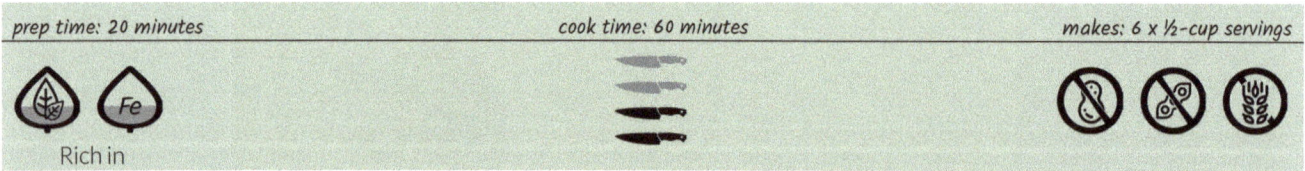

prep time: 20 minutes   cook time: 60 minutes   makes: 6 x ½-cup servings

Rich in

These granola clusters made from flaked oats, Kamut, and quinoa are splendiferous. The crunchy golden nuggets will satisfy anyone, from the meanest desperado to the sweetest southern belle. The long and the short of it is you'll never grow tired of munching on this granola because it's endlessly customizable. If you have a mind to, try mixing up different flaked grains, nuts, dried fruit, and spices for a new taste experience every time. All you need do is follow this basic formula: mix 2 cups of grain flakes with 1 cup of assorted nuts, seeds, and dried fruit along with ½ cup of liquid. Use at least four different dry ingredients for a nice balance of flavour and texture. Try various combinations of nuts (chopped cashews, almonds, hazelnuts, or walnut), seeds (hemp, sunflower, or pumpkin seeds), and dried fruit (golden berries, cranberries, goji berries, raisins, or currants). Mix ¼ cup of aquafaba with 2 tablespoons each of oil and liquid sweetener for the liquid. This combination helps your granola clump together into tasty morsels.

For wheat-free, replace Kamut flakes with oat flakes.

INGREDIENTS

Grain Flakes (makes 2 cups)
- 1½ cups rolled oats
- ¼ cup Kamut flakes
- ¼ cup quinoa flakes

½ cup raw chopped assorted nuts and seeds

¼ cup hemp hearts

¼ cup dried fruit

2 tbsp olive oil

1 tbsp raw blue agave nectar or maple syrup

1 tbsp molasses

1½ tsp ground cinnamon

1 tsp grated ginger root

½ tsp vanilla extract

½ tsp salt

¼ tsp ground nutmeg

¼ tsp ground cardamom

¼ cup aquafaba (page 14)

¼ tsp cream of tartar (optional)

DIRECTIONS

1. Place an oven rack in the centre slot and preheat oven to 300°F. Line a 9- x 9" square baking pan with parchment paper.

2. In a large bowl, combine 2 cups grain flakes (1½ cups rolled oats and ¼ cup each Kamut and quinoa flakes), ½ cup raw chopped assorted nuts and seeds, and ¼ cup each hemp hearts and dried fruit. Mix until all ingredients are evenly distributed.

3. In a separate small bowl, mix 2 tbsp olive oil, 1 tbsp each agave nectar and molasses, 1½ tsp ground cinnamon, 1 tsp grated ginger root, ½ tsp each vanilla extract and salt, and ¼ tsp each ground nutmeg and ground cardamom. Stir until well combined.

4. Pour wet mixture over dry ingredients, stirring until mixture is evenly moistened.

5. In a deep bowl, add ¼ cup aquafaba and ¼ tsp cream of tartar (optional, but it helps stabilize the aquafaba and speeds up the foaming process). Beat with an electric hand mixer for 2–3 minutes or until firm peaks form. Fold beaten aquafaba into the prepared mixture. This helps to produce granola with good-sized chunks.

6. Spread mixture evenly over parchment paper to about ½-inch thickness. Bake for 45–60 minutes. Do not stir the mixture. Cook granola until it is lightly golden on top and no longer wet. Be careful not to overcook it, as it will continue to crisp up as it cools. Remove from oven and cool completely before breaking into clusters. Enjoy immediately or store in an airtight container at room temperature for up to 10 days.

NUTRITION: PER ½-CUP SERVING: *Calories 324; Carbs 36g; Fat 16g; Protein 10g; Sodium 205mg; Sugar 9g*

Fancy Un-Omelet with Best Bechamel Sauce

prep time: 30 minutes   cook time: 50 minutes   makes: 2 un-omelets

Rich in: Ca, C, C, (leaf), K, Fe

Truth be told, this eggless omelet is hardy enough to feed a hungry crew and fancy enough to impress the in-laws. Carrot Rick decided to create a plant-based blend with a similar protein, fat, moisture, and structure as eggs. He tossed together chickpea flour, aquafaba, nutritional yeast, and black Indian salt. Then mixed it all up with a little warm water. Served with Best Bechamel Sauce, the un-omelet is tender and delectable. The trick is to heat the pan and the oil to the perfect temperature. The pan needs to be hot enough to bind the base of the un-omelet mixture but not so hot the mixture burns or toughens. The filling can be varied, but the key is to cook it beforehand and have it warm and ready to go. Anyone who tries it will smile and sing a chorus of "Mmm! Mmm! Mmm!"

For nut-free, replace cashew milk with vegan nut-free milk of your choice.
For soy-free, replace Bragg soy seasoning or tamari with coconut aminos (soy-free seasoning) (page 15) and use soy-free vegan Worcestershire sauce.

INGREDIENTS

UN-OMELET FILLING *(makes 1 cup)*

¼ cup low-sodium vegetable broth

½ cup chopped onion (about ½ small)

2 cups sliced mushroom (about 8 medium)

1½ tsp dried mushroom powder

1½ tsp Bragg soy seasoning or tamari

1 tsp Bestcestershire Sauce (vegan Worcestershire sauce)

1 tsp minced garlic (about 2 cloves)

½ cup diced tomato (about 1 small)

½ cup chopped kale

1 tbsp minced basil leaves

freshly ground black pepper, to taste

BEST BECHAMEL SAUCE *(makes 1 cup)*

2 tbsp vegan butter

¼ cup minced onion (about ¼ small)

2 tbsp whole-wheat flour

3 tbsp dry white wine

⅓ cup low-sodium vegetable broth

Milk Mixture (makes ½ cup)

⅓ oat milk

1 tbsp cashew milk

2 tsp coconut milk

1 bay leaf

¼ tsp salt

¼ tsp ground white pepper

⅛ tsp American saffron

⅛ tsp ground nutmeg

DIRECTIONS

1. Prepare ***Un-Omelet Filling:***

    a. Place frying pan on medium-high heat and add ¼ cup low-sodium vegetable broth. Once hot, add ½ cup chopped onion and sauté until translucent and beginning to darken (about 5 minutes). Let the broth cook off so onions can brown, but add a little water if they begin to stick. If they become too dry, onions may burn.

    b. Add 2 cups sliced mushroom, 1½ tsp each dried mushroom powder and Bragg seasoning, and 1 tsp each Bestcestershire Sauce and minced garlic. Cook until mushrooms start to brown and liquid cooks off (5–10 minutes). Add a little water if the ingredients start to stick.

    c. Add ½ cup each diced tomato and chopped kale, 1 tbsp minced basil leaves, and freshly ground black pepper. Cook for about 5 minutes or until tomatoes and kale start to soften. Add a little water if the ingredients start to stick. Once cooked, remove from stovetop and cover.

2. Prepare ***Best Bechamel Sauce***:

    a. Place saucepan on medium heat and add 2 tbsp vegan butter. Once hot and liquified, add ¼ cup minced onion and sauté until translucent and beginning to darken (about 5 minutes). Reduce to medium-low and slowly sprinkle in 2 tbsp whole-wheat flour, whisking continuously until flour is completely absorbed. Cook until bubbles appear, whisking to eliminate lumps and flattening out any that form.

    b. When the mixture appears thick and gummy, slowly add 3 tbsp white wine, whisking continuously. It may bubble up but continue to whisk until the wine is incorporated and the base for the sauce is smooth.

    c. Slowly add ⅓ cup low-sodium vegetable broth, whisking continuously.

    d. Once smooth, slowly add ½ cup Milk Mixture (⅓ cup oat milk, 1 tbsp cashew milk, and 2 tsp coconut milk), whisking continuously to dissolve any lumps.

    e. Once smooth, add 1 bay leaf, ¼ tsp each salt and white pepper, and ⅛ tsp each American saffron and ground nutmeg. Whisk until ingredients are well combined. Bring to a low boil. Cook for 3–5 minutes or until the mixture thickens. Add a little water if the mixture becomes too thick. Remove from stovetop and cover. Reheat if necessary and discard the bay leaf before serving.

INGREDIENTS, con't

BASIC UN-OMELET

2 tbsp ground flax seeds

1⅓ cups water, divided into ⅓ cup + 1 cup

1 cup chickpea flour

1 tbsp nutritional yeast

½ tsp black Indian salt (page 15)

½ tsp baking powder

½ tsp ground turmeric

freshly ground black pepper, to taste

½ cup aquafaba (page 14)

2 tbsp grapeseed oil, divided into 2 x 1 tbsp for greasing the pan

chopped parsley leaves for garnish

DIRECTIONS, con't

3. Prepare **Basic Un-Omelet**:

    a. In a deep bowl, mix 2 tbsp ground flax seeds with ⅓ cup water and let thicken for at least 5 minutes.

    b. In a large bowl, sift 1 cup chickpea flour, 1 tbsp nutritional yeast, and ½ tsp each black Indian salt, baking powder, and turmeric. Add freshly ground black pepper to taste and stir until well combined.

    c. Heat a 7–8-inch nonstick or cast-iron frying pan on medium heat without adding oil.

    d. To the thickened flax seed, add ½ cup aquafaba and 1 cup water. Whisk together until well combined.

    e. Pour liquid mixture into flour mixture and stir with a whisk until well combined. Mixture should have the consistency of pancake batter.

    f. Add 1 tbsp grapeseed oil to the heated frying pan and heat for 1–2 minutes before slowly pouring in half of the un-omelet mixture. Let it spread out in a thin layer over the bottom of the pan. Cook until the top is no longer shiny wet and the bottom is golden brown (about 3 minutes). Flip the un-omelet and cover with a lid. Cook an additional 3 minutes or until it is done. Remove the un-omelet from pan.

4. Place ½ cup filling and ¼ cup Best Bechamel Sauce onto half of the first un-omelet, fold the un-omelet to cover the filling and place on a warming dish. Repeat with the second un-omelet.

5. Once both omelets have been cooked and filled, pour ¼ cup hot Best Bechamel Sauce over each omelet, sprinkle on chopped parsley leaves, and serve immediately.

NUTRITION: PER UN-OMELET: Calories 627; Carbs 57g; Fat 34g; Protein 23g; Sodium 1,656mg; Sugar 14g

Chickpea Frittata with Tarragon Sauce

Chickpea Frittata: prep time: 25 minutes
Tarragon Sauce: prep time: 10 minutes

cook time: 55 minutes
cook time: 10 minutes

makes: one 9" pie (6 servings)
makes: 6 x 1/3-cup

Rich in

If you want to countrify this meal, cook and serve it up in a cast-iron frying pan, but if you don't have one handy, a pie plate will do. Either way, add some sun-dried tomatoes and whole oregano leaves over the top, and you've got yourself an impressive dish. This vegan version is extra special because it looks, feels, and tastes like a regular frittata while being eggless and totally plant-based. The chickpea flour produces an egg-like texture, while the black Indian salt helps bring out an eggy flavour. The frittata tastes excellent all on its own, but we like to add the Tarragon sauce, 'cause, according to Cashew Sue, anytime is sauce time. Besides, the Tarragon Sauce is heavenly and can be whipped up lickety-split. Serve this dish with a side salad for a hardy weekend brunch.

For nut-free, replace cashew milk with vegan nut-free milk of your choice.

INGREDIENTS

3 tbsp olive oil, divided into 2 tbsp + 1 tbsp + ¼ tsp for greasing the pan (optional)

1 cup diced onion (about ½ medium)

1½ tsp minced garlic (about 3 cloves)

1 tsp dried mushroom powder

½ tsp Spike all-purpose seasoning or Old Bay seasoning

freshly ground black pepper, to taste

3 cups chopped mushroom (about 12 medium)

1 cup chopped cooked artichoke

½ cup julienne-cut sun-dried tomato, packed in oil, undrained + 1 tsp for top of frittata

1 tbsp minced oregano or marjoram leaves + 1 tsp whole leaves for top of frittata

1 tbsp minced parsley leaves

2 tbsp ground flax seeds

⅓ cup water

1½ cups chickpea flour

1 tsp baking powder

½ tsp black Indian salt (page 15)

½ tsp turmeric

¾ cup aquafaba (page 14)

Milk Mixture (makes 1 cup)
　⅔ cup oat milk
　¼ cup cashew milk
　4 tsp coconut milk

1 tsp Dijon mustard

DIRECTIONS

1. Preheat oven to 375°F. If you are not using a cast-iron pan, spray a 9-inch pie dish with oil or, using a pastry brush, spread a thin layer of olive oil on the pan (¼ tsp oil).

2. Place 9-inch cast-iron frying pan (or a large nonstick frying pan) on medium heat for 2–3 minutes without adding any oil. Pan is hot when a splash of sprinkled water dances on it. (Using your fingertips, flick a little bit of water on the pan to test.) Add 2 tbsp olive oil and heat for 30 seconds–1 minute before adding 1 cup diced onion. Sauté until translucent and beginning to darken (about 5 minutes).

3. Add 1½ tsp minced garlic, 1 tsp dried mushroom powder, ½ tsp Spike seasoning, and freshly ground black pepper to onions. Stir in and cook for 1–2 minutes to seal the flavours into the onions.

4. Add 3 cups chopped mushroom and cook for about 10 minutes or until mushrooms start to brown. Add 1 cup chopped cooked artichoke, ½ cup julienned sun-dried tomato, and 1 tbsp each minced oregano and parsley. Continue cooking for about 5 minutes, ensure any excess liquid has cooked off. Makes about 2 cups.

5. In a deep bowl, mix 2 tbsp ground flax seeds with ⅓ cup water and let thicken for at least 5 minutes.

6. Spread the cooked mushroom mixture evenly across the bottom of the cast-iron pan or pie dish.

7. Into a large bowl, sift 1½ cups chickpea flour, 1 tsp baking powder, ½ tsp each black Indian salt and turmeric. Stir until well combined and create a well in the centre of the flour mixture.

8. To the thickened flax seed mix, add ¾ cup aquafaba, 1 cup Milk Mixture (⅔ cup oat milk, ¼ cup cashew milk, and 4 tsp coconut milk), 1 tbsp olive oil, and 1 tsp Dijon mustard. Using an electric hand mixer, beat on high for 2–3 minutes or until bubbles form and the mixture expands.

9. Pour liquid ingredients into the centre of the flour mixture and whisk until well combined and no flour lumps remain. Do not overmix.

10. Pour mixture evenly over cooked vegetables and swirl until the top is smooth. Place 1 tsp each julienne-cut sun-dried tomato and whole oregano leaves over the top.

11. Bake for 25–30 minutes or until the top starts to brown and a toothpick comes out clean when inserted into the middle.

12. When ready, remove from oven and let set for at least 10 minutes before serving. Cut into 6 even slices and serve with ⅓ cup tarragon sauce per slice.

INGREDIENTS, con't

TARRAGON SAUCE (optional, makes 2 cups)
- 3 tbsp vegan butter (or olive oil)
- 3 tbsp all-purpose flour
- 3 tbsp white wine
- Milk Mixture (makes 2 cups)
  - 1⅓ cups oat milk
  - ½ cup cashew milk
  - 2 tbsp + 2 tsp coconut milk
- 1 tbsp minced tarragon leaves
- 1 tbsp lemon juice (about ½ lemon)
- 1 tbsp nutritional yeast
- ¼ tsp black Indian salt (page 15)
- ⅛ tsp white pepper
- ⅛ tsp turmeric
- pinch of ground cloves

DIRECTIONS, con't

13. Prepare Tarragon Sauce: (While frittata cooks in the oven.)

a. Place saucepan on medium heat and add 3 tbsp vegan butter. Once hot and liquified, reduce to medium-low and slowly sift 3 tbsp all-purpose flour into the heated oil. Whisk continuously until flour is completely absorbed. Cook for a few minutes or until bubbles form, whisking to eliminate lumps and integrating any that form.

b. Slowly add 3 tbsp white wine, whisking continuously. The mixture may bubble up, but continue to whisk until the wine is incorporated and the base for the sauce is smooth.

c. Slowly add 2 cups Milk Mixture (1⅓ cups oak milk and ½ cup cashew milk, and 2 tbsp + 2 tsp coconut milk), whisking continuously. Once the mixture is smooth, add 1 tbsp each minced tarragon leaves, lemon juice, and nutritional yeast, ¼ tsp black Indian salt, ⅛ tsp each white pepper and turmeric, and a pinch of ground cloves. Whisk until well combined. Stirring continuously, bring to a low boil, and cook for 3–5 minutes or until mixture thickens.

d. Remove from stovetop and cover. Heat before serving.

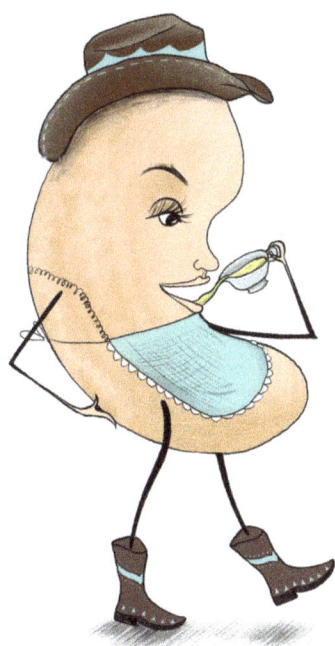

NUTRITION: FRITTATA ONLY - PER SERVING: Calories 271; Carbs 28g; Fat 13g; Protein 9g; Sodium 504mg; Sugar 6g;
TARRAGON SAUCE - PER ⅓-CUP SERVING: Calories 128; Carbs 10g; Fat 9g; Protein 2g; Sodium 201mg; Sugar 4g

Broccoli Fritters

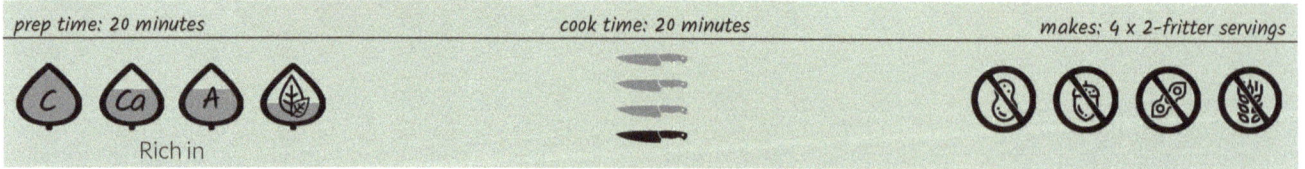

prep time: 20 minutes   cook time: 20 minutes   makes: 4 x 2-fritter servings

Rich in: C, Ca, A

Sit for a spell and chow down on Broccoli Fritters, 'cause these delightful patties provide a bonanza of flavourful delight. Made with broccoli, tahini, and other good stuff — one is just not enough. They're flat-out delicious on their own, but when served with Fresh Tomato Salsa (page 51), that extra tartness delivers a dish that's a cut above. No matter how you serve 'em, they won't last long. Even Broccoli Bandit sidles on up when he smells these tasty patties on the grill.

INGREDIENTS

4 cups chopped broccoli + water to steam

½ cup tahini

¼ cup chickpea flour

¼ cup minced Anaheim chili peppers, pulp and seeds removed

¼ cup minced parsley leaves

¼ cup sliced green onion + 1 tbsp of green portion for garnish (2–3 medium)

2 tbsp water

1 tbsp tapioca flour

1½ tsp minced garlic (about 3 cloves)

1½ tsp lemon juice (from ½ lemon)

½ tsp salt

½+ tsp grapeseed oil for greasing the pan

DIRECTIONS

1. Add an inch or two of water to your saucepan. Insert a steamer basket, cover with a lid, and heat on high heat until water comes to a boil. Add 4 cups chopped broccoli into the steamer basket, cover with a lid, reduce heat to medium, and steam until tender but not mushy (7–10 minutes). Remove from heat, drain, and immediately rinse in cool water to stop further cooking.

2. Chop steamed broccoli into small pieces and mix in a medium bowl with ½ cup tahini, ¼ cup each chickpea flour, minced Anaheim chili peppers, parsley leaves, and sliced green onion, 2 tbsp water, 1 tbsp tapioca flour, 1½ tsp each minced garlic and lemon juice, and ½ tsp salt. Stir until well combined.

3. Place griddle (flat grill) or frying pan on medium heat for a few minutes without adding oil. Pan is hot when a splash of sprinkled water dances on it. (Using your fingertips, flick a little bit of water on the pan to test.)

4. Make 8 patties. Scoop batter onto the parchment paper using a ½ cup measuring cup and form into 4-inch wide patties.

5. Spray heated pan with oil or, using a pastry brush, spread a little oil (½ tsp) on the pan and heat for 30 seconds–1 minute.

6. Add patties and cook 2–3 minutes per side. If cooking in batches, add more oil to your pan before adding additional patties. Serve immediately.

NUTRITION: *PER 2-FRITTER SERVING: Calories 256; Carbs 18g; Fat 17g; Protein 9g; Sodium 283mg; Sugar 2g*

Savoury Latke-Style Sweet Potato Cakes with Saucy Apple Compote

Sweet Potato Cakes: prep time: 20 minutes cook time: 10 minutes makes: 4 x 4-cake servings
Saucy Apple Compote: prep time: 15 minutes cook time: 15 minutes makes: 4 x ½-cup servings

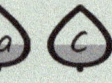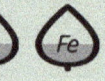 

Rich in

Strawberry Sal introduced these sweet potato cakes to the gang, and Carrot Rick named them 'cause they look like traditional latkes. But there's no way, no how, they're made the same. These lovely patties are plant-based, gluten-free, and stuffed full of nutrients. Saucy Peanut matched 'em up with Saucy Apple Compote, and a new tradition was born. These savoury veggie cakes make a great addition to any breakfast. Fry them in a small amount of oil to keep the fat content down or increase the amount of oil, so they become crispier and more decadent. It's your choice, but they're always a big winner no matter how you cook them. These savoury little patties can easily be thrown together with a variety of vegetables. Try mixing it up with russet, yellow, or sweet potatoes, yams, or even zucchini.

INGREDIENTS

SAUCY APPLE COMPOTE
(optional, makes 2 cups)

- 4 medium apples
- 1½ tbsp water
- 1½ tbsp fresh or dried whole cranberries
- 1½ tbsp maple syrup
- 1 tsp lemon juice
- ¼ tsp salt
- ¼ tsp ground cinnamon
- ⅛ tsp ground allspice
- ⅛ ground ginger
- ⅛ ground cloves

SAVOURY LATKE-STYLE SWEET POTATO CAKES

- 2 tbsp ground flax seeds
- ⅓ cup aquafaba (page 14)
- 2 medium sweet potatoes or other large veggie (about 4 cups grated)
- ¾ tsp salt, divided into ¼ tsp + ½ tsp
- ½ cup chickpea flour
- 2 tbsp grated onion
- 1 tbsp minced rosemary
- 1 tsp lemon juice
- ½ tsp Spike all-purpose seasoning or Old Bay seasoning
- ½ tsp smoked paprika
- ¼ tsp garlic powder
- ¼ tsp ground allspice
- freshly ground black pepper, to taste
- 1+ tbsp grapeseed oil for frying

DIRECTIONS

1. Prepare *Saucy Apple Compote*:

   a. Peel, core, and chop 4 medium apples (about 4 cups). Place in a medium saucepan with 1½ tbsp each water, fresh whole cranberries, and maple syrup, 1 tsp lemon juice, ¼ tsp each salt and ground cinnamon, and ⅛ tsp each ground allspice, ground ginger, and ground cloves. Stir until well combined.

   b. Cook on medium heat until the mixture starts to bubble. Reduce to medium-low and cover with a lid. Stew until apples soften (about 10 minutes). Remove from stovetop.

2. Prepare *Savoury Latke-Style Sweet Potato Cakes*:

   a. In a medium dish, mix 2 tbsp ground flax seeds with ⅓ cup aquafaba and let thicken for at least 5 minutes.

   b. Peel and grate 2 medium sweet potatoes into a large bowl (about 4 cups) and sprinkle with ¼ tsp salt. Stir until well coated.

   c. Add to thickened flax seed, ½ cup chickpea flour, 2 tbsp grated onions, 1 tbsp minced rosemary, 1 tsp lemon juice, ½ tsp each Spike seasoning and smoked paprika, ¼ tsp each garlic powder and ground allspice, and freshly ground black pepper. Mix until well combined.

   d. Place stovetop griddle (flat grill) between medium and medium-low heat for about 5 minutes without adding any oil.

   e. Drain any accumulated liquid from grated sweet potatoes before placing them into a clean, dry towel. Squeeze out any remaining water. Add drained, grated sweet potatoes to thickened flax seed mixture and stir. Using your fingertips, mix until well combined.

   f. Once pan is hot, add 1 tbsp grapeseed oil (use more oil for crispier cakes) and heat for 1–2 minutes. Pan is ready when a splash of sprinkled water dances on it. (Using your fingertips, flick a little bit of water on the pan to test.) Using a 2 tbsp measuring spoon, scoop a heaping portion of potato mixture directly onto the griddle and flatten with a spatula to about 2 inches in diameter. Cook each side until golden brown (3–4 minutes). If you cook them in batches, add more oil to your pan before grilling the remaining cakes.

   g. Serve immediately with Saucy Apple Compote as a tasty side dish.

NUTRITION: SAVOURY CAKES ONLY - *PER 4-CAKES/SERVING: Calories 269; Carbs 40g; Fat 9g; Protein 7g; Sodium 684mg; Sugar 7g;* **SAUCY APPLE COMPOTE** - *PER ¼-CUP SERVING: Calories 103; Carbs 28g; Fat 0g; Protein 0g; Sodium 146mg; Sugar 21g*

Mexican-Style Rice and Beans with Fresh Tomato Salsa

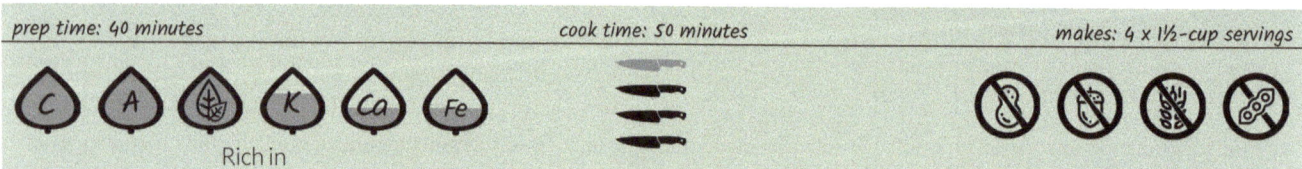

prep time: 40 minutes cook time: 50 minutes makes: 4 x 1½-cup servings

Rich in: C, A, K, Ca, Fe

Desayuno is the Spanish word for "breakfast," and this Mexican-inspired dish is a great way to break your fast. We've heard tell that eggs and beans are traditional breakfast fare in Mexico, but that just won't work here. However, Saucy Peanut, being a quick thinker, opted-out eggs and opted-in rice. The result? A heap of satisfaction in the belly, setting you up for a hunky-dory day. While it may not be a typical American brunch, it's a sure winner filled with protein and nutrients. What's more, variety is the spice of life! (Others argue the spice of life is chilies, but luckily for you, this recipe has both.) Serve it up with tortillas or toast, along with a colourful side salad, and you'll be raring to go.

You can cook the rice in a rice cooker or Instant Pot, but you will need to adjust the cooking time and reduce the liquids accordingly. For a hotter sauce leave the seeds in. If you feel lazy and don't mind sacrificing taste, substitute the Fresh Tomato Salsa for a store-bought version. If you use canned black beans, a 13.5-oz can contains 1½ cups beans. If you don't have another ½ cup beans on hand, use ½ cup corn kernels instead.
For soy-free, replace Bragg soy seasoning or tamari with coconut aminos (soy-free seasoning) (page 15) and use soy-free vegan Worcestershire sauce.

INGREDIENTS

MEXICAN-STYLE RICE *(makes 2–3 cups)*

- ½ red bell pepper (save the other half for the main dish, see below)
- ½ cup raw long-grain brown rice
- 1 cup canned low-sodium diced tomatoes (¾ of 13.5-oz can)
- ½ cup water
- ½ tsp chili powder
- ½ tsp ground cumin
- ¼ tsp salt
- 1 tbsp minced cilantro leaves

FRESH TOMATO SALSA *(makes 2 cups), divided into 2 x 1 cup*

- 1 tsp cumin seeds
- 2 large tomatoes
- ¼ small onion
- 1 medium jalapeño or serrano pepper
- 2 tbsp chopped cilantro leaves
- 2 tbsp lime juice (1–2 limes)
- ½ tsp salt

OTHER INGREDIENTS

- ½ medium onion
- 3 garlic cloves
- 12 medium mushrooms
- ½ red bell pepper
- 1 tbsp olive oil
- 1 tbsp Bragg soy seasoning or tamari
- 1 tsp Bestcestershire Sauce (vegan Worcestershire sauce)
- 1 tsp dried mushroom powder
- 2 cups cooked, drained black beans
- 1 tbsp chopped cilantro leaves
- 1 avocado, diced

DIRECTIONS

1. Prepare **Mexican-Style Rice**:

    a. Remove seeds and pulp from half of a red bell pepper and dice (about ½ cup).

    b. Wash ½ cup raw long-grain brown rice several times and drain off excess water. Place in a medium saucepan with 1 cup canned low-sodium diced tomatoes, ½ cup water, the diced red bell pepper, ½ tsp each chili powder and ground cumin, and ¼ tsp salt. Cover with a lid, bring to a boil, then reduce to medium-low and simmer until all liquid has been absorbed (about 25 minutes). Remove from stovetop and stir in 1 tbsp minced cilantro leaves. Fluff with a fork and cover.

2. Prepare **Fresh Tomato Salsa**: (Prepare while rice cooks.)

    a. Place small frying pan on medium heat and dry toast 1 tsp cumin seeds. Shake pan continuously to keep cumin seeds moving until seeds darken slightly and emit a pleasant earthy aroma (about 1 minute).

    b. Chop 2 large tomatoes (about 2 cups) and mince ¼ small yellow onion (about ¼ cup). Remove seeds and stem from jalapeño pepper and chop finely. (Use serrano peppers for a hotter salsa.)

    c. Place in a medium dish with 2 tbsp each chopped cilantro and lime juice, 1 tsp toasted cumin seeds, and ½ tsp salt. Stir until well combined, draining off any excess liquid before serving.

3. While rice cooks, prepare the rest of the ingredients. Dice ½ medium onion (about 1 cup) and mince 3 garlic cloves (about 1½ tsp). Slice 12 medium mushrooms (about 3 cups). Remove seeds and pulp from half a red bell pepper and dice (about ½ cup).

4. Place frying pan on medium heat and add 1 tbsp oil. Once hot, add the diced onions and sauté until translucent and beginning to darken (about 5 minutes). Add a little water if onions begin to stick.

5. Add 1 tbsp Bragg seasoning, the minced garlic, and 1 tsp each Bestcestershire Sauce and dried mushroom powder. Cook a few minutes before adding the sliced mushrooms and chopped red bell pepper. Sauté until brown and tender (10–15 minutes).

6. Add 2 cups each Mexican-Style Rice and cooked black beans, 1 cup Fresh Tomato Salsa, and 1 tbsp chopped cilantro. Cook until heated through.

7. Serve immediately with remaining Fresh Tomato Salsa and a diced avocado.

NUTRITION: PER 1½-CUP SERVING: *Calories 400; Carbs 63g; Fat 10g; Protein 17g; Sodium 1,041mg; Sugar 10g*

APPIES

Dips and Spreads

Herb Hummus	55
Spicy Black Bean Dip	57
Big Daddy Dip (Baba Ghanoush)	59
Emerald Dip	61
Snap'n Tapenade	63

Mushroom Bites

Cheezy Artichoke-Stuffed Mushroom Caps	65
Marinated Mushroom Bites	67
Portobello Carpaccio	69

Crunchy Appies

Krispy Kale Chips	71
Zesty Chickpeas	73

Herb Hummus

prep time: 15 minutes   cook time: 2 minutes   makes: 8 x ¼-cup servings

Rich in

It's mighty swell when Herb Hummus is close at hand, especially when you're hungry, short on time, and yearning for some good eats. The store-bought tubs may work, but they just don't do the trick. Not only are they plain and boring, but over time they'll cost you an arm and a leg. Our hummus can be made for a song (and you'll save even more when you use dried peas), plus it's quick and easy to make, and the taste is over the moon. Another reason to make your own hummus is the flexibility of using different ingredients. You can swap out the herbs, or you can create a creamy, no added oil version. For a lovely light texture and lower fat content, all you need do is replace ⅓ cup olive oil with ¼ cup aquafaba. Herb Hummus with crackers and chips go together like a wink and smile, but this spread also works wonders on sandwiches.

Cook up some dried chickpeas in advance or simply open a 19-oz can (2 cups of drained beans). Drain and save the chickpea water (aquafaba) from the can to use in this recipe or another one.
Zest the lemon before cutting and juicing.
For soy-free, replace Bragg soy seasoning or tamari with coconut aminos (soy-free seasoning) (page 15).

INGREDIENTS

1½ tbsp raw sesame seeds

2 cups cooked, drained chickpeas + a few for garnish

⅓ cup tahini

⅓ cup lemon juice (2–3 lemons)

1½ tbsp chopped oregano leaves

1 tbsp apple cider vinegar

1 tbsp chopped basil leaves + small amount for garnish

1½ tsp Bragg soy seasoning or tamari

1½ tsp minced garlic (about 3 cloves)

1 tsp lemon zest (from ½ lemon)

1 tsp paprika + small amount for garnish

½ tsp salt

freshly ground black pepper, to taste

⅓ cup olive oil or ¼ cup aquafaba (page 14) + small amount for garnish

DIRECTIONS

1. Place small frying pan on medium heat and dry toast 1½ tbsp raw sesame seeds. Shake pan continuously to keep seeds moving until they darken slightly and emit a pleasant nutty aroma (about 1 minute). Divide into 1 tbsp and 1½ tsp (for garnish).

2. Remove one or two chickpeas and set them aside for garnish (optional). In a food processor or blender, place 2 cups cooked and drained chickpeas, ⅓ cup each tahini and lemon juice, 1½ tbsp chopped oregano leaves, 1 tbsp each toasted sesame seeds, apple cider vinegar, and chopped basil, 1½ tsp each Bragg seasoning and minced garlic, 1 tsp each lemon zest and paprika, ½ tsp salt, and freshly ground black pepper. Blend until the mixture becomes smooth (3–5 minutes), scraping down sides as needed with a rubber spatula. Slowly pour ⅓ cup olive oil (or ¼ cup aquafaba for oil-free version) into the mixture and continue to blend for 3–5 minutes or until smooth and creamy.

3. Serve in a pretty dish and drizzle a small amount of oil on top along with 1½ tsp toasted sesame seeds, a sprinkle of paprika and chopped basil, and one or two whole chickpeas.

NUTRITION: PER ¼-CUP SERVING: *Calories 223; Carbs 12g; Fat 17g; Protein 7g; Sodium 209mg; Sugar 2g*

APPIES - DIPS AND SPREADS

Spicy Black Bean Dip

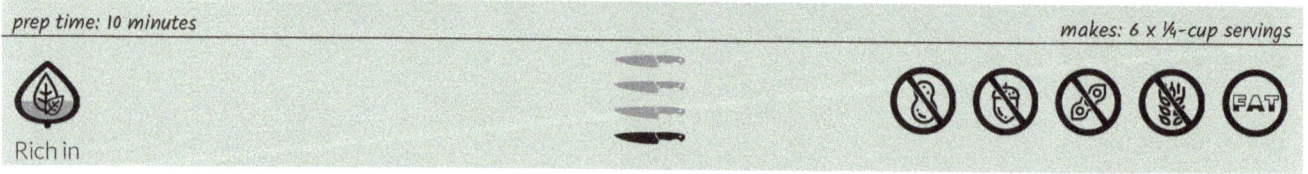

prep time: 10 minutes makes: 6 x ¼-cup servings

Rich in

Make Spicy Black Bean Dip when you're fixin' for a snack that's down-home delicious and has just the right amount of spicy. As an added boon, you'll get a protein boost. Plus, you can mix it up lickety-split. Of course, we like it best as a dip for fresh veggies, but it's also darn good when served up with fresh sourdough bread, corn chips, or even as a spread on your veggie sandwich. This toothsome appetizer is sure to please when your compadres stop by for some chitchat.

INGREDIENTS

1½ cups cooked black beans, drained and rinsed (13.5-oz can)

¼ cup Fresh Tomato Salsa (page 51), store-bought salsa, or ⅓ cup chopped fresh tomato and 1 tbsp diced onion

2 tbsp chopped cilantro leaves + small amount for garnish

1 tbsp olive oil + small amount for garnish

1 tbsp lime juice (about 1 lime)

1½ tsp ground cumin

½ tsp dried minced onion

½ tsp salt

¼ tsp black pepper

¼ tsp garlic powder

3–5 drops Tabasco sauce or hot sauce

corn kernels for garnish

DIRECTIONS

1. In a food processor or blender, add 1½ cups cooked, drained, and rinsed black beans, ¼ cup Fresh Tomato Salsa, 2 tbsp chopped cilantro, 1 tbsp each olive oil and lime juice, 1½ tsp ground cumin, ½ tsp each dried minced onion and salt, ¼ tsp each black pepper and garlic powder, and 3–5 drops Tabasco sauce. Blend until smooth.

2. To serve, garnish with corn kernels, chopped cilantro, and a drizzle of olive oil.

NUTRITION: PER ¼-CUP SERVING: *Calories 81; Carbs 12g; Fat 3g; Protein 3g; Sodium 306mg; Sugar 1g*

APPIES - DIPS AND SPREADS

Big Daddy Dip (Baba Ghanoush)

prep time: 20 minutes + time to marinate   cook time: 25 minutes   makes: 4 x ¼-cup servings

Rich in C, K

It ain't balderdash when we tell you our version of classic eggplant dip is a new twist on an ole standard. We call our creation Big Daddy Dip 'cause the big daddy of all the dips is baba ghanoush. Besides, baba is the Arabic word for "father," and ghanoush means pampered. And who wouldn't feel grand while eating this dish? Just 'cause most recipes roast then peel the eggplant, that don't mean we do. Carrot Rick is adamant that we leave the skin, seeing as that's where most of the nutrients are found. And that's just what we did, resulting in a delish dish that goes great with raw veggies and is marvellous with fresh sourdough bread.

If you don't have za'atar, use ⅛ tsp each dried thyme, oregano, and sesame seeds.
Zest the lemon before cutting and juicing.
For soy-free, replace Bragg soy seasoning or tamari with coconut aminos (soy-free seasoning) (page 15) and use soy-free vegan Worcestershire sauce.

INGREDIENTS

1 tbsp grapeseed oil + ¼ tsp for greasing the pan

1 large globe eggplant

2 tbsp minced parsley leaves + small amount for garnish

1 tbsp Bragg soy seasoning or tamari

1 tbsp minced garlic (about 6 cloves)

1 tsp Bestcestershire Sauce (vegan Worcestershire sauce)

½ tsp salt, divided into 2 x ¼ tsp

2 tbsp lemon juice (about 1 lemon)

2 tbsp tahini

2 tsp lemon zest (about ½ lemon)

¼ tsp za'atar

⅛ tsp black pepper

American saffron for garnish

olive oil for garnish

DIRECTIONS

1. Preheat oven to 400°F. Spray a large baking sheet with oil or, using a pastry brush, spread a thin layer of oil on the sheet (¼ tsp oil).

2. Slice a large globe eggplant into rounds (4–5 cups). Place in a medium bowl along with 2 tbsp minced parsley leaves, 1 tbsp each grapeseed oil, Bragg seasoning, and minced garlic, 1 tsp Bestcestershire Sauce, and ¼ tsp salt. Toss until eggplant rounds are well coated and marinate for 15–30 minutes.

3. Place the marinated eggplant rounds in a single layer on the prepared baking sheet and roast for 20 minutes (turn them at the halfway point (or cook them on a grill). Roast until tender. Once eggplant is tender, turn the broiler on high and broil each side for 1–2 minutes or until the flesh starts to char, but do not let it burn. Remove from oven and let cool.

4. In a food processor or blender, add cooked eggplant rounds (leave the skin on), 2 tbsp each lemon juice and tahini, 2 tsp lemon zest, ¼ tsp each salt and za'atar, and ⅛ tsp black pepper. Blend until smooth.

5. Put dip in a serving dish, drizzle a little olive oil over the top, and sprinkle with minced parsley and American saffron.

NUTRITION: *PER ¼-CUP SERVING:* *Calories 209; Carbs 15g; Fat 15g; Protein 7g; Sodium 634mg; Sugar 6mg*

APPIES - DIPS AND SPREADS

Emerald Dip

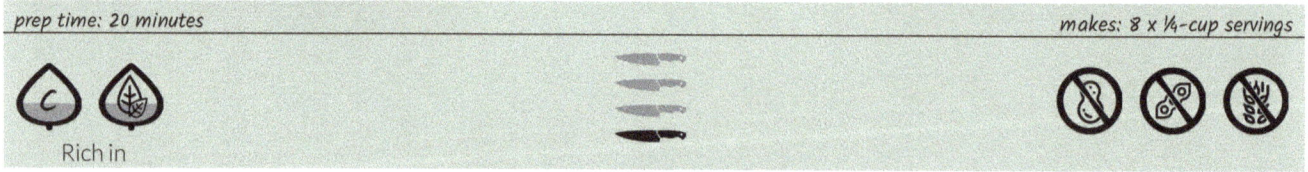

prep time: 20 minutes

makes: 8 x ¼-cup servings

Rich in

When you're all fired up for something good to snack on, look no further. Emerald Dip does the trick anytime you want something wickedly delicious yet simple and easy to throw together. The secret is blending English peas with mint, a smidgeon of nuts, and a hint of jalapeño pepper. This dazzling dip is impressive anytime, especially when served with some raw veggies and bread. Bring it along to a ho-down, or share it with your chums on a Saturday night. The green peas make it a natural to serve up for Saint Patty's Day. Plus, it's sure to be a bit hit at Christmastime, especially when you add a sprinkling of pomegranate seeds — they'll add rousing bursts of flavour along with a cheery red colour. When you're on the lookout for English peas, keep in mind they're sometimes called green peas, sweet peas, or garden peas.

INGREDIENTS

2 cups frozen English peas + boiling water for soaking

1 jalapeño pepper

2 tbsp cashews, soaked in water for at least 4 hours

2 tbsp pine nuts, soaked in water for at least 4 hours

¼ cup chopped mint leaves + a few for garnish

2 tbsp olive oil

2 tbsp lime juice (1–2 limes)

2 tbsp white balsamic vinegar

1 tsp minced garlic (about 2 cloves)

1 tsp grated ginger root

¾ tsp Spike all-purpose seasoning or Old Bay seasoning

½ tsp American saffron

½ tsp paprika

¼ tsp salt

freshly ground black pepper, to taste

1 tbsp pomegranate seeds (optional)

DIRECTIONS

1. In a medium bowl, place 2 cups frozen English peas and cover with boiling water. Let sit for at least 10 minutes. Drain and rinse.
2. Chop a jalapeño pepper, leaving the seeds in if you want a hotter dip (1–2 tbsp).
3. Drain and rinse the soaked cashews and pine nuts. Place in a food processor or blender along with 2 cups of prepared green peas, ¼ cup chopped mint leaves, the chopped jalapeño pepper, 2 tbsp each olive oil, lime juice, and white balsamic vinegar, 1 tsp each minced garlic and grated ginger root, ¾ tsp Spike seasoning, and ½ tsp each American saffron and paprika, ¼ tsp salt, and freshly ground black pepper. Process until smooth and creamy, 3–5 minutes, scraping down sides as needed with a rubber spatula.
4. To serve, garnish with 1 tbsp pomegranate seeds and a sprinkling of mint leaves.

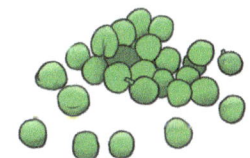

NUTRITION: PER ¼-CUP SERVING: *Calories 79; Carbs 8g; Fat 4g; Protein 2g; Sodium 169mg; Sugar 3g*

Snap'n Tapenade

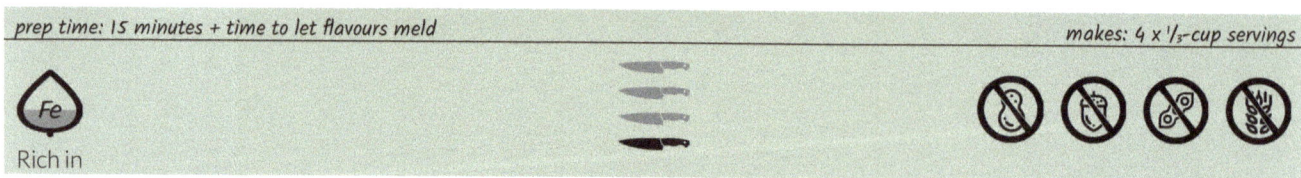

prep time: 15 minutes + time to let flavours meld

makes: 4 x 1/3-cup servings

Rich in Fe

Traditionally, tapenade is the Provençal name (from Southeastern France) for a spread of finely chopped or puréed olives, capers, and anchovies. Typically made with black olives, we have turned this traditional concoction on its head. We removed the anchovies (ya!), added a few green olives, and created a chunkier version. Ohh, sooo yummy! Plus, it's super simple to make. All you need do, is throw it all into a food processor, pulse a few times (instead of pulverizing the mixture), and you've got a dish that comes together in a snap. Serve it with fresh focaccia bread (or a baguette) and enjoy little nuggets of taste explosions. This salty treat goes well with an ice-cold beer, a refreshing spritzer, or a glass of wine and is guaranteed to produce smiles from anyone who has a nibble.

INGREDIENTS

¾ cup pitted Kalamata olives + a few for garnish

¼ cup pitted California black olives

¼ cup pitted green olives

2½ tbsp capers, divided into 2 tbsp + 1½ tsp for garnish

1 tsp minced garlic (about 2 cloves)

1 tsp lemon juice

1 tsp balsamic vinegar

freshly ground black pepper, to taste

2 tbsp olive oil

1 tbsp chopped parsley leaves + small amount for garnish

1 tbsp chopped basil leaves + a few small whole leaves for garnish

DIRECTIONS

1. In a food processor, combine ¾ cup pitted Kalamata olives, ¼ cup each pitted California black olives and pitted green olives, 2½ tbsp capers, 1 tsp each minced garlic, lemon juice, and balsamic vinegar, and freshly ground black pepper.

2. Pulse a few times until coarsely chopped and well combined. Do not over-blend. The mixture should be reasonably chunky.

3. Slowly pour in 2 tbsp olive oil as you pulse a couple more times. Remove mixture from the food processor and add 1 tbsp each chopped parsley and basil leaves, stir until well combined, and refrigerate for at least 60 minutes to let the flavours meld. Serve garnished with 1½ tsp capers, a few pitted kalamata olives, a sprinkle of minced parsley, and a couple of small whole basil leaves.

NUTRITION: PER ⅓-CUP SERVING: *Calories 176; Carbs 5g; Fat 17g; Protein 1g; Sodium 658mg; Sugar 0g*

Cheezy Artichoke-Stuffed Mushroom Caps

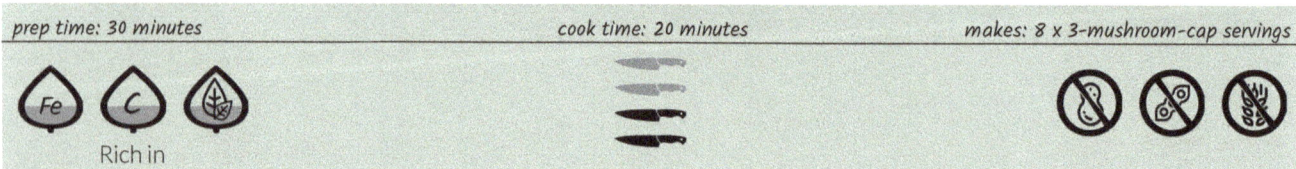

prep time: 30 minutes   cook time: 20 minutes   makes: 8 x 3-mushroom-cap servings

Rich in

These tasty stuffed mushroom caps are a fun snack anytime you've got a craving for a gooey, savoury treat. They're also great for when the gang stops by, to serve up on game day, or pretty much anytime you want to show off just how good vegan food tastes. Prepare the Cheezy Artichoke Filling in advance for a hot appetizer that's ready in less than half an hour. That way, you can quickly toss the ingredients together and throw the caps in the oven. Then serve them up to your hungry crew and sit back, basking in the praise coming your way. We recommend using two-inch-wide white button mushrooms 'cause their naturally cupped shape is just the right size. Besides, they're the perfect size to pop in your mouth and devour with just two bites.

The recipe for Garlic Cashew Creme Cheez makes 1 cup. Keep the remaining ¼ cup in the fridge and use it as a spread for veggie sandwiches, burgers, vegan hotdogs, or as a topping on potatoes.

INGREDIENTS

CHEEZY ARTICHOKE FILLING
(makes 1½ cups)

- ¾ cup Garlic Cashew Creme Cheez (page 216)
- 2 cups artichoke hearts, drained and diced (13.5-oz can or 6–8 hearts)
- 2 tbsp minced dill
- 1½ tsp lemon juice (from ½ lemon)
- ½ tsp salt
- ½ tsp ground black pepper

OTHER INGREDIENTS

- ½ tsp olive oil for greasing the pan
- 24 whole button mushrooms
- 1½ tsp minced dill for topping
- ½ tsp paprika for topping

DIRECTIONS

1. Prepare *Cheezy Artichoke Filling*: In a medium bowl, add ¾ cup Garlic Cashew Creme Cheez, 2 cups drained and diced artichoke hearts, 2 tbsp minced dill, 1½ tsp lemon juice, and ½ tsp each salt and ground black pepper. Mix with a fork until well combined.

2. Preheat oven to 375°F and prepare baking dish. We recommend using a muffin tin to keep mushrooms from toppling over. Spray baking dish with oil, or if using a muffin tin, spray each muffin hole with oil or use a pastry brush to spread a thin layer of oil (½ tsp oil).

3. Wash 24 button mushrooms and pry stems loose with a sharp knife. Remove the whole stem, creating a little crater in each. Discard or save stems for use in soups or mushroom gravy.

4. Arrange mushrooms stem side up on the baking dish. Spoon filling into each hole (about 1 tbsp per mushroom).

5. Sprinkle 1½ tsp dill and ½ tsp paprika over the top of the stuffed mushrooms.

6. Bake for 20 minutes or until mushrooms start to brown. Remove from the oven and let set for 5 minutes before serving.

NUTRITION: *PER 3-MUSHROOM-CAP SERVING: Calories 151; Carbs 12g; Fat 8g; Protein 6g; Sodium 541mg; Sugar 3g*

Marinated Mushroom Bites

prep time: 20 minutes + time to salt mushrooms   cook time: 3 minutes   makes: 6 x ¼-cup servings

Rich in

Be sure to invite these fungi to your next shindig. Super easy to make and super fun to eat on a Friday night with pals. These little treats are best made in advance, so the flavours have time to blend. As a bonus, making them ahead of time means you can just open a bottle of wine, put out your marinated 'shrooms, and have some fun times with some fun guys (and gals). Serve chilled as a side dish, an appetizer, or with crackers as a light snack, and enjoy your evening.

Salting the mushrooms in advance helps pull out excess water and softens them by breaking down the cell structure. Rinsing the salt off reduces the sodium intake.

INGREDIENTS

2 cups small button mushroom (about 16)
1 tbsp salt
¼ cup + 1 tsp olive oil, divided into 1 tsp + ¼ cup
1 tsp black peppercorns
¾ tsp fennel seeds
½ tsp black mustard seeds
½ tsp yellow mustard seeds
2 tbsp white wine vinegar
1 tbsp brown sugar
1 tbsp dried parsley
1 tsp dried tarragon leaves
1 tsp ground mustard
½ tsp dried minced onion
¼ tsp garlic powder

DIRECTIONS

1. Wash 2 cups small button mushroom. Place in a strainer over a large bowl, and sprinkle 1 tbsp salt over the mushrooms. Toss until coated with salt and leave at room temperature for 30 minutes.
2. While mushrooms sit, place small frying pan on medium-high heat and add 1 tsp olive oil. Pan is hot when a splash of sprinkled water dances on it. (Using your fingertips, flick a little bit of water on the pan to test.) Add 1 tsp black peppercorns, ¾ tsp fennel seeds, and ½ tsp each black mustard seeds and yellow mustard seeds. Cook for a few minutes until seeds start to pop. Remove from heat. Put cooked seeds into a mortar or a small bowl, and grind until coarsely crushed.
3. Rinse mushrooms well to remove any salt residue. Squeeze each one gently to remove as much water as possible but be careful not to damage the mushrooms. Pat mushrooms dry with a clean towel and place in a medium bowl.
4. To the soaked, drained, and squeezed mushrooms, add coarsely crushed seeds, ¼ cup olive oil, 2 tbsp white wine vinegar, 1 tbsp each brown sugar and dried parsley, 1 tsp each dried tarragon leaves and ground mustard, ½ tsp dried minced onion, and ¼ tsp garlic powder. Stir until mushrooms are well coated.
5. Cover and refrigerate for at least 30 minutes. Serve chilled as a tasty appetizer.

NUTRITION: *PER ¼-CUP SERVING: Calories 150; Carbs 6g; Fat 14g; Protein 3g; Sodium 199mg; Sugar 2g*

Portobello Carpaccio

prep time: 30 minutes + time to freeze and then marinate mushrooms cook time: 7 minutes   makes: 6 servings

  Rich in

Traditional carpaccio is raw fish or meat that is thinly sliced or pounded thin. (Neither of which is appreciated around here.) That's why we made our carpaccio with portobello mushroom meat which won't cause anyone to skedaddle away. Instead, folks will be clamouring to scoop up supple and succulent pieces of marinated mushrooms. This unique formula infuses the mushrooms with flavour. The acid in the vinegar and lemon juice magically transforms them into tender slices of heaven. This dish looks pretty and tastes great, served with slices of fresh bread. So, shake up some good eats and set this out for a tasty treat that's sure to be enjoyed by all.

Zest the lemon before cutting and juicing.

INGREDIENTS

3 portobello mushroom caps

2 tbsp + 1 tsp olive oil, divided into 1 tsp + 2 tbsp

2 tbsp capers, drained and dried

2 tsp black peppercorns

1½ tsp fennel seeds

1 tsp black mustard seeds

1 tsp yellow mustard seeds

2 tbsp lemon juice (about 1 lemon)

1 tbsp balsamic vinegar

¾ tsp salt, divided into ½ + ¼ tsp

½ tsp minced garlic (about 1 clove)

freshly ground black pepper, to taste

2 cups washed and dried arugula

lemon wedges and strips of red bell pepper for garnish

BASIL CASHEW CREME FRAÎCHE
(makes ½ cup)

⅓ cup raw cashews, soaked in water for at least 4 hours

1½ tbsp raw pine nuts, soaked in water for at least 4 hours

2 tbsp cashew milk

2 tbsp chopped basil leaves

1 tbsp lemon juice (about ½ lemon)

1½ tsp coconut oil

1 tsp lemon zest (from ½ lemon)

¼ tsp salt

¼ tsp dried mustard

⅛ tsp horseradish sauce

pinch of ground nutmeg

olive oil for garnish

a few pieces of sliced red bell pepper for garnish

DIRECTIONS

1. Remove stems from 3 portobello mushrooms and discard (or save for later use in soups or gravy). Put mushroom caps in the freezer until they become firm (30–60 minutes). Do not let them freeze (Cooling prepares the mushrooms so they can easily be sliced thinly.)

2. Place nonstick frying pan on medium-high heat and add 1 tsp olive oil. Oil is hot when a splash of sprinkled water dances on it. (Using your fingertips, flick a little bit of water on the pan to test.) Add 2 tbsp drained and dried capers. Cook until they crisp up (about 5 minutes). Remove capers from the pan.

3. Keep frying pan on medium-high, and add 2 tsp black peppercorns, 1½ tsp fennel seeds, and 1 tsp each black mustard seeds and yellow mustard seeds. Cook for a few minutes until seeds start to pop, then remove from heat. Put into a mortar or a small bowl and grind until coarsely crushed. Separate out a small amount to use as a garnish on the Basil Cashew Creme Fraîche.

4. In a small dish, add coarsely crushed seeds, 2 tbsp each lemon juice and olive oil, 1 tbsp balsamic vinegar, and ½ tsp each salt and minced garlic. Stir until well combined.

5. Once mushrooms are chilled and firm, remove them from the freezer and shave the mushrooms. Slice them very thinly across the top of the cap (2–3 cups). Place shaved mushrooms in a narrow dish and add crushed seed mixture. Toss until all mushrooms have been coated with the mixture and marinate at room temperature for at least 1 hour.

6. After mushrooms have marinated for at least 1 hour, they become soft, tender, and super tasty. Drain all liquid off mushrooms before serving.

7. Prepare **Basil Cashew Creme Fraîche**: (Prepare while mushrooms marinate.)

    Drain and rinse the soaked cashews and pine nuts. Place in a food processor or blender along with 2 tbsp each cashew milk and chopped basil leaves, 1 tbsp lemon juice, 1½ tsp coconut oil, 1 tsp lemon zest, ¼ tsp each salt and dried mustard, ⅛ tsp horseradish sauce, and a pinch of ground nutmeg.

    a. Process until smooth and creamy (3–5 minutes), scraping down sides as needed with a rubber spatula. Refrigerate until ready to serve.

8. Spread 2 cups washed and dried arugula on a serving dish and top with a thin layer of marinated and drained mushrooms. Garnish the Basil Cashew Creme Fraîche with a bit of olive oil, a sprinkle of crushed seeds, and a few pieces of sliced red bell pepper. Put on a plate along with marinated sliced mushrooms and sprinkle toasted capers over the mushrooms and the Basil Cashew Creme Fraîche. Add lemon wedges and strips of red bell pepper as garnish and serve with slices of fresh bread.

NUTRITION: *PER SERVING: Calories 154; Carbs 11g; Fat 12g; Protein 4g; Sodium 384mg; Sugar 2g*

Krispy Kale Chips

prep time: 20 minutes   cook time: 30 minutes   makes: 4 x 1½-cup servings

Rich in: C, Ca, C, (leaf), K

When there're folks in your kitchen stomping around and looking wildly for something amazing to eat, serve up Krispy Kale Chips. They're just perfect when your brood's craving something crunchy (like crisps) but healthier. These snackables are simple to make, taste fantastic, and are full of nutrients. Keep in mind there're plenty of choices for the look and feel of your chips, depending on the type of kale you use. Try making baked crisps with curly kale, black kale, Lacinato kale (aka: dinosaur or Tuscan kale), or red kale. They all work well. Just don't use baby kale, 'cause it's too thin and tender. Strawberry Sal's favourite is curly kale 'cause it's pretty. However, Cashew Sue prefers Lacinato kale (which has long, dark green leaves in a strap-like shape). Carrot Rick's a big advocate of any kind of kale chip because it's a tasty way to sneak a superfood into your diet.

INGREDIENTS

2 tbsp olive oil or grapeseed oil + ¼ tsp for greasing the pan

1 head of mature kale

1 tbsp raw sesame seeds

½ tsp Spike all-purpose seasoning or Old Bay seasoning

½ tsp nutritional yeast

freshly ground black pepper, to taste

DIRECTIONS

1. Preheat oven to 300°F. Spray a large baking sheet with oil or, using a pastry brush, spread a thin layer of oil on the sheet (¼ tsp oil).
2. Wash 1 head of kale, separate into leaves, remove stems, and tear into chip-sized pieces (about 8 cups). Dry in a salad spinner before placing in a medium bowl.
3. In a small dish, mix 2 tbsp olive oil, 1 tbsp raw sesame seeds, ½ tsp each Spike seasoning and nutritional yeast, and freshly ground black pepper. Stir until all ingredients are well combined.
4. Sprinkle seasoning mixture onto the kale leaves and toss until kale is well coated.
5. Spread coated kale in a single layer on the prepared baking sheet and bake until leaves start to crisp up (10–15 minutes).
6. Turn the oven off and let kale chips sit in the cooling oven for 10–15 minutes. This is crucial because it allows the kale to dry completely and become nice and crispy.
7. Serve immediately. Leftover chips can be stored overnight in an airtight container. They will retain their flavour but may lose some of their crispiness, though they are still fantastic as a slightly chewy treat.

NUTRITION: PER 1½-CUP SERVING: Calories 141; Carbs 13g; Fat 9g; Protein 6g; Sodium 132mg; Sugar 3g

Zesty Chickpeas

prep time: 10 minutes   cook time: 30 minutes   makes: 6 x ¼-cup servings

Rich in

These zesty little treats are a guaranteed winner. They make a fantastic snack and are a wickedly good addition to any meal, especially when you're on the lookout for a little extra protein. By Jiminy, but they're great when you've got a yearning for something healthy and satisfying to nibble. Sprinkle them over salads or casseroles for a bit of extra crunch, or pop them in your mouth when you're feeling peckish. This is our go-to recipe once we've opened a can of chickpeas and used up the handy, dandy aquafaba. It's a fun and easy way to use up leftover chickpeas.

Save drained chickpea water for later use as aquafaba, aka: egg white substitute (page 14).
For soy-free, replace Bragg soy seasoning or tamari with coconut aminos (soy-free seasoning) (page 15).

INGREDIENTS

2 cups cooked drained and rinsed chickpeas (19-oz can)

2 tbsp grapeseed oil

1 tbsp lemon zest (about 1 lemon) + a few strands for garnish

1 tbsp sesame seeds

1 tsp Bragg soy seasoning or tamari

1 tsp lemon & herb seasoning

½ tsp nutritional yeast

½ tsp salt

freshly ground black, to taste

DIRECTIONS

1. Preheat oven to 375°F.
2. Place 2 cups drained and rinsed chickpeas on a towel and pat dry, removing any skins that separate.
3. In a medium bowl, mix 2 cups chickpeas, 2 tbsp grapeseed oil, 1 tbsp each lemon zest and sesame seeds, 1 tsp each Bragg seasoning and lemon & herb seasoning, ½ tsp each nutritional yeast and salt, and freshly ground black pepper. Stir until chickpeas are well coated. Remove any skins that separate during the stirring process.
4. Spread coated chickpeas on a large baking sheet in a single layer and bake for 20 minutes, turning them at the 10-minute mark. For crunchier chickpeas, ensure there is space between each one. Turn off the heat and leave chickpeas in the cooling oven for 5–10 minutes to increase their crunch. (Chickpeas shrink during cooking.)
5. The chickpeas will be crispy when you first take them out of the oven and taste wonderful when served hot. Store leftovers overnight in an airtight container. They will retain their flavour but lose some of their crispiness, though they are still fantastic as a slightly chewy treat. Serve topped with a few strands of lemon zest.

 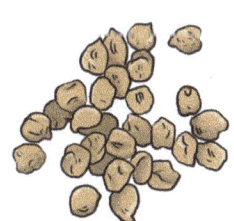

NUTRITION: *PER ¼-CUP SERVING: Calories 117; Carbs 12g; Fat 7g; Protein 4g; Sodium 303mg; Sugar 0g*

SALADS and DRESSINGS

Full-Meal Salads

On-the-Go Layered Salad with Orange-Tarragon Dressing	77
Quinoa Power Salad with Cilantro-Lime Dressing	79

Salads with Nuts

Mandarin Bliss Salad with Pecans and Slivered Almonds	81
Tasty Pear and Candied Walnut Salad with Cranberry Vinegar Dressing	83
Scrumptious Spinach Salad with Strawberries, Slivered Almonds, and Mint-Balsamic Dressing	85
Fresh Apple and Fennel Salad with Candied Pecans	87

Must-Try Salads

Vegan Caesar Salad with Tender and Crispy Croutons	89
Sweet and Complete Corn and Pea Salad	91

Easy Salads

Salad with Sliced Cabbage, Apple, Vinegar, and Caraway	93
Southwestern Salad	95

On-the-Go Layered Salad with Orange-Tarragon Dressing

prep time: 35 minutes + time to marinate   cook time: 10 minutes   makes: 4 x 3½-cup servings

    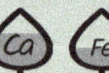   
Rich in

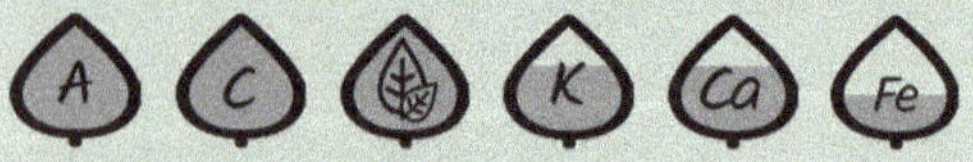

This Salad is perfect when you're headin' out on the range, going on a trek, or just need a quick lunch handy. Use wide-mouth glass jars — they look pretty and seal up tight. Plus, they don't give no back talk (not like some other big-mouth folks we know.) Put your dressing in first so it stays on the bottom of the jar until you're ready to chow down. Vary your veggies according to what you have on hand, but add the cooked veggies first. Place them directly on top of the dressing, followed by firm, non-porous veggies. From there, layer your veggies in lesser degrees of firmness. Top it all off with leafy greens. This trick of overlaying your ingredients guarantees nothing gets soggy and keeps the lettuce crisp. Finally, turn the jar upside down and shake it like crazy when you're ready to eat. That spreads the dressing throughout the salad, and then no matter where you may be, you can hunker down and enjoy a satisfying meal. You can either eat right out of the jar or spread your salad on a plate, but either way, you have an easy, healthy, and tasty lunch at your fingertips.

It is easy and fun to make your own sprouted lentils (page 22), but it does take a few days, so you'll need to start sprouting well in advance to use your own crop.

INGREDIENTS

ROASTED VEGGIES
(makes 4 cups)

- 1 tbsp grapeseed oil + ¼ tsp for greasing the pan
- ¼ cup balsamic vinegar
- 1 tbsp Bragg soy seasoning or tamari
- 1 tbsp minced garlic (about 6 cloves)
- 1 tbsp minced tarragon leaves
- ¼ tsp Spike all-purpose seasoning or Old Bay seasoning
- 1 medium butternut squash
- 1 small globe eggplant

ORANGE-TARRAGON DRESSING
(makes 1 cup)

- ¼ cup orange juice (about 1 orange)
- ¼ cup apple juice
- ¼ cup apple cider vinegar
- 2 tbsp minced tarragon leaves
- 1 tbsp grated ginger root
- 1 tbsp lime juice (about 1 lime)
- ¼ tsp Spike all-purpose seasoning or Old Bay seasoning
- freshly ground black pepper, to taste
- ¼ cup olive oil

OTHER INGREDIENTS

- 1 cup frozen shelled edamame beans + boiling water for soaking
- 1 medium carrot
- 1 medium red bell pepper
- ¼ head of cauliflower
- 2 cups sprouted lentils (page 22) or mixed bean sprouts
- 4 cups mixed salad greens, torn into bite-sized pieces

DIRECTIONS

1. Prepare **Roasted Veggies**:

    a. Preheat oven to 400°F. Spray baking sheet with oil or, using a pastry brush, spread a thin layer of oil on the sheet (¼ tsp oil).

    b. In a small dish, mix ¼ cup balsamic vinegar, 1 tbsp each grapeseed oil, Bragg seasoning, minced garlic, and minced tarragon leaves, and ¼ tsp Spike seasoning. Set marinade aside.

    c. Remove seeds and skin from 1 medium butternut squash and cut into bite-sized cubes (about 3 cups). Cut 1 small globe eggplant into cubes (about 2 cups). Place cut veggies into a medium bowl.

    d. Add marinade and toss veggies until they are well coated. Let sit for 10 minutes before cooking.

    e. Spread marinated veggies in a single layer on prepared baking sheet and cook for 10 minutes or until starting to brown and soften. Butternut squash will be on the firm side, which adds a nice crunchy texture.

2. Prepare **Orange-Tarragon Dressing**:

    a. In a medium bowl, mix ¼ cup each orange juice, apple juice, and apple cider vinegar, 2 tbsp minced tarragon leaves, 1 tbsp each grated ginger root and lime juice, ¼ tsp Spike seasoning, and freshly ground black pepper. While whisking, slowly drizzle in ¼ cup olive oil and whisk until the oil emulsifies with the remaining ingredients. Pour into a small jar, seal, and shake, then set aside to intensify the flavours. Shake before using.

    b. If you refrigerate the dressing, remove it a few hours before use to allow the oil to properly liquify. Shake before using.

3. In a small bowl, add 1 cup frozen shelled edamame beans and cover with boiling water. Let sit for 10 minutes, drain, and rinse.

4. While the beans soak, prepare the remaining ingredients. Peel and dice 1 medium carrot (about 1 cup), remove seeds and pulp from 1 medium red bell pepper and dice pepper (about 1 cup), and cut ¼ head of cauliflower into florets (about 1 cup). Place cut veggies into separate piles.

5. Wash and drain 2 cups sprouted lentils. Wash and dry 4 cups mixed salad greens.

6. Set aside 4 large (4-cup size) wide-mouth glass jars with lids: In the bottom of each jar, add ¼ cup salad dressing. (Shake dressing before pouring.) Then layer vegetables in each jar in this order: 1 cup roasted veggies, ¼ cup each diced carrot, cauliflower florets, diced red bell peppers, edamame, and ½ cup sprouted lentils. Top with 1 cup mixed salad greens.

7. Seal each jar with a lid and refrigerate until you are ready to enjoy a tasty salad. The prepared jars can be stored for several days.

8. When ready to eat, turn the jar upside down and shake to spread the dressing throughout the salad.

NUTRITION: PER 3½-CUP SERVING: *Calories 447; Carbs 60g; Fat 18g; Protein 17g; Sodium 491mg; Sugar 17g*

Quinoa Power Salad with Cilantro-Lime Dressing

prep time: 25 minutes + overnight soaking for stovetop method   cook time: 30 minutes + 90 minutes for stovetop method   makes: 4 x 2-cup servings

Rich in

When the crew is hankering for a tasty lunch, Quinoa Power Salad is a dang good option. Quinoa and black beans are mighty fine partners and, when rounded up together, provide a great source of plant protein. Paired with green bell peppers, tomatoes, and a zingy Cilantro-Lime Dressing, you'll have a meal that'll fire you up to face the day. Cooking dried beans takes a little longer than canned, but the effort is worth it. To save time, prepare the quinoa and beans the day before, then quickly toss the salad together just before lunch. Cuban-Style Black Beans make a satisfying side to any meal when you're looking for a little extra protein.

Bruising whole cloves of garlic releases a robust flavour. Simply use the flat side of a knife to press down on the cloves until they split.
Refrigerate any salad leftovers in an airtight container for a day or two.

INGREDIENTS

CUBAN-STYLE BLACK BEANS
(makes 2 cups)

- ¾ cup dried black beans or 19-oz can, cooked, drained, and rinsed
- ¼–¾ cup low-sodium vegetable broth
- ½–¾ cup water
- ½ cup chopped onion (about ½ small)
- 1 tbsp tomato paste
- 1 tsp dried mushroom powder
- ½ tsp ground cumin
- ½ tsp ground oregano
- ½ tsp salt
- ¼ tsp chili powder
- ¼ tsp dried chipotle pepper
- ¼ tsp ground black pepper
- 3 peeled and bruised garlic cloves
- 1 bay leaf
- 1 tbsp chopped cilantro leaves

CILANTRO-LIME DRESSING
(makes ½ cup)

- ¼ cup lime juice (3–4 limes)
- ¼ cup chopped cilantro leaves
- 1 tbsp maple syrup or raw blue agave nectar
- ½ tsp onion powder
- ½ tsp ground cumin
- ½ tsp salt
- ½ tsp Sriracha sauce or chili garlic sauce
- ¼ tsp garlic powder
- ¼ tsp chili powder
- ¼ cup olive oil

OTHER INGREDIENTS

- 1 cooked ear of corn or ¾ cup frozen corn kernels + boiling water for soaking
- 2 cups cooked tri-coloured quinoa
- 2 cups diced heirloom or field tomato, divided into 1½ cups + ½ cup (about 1 large)
- 1 cup diced green bell pepper (about 1 medium)
- ¼ cup sliced green onion (about 2 medium)
- 1 avocado
- cilantro leaves for garnish

DIRECTIONS

1. Prepare **Cuban-Style Black Beans**:

   a. Pressure cooker option: In an Instant Pot or pressure cooker, place ¾ cup dried black beans, ½ cup each low-sodium vegetable broth and water, ½ cup chopped onion, 1 tbsp tomato paste, 1 tsp dried mushroom powder, ½ tsp each ground cumin, ground oregano, and salt, ¼ tsp each chili powder, dried chipotle pepper, and ground black pepper, 3 peeled and bruised garlic cloves, and 1 bay leaf. Cook under pressure for 30 minutes and let the pressure release slowly (natural release) for at least 20 minutes.

   b. Stovetop option: Soak ¾ cup dried black beans overnight. Rinse well and add soaked beans to a medium pot. Add ¾ cup each low-sodium vegetable broth and water, along with the onion, tomato paste, dried mushroom powder, garlic, and all the dried herbs and spices (as per the Instant Pot option above). Bring to a boil, cover with a lid, and simmer for 1½–2 hours. Add more water during cooking as needed so beans do not dry out.

   c. Canned or pre-cooked beans option: In a medium frying pan on medium-high heat, cook ½ cup chopped onions in ¼ cup low-sodium vegetable broth until soft. Add 2 cups (19-oz can) drained and rinsed black beans, tomato paste, dried mushroom powder, garlic (mince the garlic first), and all the dried herbs and spices (as per the Instant Pot option above). Heat through, adding a little water if beans seem too dry.

   d. When the beans are done, add 1 tbsp chopped cilantro and remove from the heat source. Discard the bay leaf before serving.

2. Prepare **Cilantro-Lime Dressing**:

   a. In a medium bowl, mix ¼ cup each lime juice and chopped cilantro leaves, 1 tbsp maple syrup, ½ tsp each onion powder, ground cumin, salt, and Sriracha sauce, and ¼ tsp each garlic powder and chili powder. Whisk until well combined. While whisking, slowly drizzle in ¼ cup olive oil and continue whisking until the oil emulsifies with the remaining ingredients. Pour into a small jar, seal, and shake, then set aside to intensify the flavours. Shake before using.

   b. If you refrigerate the dressing, remove it a few hours before use to allow the oil to properly liquify. Shake before using.

3. Prepare corn kernels. If using fresh corn, stand an ear of cooked corn on a cutting board and cut down the sides of the cob to remove the kernels. If using frozen corn, place ¾ cup frozen kernels in a small bowl, cover with boiling water, and let sit for at least 10 minutes before draining and rinsing.

4. In a large bowl, mix 2 cups each cooked quinoa and prepared Cuban-Style Black Beans, 1½ cups diced heirloom tomatoes, 1 cup diced green bell pepper, ¾ cup prepared corn kernels, and ¼ cup sliced green onion. Pour Cilantro-Lime Dressing over the top and toss until well combined. Cut avocado in half, remove the pit, and slice.

5. Serve immediately. Divide salad among 4 bowls and garnish each serving with 2 tbsp diced tomato, avocado slices, and cilantro leaves.

NUTRITION: *PER 2-CUP SERVING:* Calories 628; Carbs 90g; Fat 26g; Protein 20g; Sodium 560mg; Sugar 10g

Mandarin Bliss Salad with Pecans and Slivered Almonds

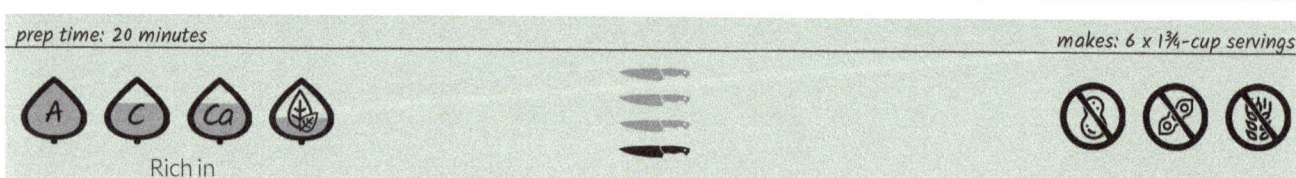

prep time: 20 minutes

Rich in

makes: 6 x 1¾-cup servings

Looking for a great way to wind down after a bustling day? Take a few bites of this delightful salad and bliss out in pure delight. Sink your teeth into hardy romaine lettuce, sweet mandarin oranges, crunchy nuts, and chewy cranberries to experience a bonanza of flavour. The tartness of the apple cider vinegar is balanced nicely with the sweetness of the Mandarin oranges and agave nectar, delivering a bounty of contrasting taste experiences. The Mandarin oranges are great to use in the winter, but in the summer, and just for fun, Cashew Sue's a fan of swapping out the orange sections for chopped, sweet mango. Potato Pat likes to serve the salad in chilled bowls — not only does it impress the townies, but the salad tastes better.

Instead of canned mandarin oranges, you can use 2 cups fresh chopped mango with ¼ cup fresh orange juice in the dressing. A Bermuda onion is a sweet, slightly flattish onion. Use any colour of Bermuda onion — the red one looks the nicest — or any other sweet onion.

INGREDIENTS

2 x 10-oz cans mandarin orange sections (about 2 cups), drained with juice reserved for dressing

SWEET APPLE CIDER VINEGAR DRESSING (makes ¾ cup)

¼ cup orange juice (from canned mandarin oranges)

¼ cup apple cider vinegar

¼ cup olive oil

1½ tbsp raw blue agave nectar

1 tbsp chopped green onion or 2 tbsp chopped chives (about ½ medium green onion)

2 tsp dry mustard

½ tsp Spike all-purpose seasoning or Old Bay seasoning

¼ tsp Tabasco or hot sauce

freshly ground black pepper, to taste

2 heads of romaine lettuce

½ cup pecan halves

½ cup slivered almonds

½ cup dried cranberries

¼ cup thinly sliced red Bermuda or other sweet onion

DIRECTIONS

1. Open 2 x 10-oz cans mandarin oranges. Set aside 2 cups mandarin orange sections. Drain and save the liquid in a separate bowl to use in the dressing (see below).

2. Prepare *Sweet Apple Cider Vinegar Dressing*:

    a. In a small jar or container with a lid, add ¼ cup each orange juice, apple cider vinegar, and olive oil, 1½ tbsp agave nectar, 1 tbsp chopped green onion, 2 tsp dry mustard, ½ tsp Spike seasoning, ¼ tsp Tabasco, and freshly ground black pepper.

    b. Seal and shake until ingredients are well combined, then set aside to intensify the flavours.

    c. If you refrigerate the dressing, remove it a few hours before use to allow the oil to properly liquify. Shake before using.

3. Wash, dry, and tear 2 heads of romaine lettuce into bite-sized pieces (about 8 cups) and place in a large salad bowl.

4. Add to the lettuce 2 cups drained mandarin orange sections, ½ cup each pecan halves, slivered almonds, and dried cranberries, and ¼ cup thinly sliced sweet onion.

5. If you are serving the entire salad, pour all the dressing over the salad and toss to mix before serving in the chilled bowls. However, if you are keeping some of the salad for another meal, add 2 tbsp salad dressing per bowl of salad and toss well. Refrigerate leftover salad and dressing separately.

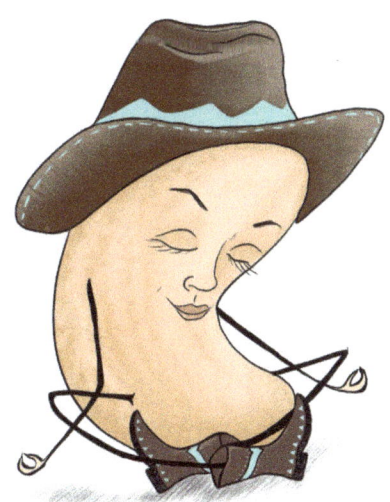

NUTRITION: PER 1¾-CUP SERVING: *Calories 353; Carbs 39g; Fat 22g; Protein 5g; Sodium 65mg; Sugar 30g*

Tasty Pear and Candied Walnut Salad with Cranberry Vinegar Dressing

prep time: 20 minutes   cook time: 10 minutes   makes: 6 x 2-cup servings

Rich in C K

When you're fixin' to serve up a fancy salad, this one fits the bill, and best of all, it's quick to make. The tangy Cranberry Vinegar Dressing perfectly matches the crispy, crunchy sweetness of green pears and candied walnuts over tender greens. The Candied Walnuts are always a favourite and are a pleasant surprise when hidden inside a bite of salad. These little nuggets are made in a cinch, but since they taste so good, you might be tempted to snack on them while tossing everything together. If that's the case, double the recipe so you can snack and still have enough candied walnuts for the salad.

Candied Walnuts can be made on their own and served as a sweet treat at the end of any meal. You can substitute with either cranberry or apple juice if you don't have frozen concentrated cranberry juice.

INGREDIENTS

CANDIED WALNUTS
(makes ½ cup)
- ½ cup raw walnuts
- 2 tbsp sugar
- 2 tbsp water

CRANBERRY VINEGAR DRESSING
(makes ⅔ cup)
- ⅓ cup olive oil
- ¼ cup red wine vinegar
- 2 tbsp frozen concentrated cranberry juice
- 1 tsp Dijon mustard
- ½ tsp Spike all-purpose seasoning or Old Bay seasoning
- ½ tsp ground allspice

OTHER INGREDIENTS
- 3 medium green pears
- 1 tbsp lemon juice (about ½ lemon)
- 1 tsp salt
- 10 cups mixed salad greens, torn into bite-sized pieces
- ½ cup dried cranberries

DIRECTIONS

1. Prepare **Candied Walnuts**:

   a. In a small saucepan, mix ½ cup raw walnuts with 2 tbsp each sugar and water. Cook on medium-high heat until sugar starts to dissolve.

   b. When mixture starts to boil, reduce to medium and cook for 10–20 minutes, stirring frequently. Cook until all liquid is absorbed.

   c. Line a baking sheet with parchment paper and arrange nuts in a single layer, well separated from each other. Let them dry.

2. Prepare **Cranberry Vinegar Dressing**:

   a. In a small jar or container with a lid, add ⅓ cup olive oil, ¼ cup red wine vinegar, 2 tbsp frozen concentrated cranberry juice, 1 tsp Dijon mustard, and ½ tsp each Spike seasoning and ground allspice.

   b. Seal and shake until ingredients are well combined, then set aside to intensify the flavours. Shake before using.

   c. If you refrigerate the dressing, remove it a few hours before use to allow the oil to properly liquify. Shake before using.

3. Peel, core, and slice 3 medium green pears (about 3 cups) and place in a medium bowl. Cover with 1 tbsp lemon juice and 1 tsp salt. Toss until pears are well coated. (This will ensure they do not oxidize and become brown.)

4. In a large salad bowl, combine 10 cups torn mixed salad greens, about 3 cups sliced pears, and ½ cup each candied walnuts and dried cranberries.

5. If you are serving the entire salad, pour all the dressing over the salad and toss to mix before dividing into 6 individual bowls. However, if keeping some of the salad for another meal, add 1½ tbsp salad dressing per bowl and toss well. Refrigerate leftover salad and dressing separately.

NUTRITION: *PER 2-CUP SERVING: Calories 284; Carbs 28g; Fat 19g; Protein 4g; Sodium 416mg; Sugar 21g*

Scrumptious Spinach Salad with Strawberries, Slivered Almonds, and Mint-Balsamic Dressing

prep time: 20 minutes   cook time: 5 minutes   makes: 4 x 2¼-cup servings

Rich in: A, C, Ca, (leaf), K

This salad's always a winner no matter how often it's served. The abundance of fresh ingredients and rip-roaringly delightful flavours create a darn delicious salad. By good rights, the dressing pulls it all together — the heavenly mix of earthy mint and sweetly acidic balsamic vinegar really sets off the delectable strawberries and tender spinach. (Baby spinach leaves and freshly toasted almonds are a must.) Serve this salad in chilled bowls for the pink of perfection.

A Bermuda onion is a sweet, slightly flattish onion. Use any colour of Bermuda onion — the red one looks the nicest. If not available, use any other sweet onion.
If you are not using the other half avocado right away, keep the pit intact, coat the avocado with a bit of lemon juice, and refrigerate for up to a day.

INGREDIENTS

MINT-BALSAMIC DRESSING
(makes ½ cup)

- 3 tbsp olive oil
- 2 tbsp orange juice (about half orange)
- 2 tbsp white balsamic vinegar
- 2 tbsp chopped mint leaves
- 1 tbsp lemon juice (about ½ lemon)
- 1 tsp cacao nibs or cocoa powder
- ¼ tsp salt
- ⅛ tsp ground cardamom
- freshly ground black pepper, to taste

OTHER INGREDIENTS

- ½ cup raw slivered almonds
- 6 cups baby spinach
- ½ slightly soft avocado
- 1 tsp lemon juice
- 3 cups sliced strawberries (about 36)
- ¼ cup thinly sliced red Bermuda or other sweet onion, divided into 3 tbsp + 1 tbsp

DIRECTIONS

1. Prepare *Mint-Balsamic Dressing*:

   a. In a small jar or container with a lid, mix 3 tbsp olive oil, 2 tbsp each orange juice, white balsamic vinegar, and chopped mint leaves, 1 tbsp lemon juice, 1 tsp cacao nibs, ¼ tsp salt, ⅛ tsp ground cardamom, and freshly ground black pepper.

   b. Seal and shake until ingredients are well combined, then set aside to intensify the flavours. Shake before using.

   c. If you refrigerate the dressing, remove it a few hours before use to allow the oil to properly liquify. Shake before using.

2. Preheat oven to 375°F.

3. Place ½ cup slivered almonds in a small roasting pan. Roast almonds for 5 minutes or until they start to brown. Remove from the oven and let cool.

4. Wash and drain 6 cups baby spinach. Tear into bite-sized pieces and place in a large salad bowl.

5. Remove the skin and pit from half of a slightly soft avocado. Dice into ¼-inch cubes, place in a separate bowl, and stir in 1 tsp lemon juice.

6. To the spinach leaves, add 3 cups sliced strawberries, ½ cup toasted slivered almonds, and 3 tbsp thinly sliced Bermuda onion. Gently toss to combine.

7. If you are serving the entire salad, pour all the dressing over the salad and toss gently before dividing into 4 individual bowls. Top each serving with 1 tbsp each diced avocado and sliced red onion. However, if keeping some of the salad for another meal, add 2 tbsp salad dressing per bowl and toss well. Garnish with the toppings. Refrigerate leftover salad, dressing, and toppings separately.

NUTRITION: PER 2¼-CUP SERVING: *Calories 279; Carbs 18g; Fat 21g; Protein 6g; Sodium 198mg; Sugar 10g*

Fresh Apple and Fennel Salad with Candied Pecans

prep time: 30 minutes + time to marinate   cook time: 10 minutes   makes: 4 x 2-cup servings

Rich in: A, C, [leaf], K, Fe

This fresh salad is sooo good that it oughta be forbidden. The Fuji apple is crisp and juicy with pretty pink speckled flesh and a flavour that walks a perfect line between sweet and tart. The combination of marinated Fuji apples with sweet butter lettuce, fresh fennel bulb, and candied pecans is so tempting fights may break out if there's not enough to go 'round. It's a nice touch to serve the salad in chilled bowls, which, without a doubt, highlight its crisp texture and bold flavours. This lovely late summer or early fall salad is quite simply second to none.

*Candied Pecans can be served on their own as a sweet treat at the end of any meal.
Zest the lemon before cutting and juicing.*

INGREDIENTS

LEMON-TARRAGON DRESSING
(makes ½ cup)
- 3 tbsp olive oil
- 2 tbsp lemon juice (about 1 lemon)
- 2 tbsp water
- 1 tbsp apple cider vinegar
- 1 tbsp minced tarragon leaves
- 1½ tsp lemon zest (about ½ lemon)
- ½ tsp sugar
- ¼ tsp salt
- ¼ tsp American saffron
- ¼ tsp white pepper
- pinch of chili powder

1 medium Fuji apple

CANDIED PECANS
(makes ½ cup)
- ½ cup raw pecans
- 2 tbsp sugar
- 2 tbsp water

1 large head of butter lettuce
1 small fennel bulb

DIRECTIONS

1. Prepare **Lemon-Tarragon Dressing**:

   a. In a small jar or container with a lid, add 3 tbsp olive oil, 2 tbsp each lemon juice and water, 1 tbsp each apple cider vinegar and minced tarragon, 1½ tsp lemon zest, ½ tsp sugar, ¼ tsp each salt, American saffron, and white pepper, and a pinch of chili powder.

   b. Seal and shake until ingredients are well combined, then set aside to intensify the flavours. Shake before using.

   c. If you refrigerate the dressing, remove it a few hours before use to allow the oil to properly liquify. Shake before using.

2. Peel, core, and slice a medium Fuji apple (about 1 cup) into a bowl. Pour the Lemon-Tarragon Dressing over the apples and toss until the fruit is well coated. Let marinate for about 30 minutes.

3. Prepare **Candy Pecans**: (Make these while the apples marinate.)

   a. In a small saucepan, mix ½ cup raw pecans and 2 tbsp each sugar and water. Cook on medium-high heat until sugar starts to dissolve.

   b. When the mixture starts to a boil, reduce to low, and cook for 7–10 minutes, stirring frequently. Cook until all liquid is absorbed.

   c. Line a baking sheet with parchment paper and arrange nuts in a single layer, well separated from each other. Let them dry.

4. Prepare other veggies. Wash a large head of butter lettuce and tear it into bite-sized pieces (about 6 cups). Thinly slice a small fennel bulb (about 1 cup). Place in a large salad bowl along with candied pecans, the marinated apples, and the dressing they were marinating in.

5. Toss until all ingredients are well coated. Divide equally among 4 chilled bowls. Serve immediately.

NUTRITION: *PER 2-CUP SERVING: Calories 270; Carbs 25g; Fat 20g; Protein 3g; Sodium 182mg; Sugar 17g*

Vegan Caesar Salad with Tender and Crispy Croutons

Vegan Caesar Salad: prep time: 25 minutes		makes: 4 x 2-cup servings
Tender and Crispy Croutons: prep time: 10 minutes	cook time: 15 minutes	makes: 4 x ½-cup servings
Farmesan: prep time: 5 minutes	cook time: 10 minutes	makes: 4 x 4-tsp servings

Rich in

There's simply no contest. This here Vegan Caesar Salad is hands down the best. Everyone loves it! Whenever there's even so much as a rumour that this salad is about to be tossed, anyone nearby'll start gathering 'round. Then they'll be laughing and jostling to get the best spot so they can be the first to dig in. Broccoli Bandit says the croutons are mandatory. Potato Pat is adamant it's the Farmesan that makes this salad the unanimous winner. However, Cashew Sue knows it's the dressing that's the star of this dish. Believe it! We have stumbled upon the perfect combination of flavours.

We like to double or triple the Farmesan and freeze the extra for up to 6 months until needed. Use Farmesan in place of parmesan cheese; it does not melt, but it adds a nice flavour and texture; we especially like it on pasta.
For soy-free, use soy-free vegan Worcestershire sauce and omit the Fake'n Bacon.
It can be Gluten-free, depending on what type of bread you use to make the croutons.

INGREDIENTS

VEGAN CAESAR DRESSING
(makes ¾ cup)

- ¼ cup raw cashews, soaked in water for at least 4 hours
- 2 tbsp cooked chickpeas
- 2 tbsp aquafaba (page 14)
- 2 tbsp olive oil
- 2 tbsp lemon juice (about 1 lemon)
- 1 tsp minced garlic (about 2 cloves)
- 1 tsp Bestcestershire Sauce (vegan Worcestershire sauce)
- 1 tsp capers, including caper liquid
- ½ tsp dry mustard
- ½ tsp nutritional yeast
- ¼ tsp salt
- freshly ground black pepper, to taste

TENDER CRISPY CROUTONS
(makes 2 cups)

- 4–6 slices stale whole-wheat French bread
- 2 tbsp olive oil
- 1½ tsp minced basil, parsley, or oregano leaves
- ¼ tsp garlic powder
- ¼ tsp dried minced onion
- ¼ tsp Spike all-purpose seasoning or Old Bay seasoning

FARMESAN *(makes ⅓ cup)*

- 3 tbsp raw slivered almonds
- 1½ tbsp raw pine nuts
- 1½ tbsp raw sesame seeds
- 1½ tsp nutritional yeast
- 1 tsp lemon zest (from ½ lemon)
- ⅛ tsp salt

OTHER INGREDIENTS

- 2 heads of romaine lettuce
- Fake'n Bacon (page 147) (optional)
- lemon wedges for garnish

DIRECTIONS

1. Prepare *Vegan Caesar Dressing*:

    a. Drain and rinse the soaked cashews. Place in a food processor or blender along with 2 tbsp each cooked chickpeas, aquafaba, olive oil, and lemon juice, 1 tsp each minced garlic, Bestcestershire Sauce, and capers (including caper liquid), ½ tsp each dry mustard and nutritional yeast, ¼ tsp salt, and freshly ground black pepper. Process until the dressing is smooth and creamy (3–5 minutes), scraping down sides as needed with a rubber spatula.

    b. If you refrigerate the dressing, remove it a few hours before use to allow the oil to properly liquify. Shake before using.

2. Prepare *Tender Crispy Croutons*:

    a. Preheat oven to 350°F.

    b. Tear 4–6 pieces of stale bread into bite-sized pieces (about 3 cups) and place in a large bowl. (The bread shrinks during cooking.)

    c. In a small bowl, mix 2 tbsp olive oil, 1½ tsp minced basil, and ¼ tsp each garlic powder, dried minced onion, and Spike seasoning. Stir until well combined, pour over bread pieces, and toss until well coated.

    d. Place bread in a single layer on a baking sheet and cook until crispy but not browned (10–15 minutes). You want your croutons to be tender and crispy but not too hard. Remove from the oven.

3. Prepare *Farmesan*: (Cook nuts and seeds at the same time as the croutons.)

    a. In a small roasting pan, mix 3 tbsp raw slivered almonds and 1½ tbsp each raw pine nuts and raw sesame seeds. Roast in preheated 350°F oven for 5–10 minutes or until brown. Remove from the oven and let cool.

    b. Place in a small food processor or blender and pulse until crumbly. Add 1½ tsp nutritional yeast, 1 tsp lemon zest, and ⅛ tsp salt, and pulse until everything turns to crumbs.

4. Remove the core from 2 heads of romaine lettuce. Tear the leaves lengthwise into 1-inch strips (about 8 cups). Wash and then dry the leaves before placing them into a large bowl.

5. If you are serving the entire salad, add 2 cups Tender and Crispy Croutons to the lettuce leaves, and pour ¾ cup Vegan Caesar Dressing over the lettuce. Toss well, divide the salad among 4 bowls, and garnish each serving with Farmesan and Fake'n Bacon (if using) and a couple of lemon wedges. Serve immediately. If you want to keep some of the salad for another meal, mix each serving separately with ½ cup croutons, 3 tbsp salad dressing, and the garnishes. Refrigerate leftover salad and toppings separately, and store croutons in an air-tight container at room temperature.

NUTRITION: SALAD ONLY (no croutons, Farmasen, or Fake'n Bacon) - *PER 2-CUP SERVING:* Calories 147; Carbs 10g; Fat 11g; Protein 4g; Sodium 195mg; Sugar 3g; **TENDER AND CRISPY CROUTONS** - *PER ½-CUP SERVING:* Calories 369; Carbs 55g; Fat 13g; Protein 12g; Sodium 350mg; Sugar 2g; **FARMESAN** - *PER 4-TBSP SERVING:* Calories 86; Carbs 2g; Fat 8g; Protein 3g; Sodium 73mg; Sugar 0g

Sweet and Complete Corn and Pea Salad

prep time: 30 minutes   cook time: 15 minutes   makes: 4 x 1½-cup servings

Rich in: C, (leaf), A, Fe, K

When someone your sweet on is heading over, and you want to serve up something special, this salad's sure to win the day. It's sweet, complete, and packs a punch. Not only 'cause the salad taste great, but it also provides a burst of complete protein — plus, it's pretty. The peas look beautiful against the yellow corn. In case you didn't already know, snow peas are sweet and flat, and you can eat them whole. Blanching the peas ensures they stay bright green and perfectly tender-crisp. To save time, put the corn on to boil while making the dressing and preparing the snow peas. Since corn on the cob is always a favourite, especially 'round here, we always make extra (which we enjoy with a dab of vegan butter and a sprinkle of salt).

If you do not use fresh corn on the cob, you can use 3 cups of frozen corn kernels. Cover with boiling water and let sit for 10 minutes before draining and rinsing.

A Bermuda onion is a sweet, slightly flattish onion. Use any colour of Bermuda onion — the red one looks the nicest. If not available, use any other sweet onion.

INGREDIENTS

GINGER-MINT DRESSING
(makes ½ cup)
- ¼ cup minced mint leaves
- 3 tbsp olive oil
- 2 tbsp lime juice (1–2 limes)
- 1 tbsp white balsamic vinegar
- 1 tbsp minced jalapeño pepper
- ½ tsp American saffron
- ½ tsp grated ginger root
- ¼ tsp salt
- freshly ground black pepper, to taste

OTHER INGREDIENTS
- 4 ears of shucked raw corn + water for cooking
- ½ tsp raw blue agave nectar
- 2 cups snow peas
- 2 bowls of iced water for cooling the corn and the peas
- 1 cup fresh or frozen green peas + boiling water for soaking
- 2 tbsp thinly sliced red Bermuda or other sweet onion
- sprig of mint for garnish

DIRECTIONS

1. Prepare **Ginger-Mint Dressing**:

    a. In a small jar or container with a lid, add ¼ cup minced mint leaves, 3 tbsp olive oil, 2 tbsp lime juice, 1 tbsp each white balsamic vinegar and minced jalapeño pepper, ½ tsp each American saffron and grated ginger root, ¼ tsp salt, and freshly ground black pepper.

    b. Seal and shake until ingredients are well combined, then set aside to intensify the flavours. Shake before using.

    c. If you refrigerate the dressing, remove it a few hours before use to allow the oil to properly liquify. Shake before using.

2. Place 4 ears of shucked raw corn in a large pot, cover with water, and add ½ tsp agave nectar. Cover with a lid and bring to a boil. Once the water starts to boil, turn off the heat and let the corn sit in the boiled water for 10 minutes.

3. While corn cooks, remove the end piece from 2 cups of snow peas.

4. Prepare 2 bowls of iced water to cool the corn and the peas.

5. Use tongs to remove cooked corn and submerge in a bowl of ice water to cool.

6. Bring the same large pot of water to a boil (you can use the same water). Put 2 cups of prepared peas into a large metal colander, lower into boiling water, turn off the heat, and blanch peas in hot water for 2 minutes. Remove the colander from the pot and empty the peas into a separate ice bath to stop further cooking.

7. Shuck 1 cup fresh green peas or place 1 cup frozen green peas in a small dish and cover with boiling water. Let sit for 10 minutes before draining and rinsing.

8. While the green peas soak, slice the kernels off the corncobs. Stand each ear of cooked corn on a cutting board and cut down the side of the cob to remove the kernels (about 3 cups). The kernels will naturally stay in clumps; if so, leave them intact.

9. In a large serving bowl, add about 3 cups sliced corn kernels, 2 cups blanched snow peas, 1 cup prepared green peas, and 2 tbsp sliced red Bermuda onion. Pour on the Ginger-Mint Dressing and toss until veggies are well coated.

10. Serve immediately or refrigerate until ready to eat. To serve, divide into 4 x 1½ cup servings and garnish each with a couple of mint leaves.

NUTRITION: *1½-CUP SERVING: Calories 317; Carbs 42g; Fat 13g; Protein 9g; Sodium 154mg; Sugar 14g*

Salad with Sliced Cabbage, Apple, Vinegar, and Caraway

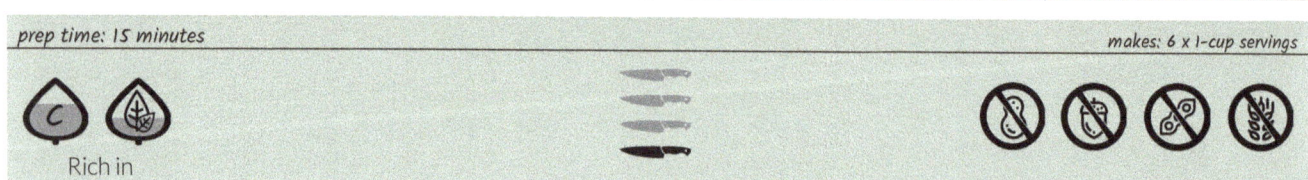

prep time: 15 minutes

makes: 6 x 1-cup servings

Rich in

Our Sliced Cabbage and Apple Salad with Vinegar and Caraway is what we call a "just 'cause" salad, just 'cause it's easy to make, easy to eat, and tastes great. This combination of ingredients blends together perfectly, creating a low-calorie snack or sensational addition to any meal. Carrot Rick, who is always looking for a healthier alternative, will often skip the oil just 'cause it still tastes great but has fewer calories. Keep the skin on the apple when you slice it so you don't miss out on all the beneficial nutrients hidden in the peel.

INGREDIENTS

½ head of green cabbage
1 large Red Delicious apple, unpeeled
¼ cup white vinegar
2 tbsp olive oil
2 tbsp apple cider vinegar
2 tbsp raw sunflower seeds
2 tbsp dried cranberries + a few for garnish
½ tsp ground allspice
½ tsp caraway seeds
½ tsp salt
freshly ground black pepper, to taste

DIRECTIONS

1. In a medium bowl, thinly slice ½ head of green cabbage (about 5 cups) and shred 1 large apple, excluding the core (about 1 cup).

2. Add ¼ cup white vinegar, 2 tbsp each olive oil, apple cider vinegar, sunflower seeds, and dried cranberries, ½ tsp each ground allspice, caraway seeds, and salt, and freshly ground black pepper.

3. Toss until well coated and serve immediately. Top each serving with a few dried cranberries. Refrigerate any leftovers.

NUTRITION: *PER 1-CUP SERVING: Calories 102; Carbs 12g; Fat 6g; Protein 2g; Sodium 223mg; Sugar 4g*

Southwestern Salad

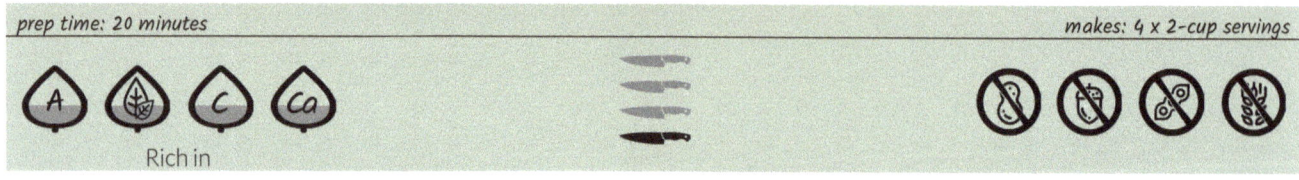

prep time: 20 minutes | makes: 4 x 2-cup servings

Rich in

Make this Southwestern Salad just 'cause it tastes soo good! The curly lettuce is deemed essential, as it provides a crunchy base where little pockets of Cilantro-Lime Dressing can gather. We love to top this salad with Fresh Tomato Salsa and Easy Guacamole. This dish is one of our go-tos when we're craving a satisfying side dish. But it also works as an above-board full-meal deal when you and your kinfolk are dreadful hungry. Especially when paired with Chipotle Cornbread (page 137) and blue corn chips.

INGREDIENTS

1 cooked ear of corn or ¾ cup frozen corn kernels + boiling water for soaking

1 head of green or red curly lettuce

1 cup cooked black beans

1 cup chopped tomato (about 1 large)

1 cup sliced green cabbage (about ⅛ head)

⅓ cup sliced green onion (about 3 medium)

½ cup Cilantro-Lime Dressing (page 79)

¼ cup broken blue corn chips

Fresh Tomato Salsa (page 51) (optional)

Easy Guacamole (page 183 (optional)

DIRECTIONS

1. Prepare corn kernels. If using fresh, slice the kernels off the cob. Stand an ear of the cooked corn on a cutting board and cut down the side of the cob to remove the kernels. The kernels will stay in clumps naturally. If so, leave them intact (about ¾ cup). If using frozen, place ¾ cup frozen corn in a small bowl and cover with boiling water. Let sit for 10 minutes before draining and rinsing.

2. Wash and dry 1 head of green curly lettuce and tear leaves into bite-sized pieces (about 4 cups). Place in a large salad bowl along with 1 cup each cooked black beans, chopped tomato, and sliced green cabbage, ¾ cup corn kernels, and ⅓ cup sliced green onion. Pour ½ cup Cilantro-Lime Dressing over the salad and toss to coat. Top with Fresh Tomato Salsa, Easy Guacamole, and a sprinkling of broken blue corn chips.

NUTRITION: SOUTHWESTERN SALAD ONLY (no tomato salsa or guacamole) - *PER 2-CUP SERVING: Calories 258; Carbs 27g; Fat 16g; Protein 6g; Sodium 495mg; Sugar 8g*

SOUPS

Creamy Soups

Hardy Mushroom Soup with Tender and Crispy Croutons	99
Broccoli Bandit Soup with Cashew Creme Fraîche	101
Roasted Pumpkin Soup	103

Lentil Soups

Lentil and Vegetable Medley Soup	105
Nuggets from Heaven: Squash, Lentil, and Chickpea Soup	107

Other High-Protein Soups

Badass Black Bean Soup	109
Fasolada Greek-Style Bean Soup	111

Comfort Soups

Infamous Ramen	113
Mighty Minestrone	115

Hardy Mushroom Soup with Tender and Crispy Croutons

prep time: 25 minutes   cook time: 40 minutes   makes: 4 x 2-cup servings

Rich in: A, Ca, (leaf), Fe, K

"Woohoo!" That's what we always hear when this creamy mushroom soup is brewing. The magnificent melding of flavours comes from the perfect combination of mushrooms, herbs, and wine, and it's not to be missed. Never mind the fact that you can eat it guilt-free (not only 'cause it's vegan, but also 'cause it's got no added oil, and it's chock-full of healthy stuff). If you're looking to serve up a meal to remember, garnish the soup with a few slices of fresh mushroom, a little minced thyme, and Tender and Crispy Croutons. Then serve it up with sourdough bread and be greeted by happy smiles and groans of delight.

For nut-free, replace cashew milk with vegan nut-free milk of your choice.
For soy-free, replace Bragg soy seasoning or tamari with coconut aminos (soy-free seasoning) (page 15).
For gluten-free, use gluten-free flour as a thickener, and omit the croutons.
For low-fat, replace coconut milk with vegan milk of your choice.

INGREDIENTS

3¼ cups mushroom broth, divided into ¼ cup + ½ cup + 2½ cups

1 cup diced onion (about ½ medium)

¼ cup Bragg soy seasoning or tamari

1 tbsp paprika

1 tbsp dried mushroom powder

½ tsp Spike all-purpose seasoning or Old Bay seasoning

¼ tsp ground allspice

freshly ground black pepper, to taste

8 cups sliced mushroom (about 32 medium) + a few slices for garnish

⅓ cup all-purpose flour

2 tbsp arrowroot powder

½ cup red wine (medium-bodied, like a merlot)

Milk Mixture (makes 3 cups)
   2 cups oat milk
   ¾ cup cashew milk
   ¼ cup coconut milk

1 tbsp minced thyme leaves + a small amount for garnish

20–24 Tender Crispy Croutons (page 89) (optional for garnish)

DIRECTIONS

1. Place a large soup pot on medium-high heat and add ¼ cup mushroom broth. Once hot, add 1 cup diced onion and sauté until translucent and beginning to darken (about 5 minutes). Add a little water if onions begin to stick, but let the broth cook off so onions can brown. If they become too dry, onions may burn.

2. Add ¼ cup Bragg seasoning, 1 tbsp each paprika and dried mushroom powder, ½ tsp Spike seasoning, ¼ tsp ground allspice, and freshly ground black pepper. Stir until well combined and cook for 1–2 minutes to enhance the flavour. Add a little water if the ingredients start to stick.

3. Add 8 cups sliced mushroom, stir until well combined, and reduce to medium heat. Continue to sauté until all liquid has cooked off and mushrooms are tender and brown (about 10 minutes). Remove from heat.

4. In a sealable container, sift ⅓ cup all-purpose flour and 2 tbsp arrowroot powder. Slowly add ½ cup mushroom broth and stir continuously to create a paste. Seal the container and shake well to continue mixing, removing any lumps. This is crucial to ensure you have a smooth, lump-free soup. Once the mixture is smooth and creamy, slowly pour into cooked mushrooms, stirring continuously until well combined.

5. Slowly add ½ cup red wine and stir until well combined. Pour in the remaining 2½ cups mushroom broth and stir until well combined.

6. Return the pot to medium heat and bring to a low boil. Continue to cook for an additional 5–7 minutes or until the soup thickens and the flour is fully cooked.

7. Add 3 cups Milk Mixture (2 cups oat milk, ¾ cup cashew milk, and ¼ cup coconut milk) and 1 tbsp minced thyme leaves. Stir until well combined. Simmer until heated through (8–10 minutes).

8. Serve immediately and garnish each bowl with a few slices of fresh mushrooms, a sprinkle of minced thyme, and 5–6 Tender Crispy Croutons.

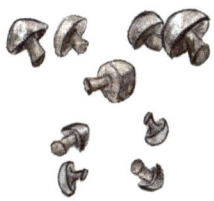

NUTRITION: *PER 2-CUP SERVING (without croutons): Calories 181; Carbs 24g; Fat 5g; Protein 10g; Sodium 1,483mg; Sugar 4g*

Broccoli Bandit Soup with Cashew Creme Fraîche

Broccoli Bandit Soup: prep time: 15 minutes	cook time: 40 minutes	makes: 6 x 1⅔-cup servings
Cashew Creme Fraîche: prep time: 15 minutes		makes: 6 x 1⅓-tbsp servings

Rich in

Jump on the broccoli bandwagon and head over to healthy street. Broccoli Bandit, Cashew Sue, and their friends Sweet Potato and Herbs — who are always up for some fun — turn the typical, humdrum cream of broccoli soup into a super tasty, nutritious, and outstandingly rich soup. When served hot with a heaping teaspoonful of Cashew Creme Fraîche and Garlic Parsley Bread (page 139) (or a nice loaf of whole-wheat sourdough bread), you'll experience for yourself the true meaning of warm and hardy comfort food.

Cashew Creme Fraîche makes a good base for a dip, or you can scoop it on vegan chili for a nice treat. Double or triple the recipe and then freeze for up to 6 months in ½-cup containers for easy use when you need it.
For low-fat, omit Cashew Creme Fraîche.

INGREDIENTS

CASHEW CREME FRAÎCHE
(makes ½ cup)

- ⅓ cup raw cashews, soaked for at least 4 hours
- 2 tbsp raw pine nuts, soaked for at least 4 hours
- 4+ tsp cashew milk
- 4 tsp lemon juice (½–1 lemon)
- 4 tsp coconut oil
- ¼ tsp salt
- pinch of ground nutmeg

OTHER INGREDIENTS

- 5¼ cups low-sodium vegetable broth, divided into ¼ cup + 5 cups
- 2 cups diced onion (about 1 medium)
- 1½ tsp minced garlic (about 3 cloves)
- ½ tsp dried dill
- 4 cups diced potato, use a combination of white and sweet potato (about 3 medium)
- 1 tsp salt
- 4 cups chopped broccoli, florets and stalks + a few florets for garnish
- ¼ cup chopped mint leaves
- 2 tbsp chopped tarragon leaves + a small amount for garnish
- freshly ground black pepper, to taste

DIRECTIONS

1. Prepare *Cashew Creme Fraîche*:

    a. Drain and rinse the soaked cashews and pine nuts. Place in a food processor or blender with 4 tsp each cashew milk, lemon juice, and coconut oil, ¼ tsp salt, and a pinch of ground nutmeg. Process until smooth and creamy (10–15 minutes), scraping down sides as needed with a rubber spatula.

    b. If you feel the Cashew Creme Fraîche is too thick, you can add more cashew milk, 1 tsp at a time, to adjust the thickness to the desired consistency.

2. Place a large soup pot on medium-high heat and add ¼ cup low-sodium vegetable broth. Once hot, add 2 cups diced onion and sauté until translucent and beginning to darken (about 5 minutes). Let the broth cook off so onions can brown, but add a little water if they begin to stick. If they become too dry, onions may burn.

3. Add 1½ tsp minced garlic and ½ tsp dried dill. Stir until well combined before adding 4 cups diced potatoes and 1 tsp salt. Cook until potatoes soften (about 15 minutes). Stir often, and add a little water if potatoes start to stick.

4. Add 4 cups chopped broccoli and cook an additional 10 minutes or until broccoli softens.

5. Add 5 cups low-sodium vegetable broth, ¼ cup chopped mint leaves, 2 tbsp chopped tarragon leaves, and freshly ground black pepper. Cook for another 10 minutes. Remove from heat and, using an immersion blender, blend about a third of the mixture. Alternatively, place a third of the mixture in a food processor or blender, process it, and return the blended portion to the pot.

6. Add ⅓ cup Cashew Creme Fraîche and stir until well combined. If you don't have Cashew Creme Fraîche and don't feel like making any the soup still tastes great, but lacks the creamy texture.

7. Divide among bowls and serve hot. Garnish each serving with a heaping teaspoonful of Cashew Creme Fraîche, a couple of broccoli florets, and a sprinkling of chopped tarragon.

NUTRITION: SOUP ONLY (without Cashew Creme Fraîche) - *PER 1⅔-CUP SERVING: Calories 120; Carbs 25g; Fat 0g; Protein 5g; Sodium 565mg; Sugar 6g;* **CASHEW CREME FRAÎCHE** - *PER 1⅓-TBSP SERVING: Calories 89; Carbs 3g; Fat 8g; Protein 2g; Sodium 377mg; Sugar 0g*

Roasted Pumpkin Soup

prep time: 20 minutes   cook time: 30 minutes   makes: 4 x 1½-cup servings

Rich in: A, C, Ca, K

This mouthwatering soup is creamy, spicy, and savoury. Everyone loves it. We like to roast sweet cooking pumpkins when they're readily available (usually in October) to make Creamy Pumpkin Pie (page 219). But we always have extra roasted meat. So, if you're feeling peckish and want something delicious to eat, grab the leftover pumpkin flesh and stew up a special treat. But don't let the lack of pumpkin stop you from enjoying the deep rich flavour of this dish. You can always substitute with roasted butternut squash. If you want a little extra protein or something you can sink your teeth into, throw in a cup of cooked chickpeas, but hold off adding them until all the blending's done. The type of squash you use has a significant impact on your end result, so be sure to use the flesh from sweet cooking pumpkins and not the jack-o'-lantern type.

INGREDIENTS

2 cups low-sodium vegetable broth, divided into ¼ cup + ½ cup + 1¼ cups

2 cups diced onion (about 1 medium)

2 tbsp water

1 tbsp grated ginger root

1 tsp garam masala

½ tsp turmeric

¼ tsp chili powder

2 medium Golden Delicious apples, peeled, cored, and chopped (about 2 cups)

2 cups roasted pumpkin purée (page 21)

2 cups coconut milk, divided into 1¾ cups + ¼ cup for garnish

1 tsp salt

3 lime leaves, divided into 2 leaves + 1 snipped leaf for garnish (page 19)

2 tbsp roasted pumpkin seeds for garnish

DIRECTIONS

1. Place a large soup pot on medium-high heat and add ¼ cup low-sodium vegetable broth. Once hot, add 2 cups diced onion and sauté until translucent and beginning to darken (about 5 minutes). Let the broth cook off so onions can brown, but add a little water if they begin to stick. If they become too dry, onions may burn.

2. In a small dish, add 2 tbsp water, 1 tbsp grated ginger root, 1 tsp garam masala, ½ tsp turmeric, and ¼ tsp chili powder. Mix into a paste.

3. Add spice paste to onions and cook for a few minutes. Add a little water if the ingredients begin to stick.

4. Add about 2 cups of chopped apples and cook for 5 minutes. Add ½ cup low-sodium vegetable broth and cook for an additional 10 minutes or until apples soften.

5. Add 2 cups roasted pumpkin purée, 1¾ cups coconut milk, 1¼ cups low-sodium vegetable broth, and 1 tsp salt. Remove from heat.

6. Purée with an immersion blender. Alternatively, place the mixture in a food processor or blender, process it, and return the blended mixture to the pot.

7. Add 2 lime leaves and simmer on medium-low heat for 5–10 minutes or until soup is heated through. Stir until heated, and add a little low-sodium vegetable broth if it is too thick. Remove lime leaves before serving.

8. Divide soup into 4 bowls, top each with a dab of coconut milk, a couple of roasted pumpkin seeds, and a few snips of lime leaf.

NUTRITION: PER 1½-CUP SERVING: *Calories 305; Carbs 25g; Fat 21g; Protein 3g; Sodium 683mg; Sugar 12g*

Lentil and Vegetable Medley Soup

prep time: 25 minutes   *cook time: 35 minutes*   *makes: 4 x 2-cup servings*

Rich in: C, A, (leaf), Fe, K

This soup's so good it'll make you sing. Whenever Cashew Sue stews up a pot of this savoury dish, you can hear her humming notes of joy. The combined flavours of ginger and turmeric mingling with red lentils, potatoes, and cauliflower create a medley of hardy satisfaction. Turmeric lifts the soup to a nifty yellow, the kale and cilantro add lovely green flecks, and the red bell pepper and tomato deliver a few bright notes. Cook up a big pot and refrigerate any leftovers. The flavour just keeps intensifying over time. Enjoy with Parsley Garlic Bread (page 139), sourdough bread, or crackers. Since this soup freezes well, make up a pot ahead of time and then pop it in the freezer. That way, it's ready anytime for a quick meal or to serve up when the neighbour folk stop over for a last-minute visit.

For soy-free, replace Bragg soy seasoning or tamari with coconut aminos (soy-free seasoning) (page 15) and use soy-free vegan Worcestershire sauce.

INGREDIENTS

- 4¼ cups low-sodium vegetable broth, divided into ¼ cup + 4 cups
- 1 cup diced onion (about ½ medium)
- 1 tbsp Bragg soy seasoning or tamari
- 1 tbsp grated ginger root
- 1½ tsp minced garlic (about 3 cloves)
- 1 tsp Bestcestershire Sauce (vegan Worcestershire sauce)
- 1 tsp turmeric
- 1 tsp cumin seeds
- ½ tsp red pepper flakes
- 2 cups diced yellow potatoes (1–2 medium)
- 1 tsp salt, divided into 2 x ½ tsp
- 2 cups chopped cauliflower (about ½ large head)
- 1 cup chopped leek (about 1 medium)
- 1 cup dried red lentils
- 1 cup chopped kale or spinach (or combination of both)
- 1 cup diced tomato (about 1 large)
- 1 cup water
- 1 cup diced red bell pepper (about 1 medium) + a few for garnish
- 2 tbsp chopped cilantro leaves + a small amount for garnish
- 1 tbsp lemon juice (about ½ lemon)

DIRECTIONS

1. Place a large soup pot on medium-high heat and add ¼ cup low-sodium vegetable broth. Once hot, add 1 cup diced onion and cook until translucent and beginning to darken (about 5 minutes). Let the broth cook off so onions can brown, but add a little water if they begin to stick. If they become too dry, onions may burn.

2. Add 1 tbsp each Bragg seasoning and grated ginger root, 1½ tsp minced garlic, 1 tsp each Bestcestershire Sauce, turmeric, and cumin seeds, and ½ tsp red pepper flakes. Cook for 1–2 minutes to let flavours meld and for the ginger and garlic to soften. Add a little water if the ingredients start to stick.

3. Add 2 cups diced potato and ½ tsp salt. Cook until potatoes start to soften (about 10 minutes), stirring often. Add a little water if they begin to stick.

4. Add 2 cups chopped cauliflower and 1 cup chopped leek. Cook until veggies start to soften (about 5 minutes). Add a little water if the ingredients start to stick.

5. Add 1 cup each dried red lentils, chopped kale, and diced tomato, and ½ tsp salt. Stir until well combined and cook for 1–2 minutes to let the flavours meld and the lentils start to soften. Add a little water if the ingredients begin to stick.

6. Add 4 cups low-sodium vegetable broth and 1 cup water and bring to a boil. Reduce to medium-low, cover with a lid, and simmer for 15–20 minutes or until vegetables and lentils are soft.

7. Stir in 1 cup diced red peppers, 2 tbsp chopped cilantro, and 1 tbsp lemon juice. Remove from stovetop. Let sit 5 minutes before serving, garnishing each portion with diced red pepper and a sprinkling of chopped cilantro.

NUTRITION: *PER 2-CUP SERVING: Calories 314; Carbs 59g; Fat 1g; Protein 20g; Sodium 1,000mg; Sugar 12g*

Nuggets from Heaven: Squash, Lentil, and Chickpea Soup

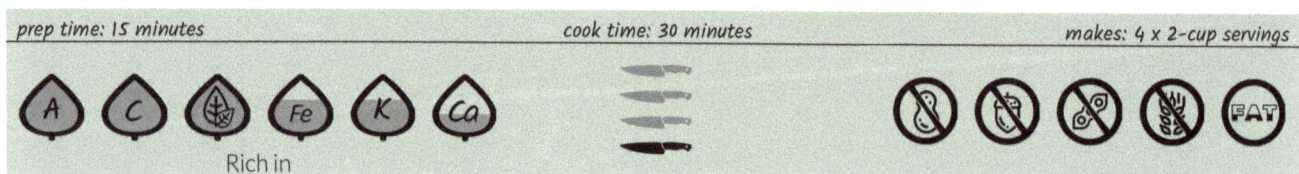

prep time: 15 minutes • cook time: 30 minutes • makes: 4 x 2-cup servings

Rich in: A, C, (leaf), Fe, K, Ca

This squash, lentil, and chickpea soup is filled with healthy nuggets of heavenly delight. This soup looks pretty, tastes terrific, and is sure to tempt any doubter 'cause it's filled with bountiful morsels that feed the body and satisfy the soul. With the addition of parsley, lemon, and a few spices, you'll discover a divine soup that'll have you and your posse revelling in delight. Potato Pat loves to serve it with Garlic Parsley Bread (page 139) and a spot of light-bodied red wine.

Cook up some dried chickpeas in advance or simply open a 13.5-oz can (which is 1½ cups of drained beans). Drain and save the chickpea water from the can for later use as aquafaba (aka: egg white substitute) (page 14).

INGREDIENTS

4¼ cups low-sodium vegetable broth, divided into ¼ cup + 4 cups

½ cup minced onion

1 tsp minced garlic (about 2 cloves)

1 tsp cumin seeds

1 small butternut squash

½ tsp cayenne pepper

½ tsp salt, divided into 2 x ¼ tsp

1 lemon

¼ cup tomato paste

2 cups cooked brown or black lentils

1½ cups cooked chickpeas

¼ cup chopped parsley leaves + a few for garnish

DIRECTIONS

1. Place a large soup pot on medium-high heat and add ¼ cup low-sodium vegetable broth. Once hot, add ½ cup minced onion and cook until translucent and beginning to darken (about 5 minutes). Let the broth cook off so onions can brown, but add a little water if they begin to stick. If they become too dry, onions may burn.

2. Add 1 tsp each minced garlic and cumin seeds and cook 1–2 minutes. Add a little water if they start to stick.

3. Peel, seed, and chop 1 small butternut squash (about 2 cups). Then add to cooked onions along with ½ tsp cayenne pepper and ¼ tsp salt. Cook until squash starts to soften (5–10 minutes). Add a little water if the ingredients begin to stick.

4. While the squash cooks, wash and cut lemon into wedges.

5. Add ¼ cup tomato paste to the soup pot and stir until the squash is well coated. Add 2 cups cooked lentils, 1½ cups cooked chickpeas, 4 cups low-sodium vegetable broth, ¼ tsp salt, and a couple of lemon wedges. Stir until well combined, cover with a lid, reduce heat, and simmer until squash is tender (about 15 minutes).

6. Discard lemon wedges, then add ¼ cup chopped parsley leaves. Serve immediately with remaining lemon wedges and a sprinkling of chopped parsley.

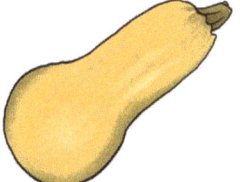

NUTRITION: *PER 2-CUP SERVING: Calories 290; Carbs 55g; Fat 2g; Protein 15g; Sodium 574mg; Sugar 7g*

SOUPS - LENTIL SOUPS

Badass Black Bean Soup

prep time: 20 minutes cook time: 50 minutes makes: 6 x 2-cup servings

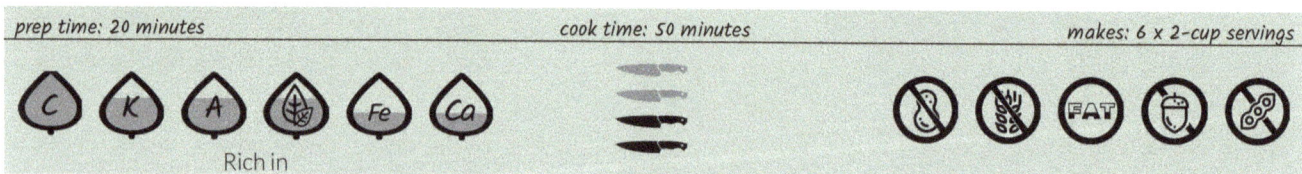

Rich in

A badass is the best of the best, and this Badass Black Bean Soup is the boss with the biggest flavour and the perfect blend of spices. Hardy black beans, mildly sweet zucchini, and earthy broccoli join forces to deliver a tasty base. Jalapeño pepper adds a little heat, especially if you include the seeds. For less hotness, remove the seeds before chopping. For a milder soup, replace the jalapeño with ¼ cup chopped poblano, and for no heat, use ¼ cup green bell pepper. Sweet, tangy sun-dried tomatoes add depth, and fresh diced tomatoes and minced oregano create a satisfying freshness. If you are in the mood and want a creamier soup, add a dollop of Cashew Creme Fraîche or Easy Guacamole. The long and the short of it is that you won't want to miss serving up this soup to your hungry gang.

You can easily substitute sun-dried tomatoes packed in olive oil for the dry-packed version, but this will slightly increase the fat grams.
For nut-free, omit Cashew Creme Fraîche.
For soy-free, replace Bragg soy seasoning or tamari with coconut aminos (soy-free seasoning) (page 15) and use soy-free vegan Worcestershire sauce.

INGREDIENTS

- 4¼ cups low-sodium vegetable broth, divided into ¼ cup + 4 cups
- 1 cup diced onion (about ½ medium)
- 1 medium jalapeño pepper or ¼ cup chopped poblano or green bell pepper
- 1 tsp cumin seeds
- ¼ cup tomato paste
- 1 tbsp Bragg soy seasoning or tamari
- 1 tbsp minced garlic (about 6 cloves)
- 1 tsp Bestcestershire Sauce (vegan Worcestershire sauce)
- 1 tsp paprika
- ½ tsp ground cumin
- ½ tsp cayenne pepper
- ½ tsp Spike all-purpose seasoning or Old Bay seasoning
- 2 medium zucchinis, diced (about 2 cups)
- 1 medium broccoli crown, florets and stems cut into bite-sized pieces (about 2 cups)
- ⅓ cup chopped sun-dried tomato, dry-packed
- ½ tsp salt
- 2 cups cooked, drained, and rinsed black beans
- 1 large red bell pepper, diced, pulp and seeds removed (1½ cups), divided into about 1 cup + ½ cup
- 4 cups water
- ¼ cup chopped oregano or marjoram leaves + 1 tbsp for garnish
- 1 small tomato, diced (about ½ cup)
- Cashew Creme Fraîche (page 101) (optional)
- Easy Guacamole (page 183) (optional)

DIRECTIONS

1. Place a large soup pot on medium-high heat and add ¼ cup low-sodium vegetable broth. Once hot, add 1 cup diced onion and cook until translucent and beginning to darken (about 5 minutes). Add a little water if onions start to stick, but let the broth cook off a bit so onions can brown. If they become too dry, onions may burn.

2. While onions cook, chop 1 jalapeño pepper (makes about 2 tbsp). Remove the seeds first if you do not like too much heat (or use ¼ cup of a milder green pepper).

3. To the cooked onions, add 1 tsp cumin seeds and cook for a few minutes. Add a little water if the ingredients begin to stick.

4. Add ¼ cup tomato paste, about 2 tbsp minced jalapeño, 1 tbsp each Bragg seasoning and minced garlic, 1 tsp each Bestcestershire Sauce and paprika, and ½ tsp each ground cumin, cayenne pepper, and Spike seasoning. Stir until well combined and cook for 1–2 minutes to let the flavours seal into onions. Add a little water if the ingredients start to stick.

5. Add about 2 cups each diced zucchini and cut broccoli, ⅓ cup chopped sun-dried tomato, and ½ tsp salt. Stir well and cook for 5–10 minutes. Add a little water if the ingredients begin to stick.

6. Add 2 cups cooked black beans and about 1 cup diced red pepper. Stir until well combined and cook for 1–2 minutes before adding 4 cups each low-sodium vegetable broth and water and ¼ cup chopped oregano leaves. Bring to a boil, then reduce heat and simmer for 30 minutes or until vegetables are tender.

7. Using an immersion blender, purée about a quarter of the ingredients. Alternatively, place a quarter of the mixture in a food processor or blender, process, and return the blended portion to the pot.

8. Stir until well combined and let sit for at least 30 minutes to allow the flavour to fully develop.

9. Divide evenly among six bowls. Garnish each serving with 1 tbsp of fresh diced tomato and diced red pepper, a dollop of Cashew Creme Fraîche and Easy Guacamole (if using), and a sprinkle of oregano leaves.

NUTRITION: *PER 2-CUP SERVING (without toppings):* Calories 168; Carbs 34g; Fat 1g; Protein 8g; Sodium 619mg; Sugar 8g

Fasolada Greek-Style Bean Soup

prep time: 30 minutes | cook time: 40 minutes | makes: 4 x 2-cup servings

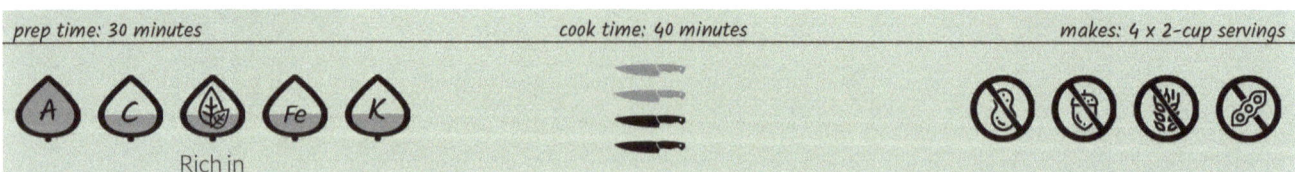

Rich in: A, C, (plant), Fe, K

Here in the village of Livewood, we open our hearts to everyone, and we love creating dishes that honour different cultures. Saucy Peanut is a big fan of fasolada, a fulfilling and nurturing bean soup that's a staple in Greece. This here is our version, and keeping in mind that Fasolada means "bean," we've *been* able to create a delicious, nutritious recipe that honours the Greek tradition. This one's a true winner, made by simmering white beans with tomatoes and vegetables, then serving it topped with olive oil and a sprinkling of herbs. It warms not only the tummy but also the heart and the soul. We recommend you make a big pot, refrigerate the leftovers, and enjoy it over several days as the flavour just keeps improving over time. Serve with Greek salad, mixed olives, and warm sourdough bread for a mighty fine meal. Another sure-fire notion is cooking up extra, then freezing the leftovers so you can enjoy it all over again in a few weeks.

For soy-free, replace Bragg soy seasoning or tamari with coconut aminos (soy-free seasoning) (page 15).

INGREDIENTS

¼ cup olive oil, divided into 1 tbsp + 2 tbsp + 4 x ¾ tsp

¾ cup diced onion (about ⅓ large)

1 tbsp tomato paste

2 tsp Bragg soy seasoning or tamari

1 tsp minced garlic (about 2 cloves)

½ tsp paprika

3 medium carrots, cut into half circles (about 1½ cups)

3 stalks celery including leaves, diced (about 1½ cups)

4 cups water

2 cups cooked, drained, and rinsed white navy beans

1 cup low-sodium vegetable broth

1 medium tomato, diced (about ¾ cup)

2 tbsp minced parsley leaves + small amount to use as garnish

1 tbsp minced mint leaves

1 tsp salt

1 bay leaf

2 tbsp lemon juice, divided into 1 tbsp + 4 x ¾ tsp (about 1 lemon)

2 tsp balsamic vinegar

freshly ground black pepper, to taste

DIRECTIONS

1. Place a large soup pot on medium-high heat and add 1 tbsp olive oil. Once hot, add ¾ cup diced onion and sauté until translucent and beginning to darken (about 5 minutes).

2. Add 1 tbsp tomato paste, 2 tsp Bragg seasoning, 1 tsp minced garlic, and ½ tsp paprika. Cook for 1–2 minutes before adding about 1½ cups each cut carrots and diced celery. Cook for about 5 minutes or until veggies start to soften.

3. Add 4 cups water, 2 cups cooked white navy beans, 1 cup low-sodium vegetable broth, about ¾ cup diced tomato, 2 tbsp minced parsley leaves, 1 tbsp minced mint leaves, 1 tsp salt, and 1 bay leaf. Reduce heat and simmer for another 20–30 minutes until everything is soft and tender.

4. Just before serving, remove the bay leaf. Add 2 tbsp olive oil, 1 tbsp lemon juice, 2 tsp balsamic vinegar, and freshly ground black pepper. Mix until creamy.

5. For each 2-cup serving, drizzle on ¾ tsp each lemon juice and olive oil and a sprinkling of minced parsley leaves.

NUTRITION: *PER 2-CUP SERVING: Calories 204; Carbs 25g; Fat 10g; Protein 7g; Sodium 546mg; Sugar 6g*

Infamous Ramen

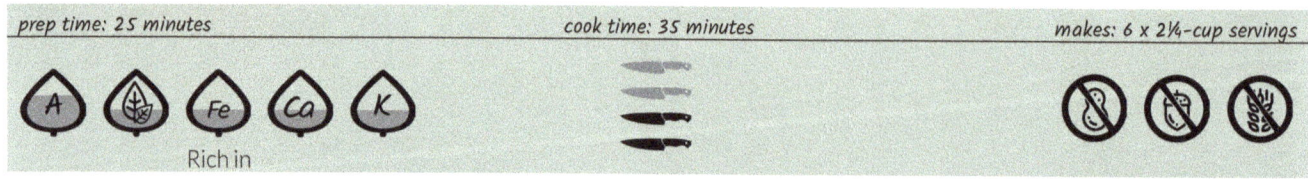

prep time: 25 minutes | cook time: 35 minutes | makes: 6 x 2¼-cup servings

Rich in: A, 🌱, Fe, Ca, K

Throughout the town, county, and beyond, our ramen is infamous. Veggieroos from all across the nation come a-knocking at Cashew Sue's door seeking a nibble of this soul-satisfying meal. 'Cause delicious ramen is true comfort food, making it a must-have on a cold, rainy day. Or pretty much anytime you're needing to fill your belly with something warm and savoury. Even more comforting is the fact that you can eat this version guilt-free, seeing as how it's 100% plant-based. The wonderful umami flavour comes from toasted sesame paste, dried mushroom powder, and white miso paste. To add to the perfection, we top each bowl with a bit of roasted seaweed, chopped green onion, and a sprinkling of sesame seeds. You'll be a star when you make it, and everyone gobbles it down. But be forewarned, don't add the noodles until just before you eat the soup, 'cause no one likes soggy noodles.

INGREDIENTS

4 tbsp toasted sesame oil, divided into 4 x 1 tbsp

½ cup sliced green onion (about 4 medium), divided into 6 tbsp + 6 x 2 tsp green portion only

1½ tsp minced garlic (about 3 cloves)

1½ tsp grated ginger root

1 tbsp tamari or Bragg soy seasoning, divided into 2 x 1 tbsp

2 tbsp dried mushroom powder

2 tsp nutritional yeast

2 tbsp rice wine vinegar

2 cups thinly sliced shiitake or brown mushroom (about 8 medium)

2 cups chopped bok choy (about 4 small)

2 cups washed bean sprouts

½ cup grated carrot (1–1 ½ medium)

¼ cup raw sesame seeds

¼ cup white miso paste

¾ cup hot water

1 cup thinly sliced extra-firm tofu (about ½ of 12-oz package)

¾ tsp shichimi togarashi or equivalent Japanese spice blend, divided into ½ tsp + ¼ tsp

½ tsp Spike all-purpose seasoning or Old Bay seasoning

4 cups low-sodium vegetable broth

½ cup soy milk

4 cups hot cooked brown rice ramen noodles (about 10-oz dry)

2 tbsp thinly sliced roasted seaweed

DIRECTIONS

1. Place saucepan on medium heat and add 1 tbsp toasted sesame oil. Once hot, add 6 tbsp sliced green onion and sauté until they start to brown (about 5 minutes). Add 1½ tsp each minced garlic and grated ginger root and cook an additional minute or two, or until garlic and ginger start to soften. Then, add 1 tbsp tamari and stir until well combined.

2. To cooked onions, add 2 tbsp dried mushroom powder and 2 tsp nutritional yeast. Sauté for a few minutes before adding 2 tbsp rice wine vinegar and 1 tbsp toasted sesame oil. Stir until well combined. Add 2 cups each thinly sliced mushroom, chopped bok choy, and bean sprouts, and ½ cup grated carrot. Cook until vegetables are tender (about 15 minutes).

3. Dry toast ¼ cup sesame seeds on medium heat in a small frying pan. Shake the pan continuously to keep seeds moving until they darken slightly and emit a pleasant nutty aroma (1–2 minutes). Remove from heat, let cool, and divide into 2 x 2 tbsp.

4. In a spice grinder, grind 2 tbsp toasted sesame seeds into a paste.

5. In a small bowl, mix ¼ cup miso paste with ¾ cup hot water and stir until well combined.

6. In a medium bowl, mix 1 cup thinly sliced tofu, 1 tbsp toasted sesame oil, and ½ tsp each shichimi togarashi and Spike seasoning. Toss until tofu is well coated. Place nonstick frying pan on medium heat. Once hot, add tofu in a single layer and cook each side until brown and crispy (about 5 minutes per side). Keep warm until noodles are cooked.

7. To cooked veggies, add 4 cups low-sodium vegetable broth, miso mixture, ½ cup soy milk, and sesame paste. Stir until well combined. Keep hot while noodles cook, but do not bring to a boil.

8. Add 1 tbsp toasted sesame oil to 4 cups hot cooked rice noodles, stirring until noodles are well coated in oil.

9. Divide ingredients into 6 big bowls. First, add ⅔ cup cooked and prepared noodles, then 1⅓ cups of veggie and broth mixture. Top each bowl with 2 heaping tbsp fried tofu and 1 tsp each green portion of sliced green onion, toasted sesame seeds, and sliced roasted seaweed. Serve immediately.

NUTRITION: PER 2¼-CUP SERVING: *Calories 354; Carbs 37g; Fat 16g; Protein 13g; Sodium 857mg; Sugar 5g*

Mighty Minestrone

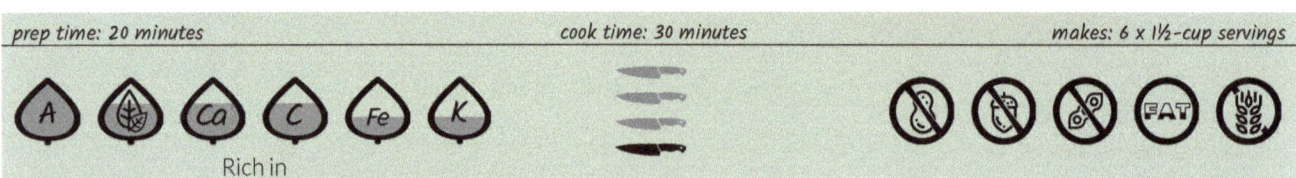

prep time: 20 minutes　　　cook time: 30 minutes　　　makes: 6 x 1½-cup servings

Rich in: A, Ca, C, Fe, K

Mighty Minestrone is mighty tasty, mighty hardy, and mighty versatile. Plus, Carrot Rick loves it, seeing as how it's loaded with nutrients. When we say there're plenty of options in making this soup, we're not kidding. For example, carrots, celery, and green beans are a natural choice but can easily be replaced by whatever veggies you find hiding in the fridge. Not only that, you can also swap out the pinto beans for garbanzo, cannellini, or even borlotti beans. In case you weren't aware, the borlotti bean is commonly found in Italy; aka: the cranberry bean, it's dappled red with white and is related to kidney and pinto beans. The fresh tomato and herbs are part of the secret to making this one mighty fine dish. Serve it up with fresh whole-grain sourdough bread, and you've got yourself a fulfilling and deeply satisfying meal.

If opening a 13.5-oz can of red kidney beans and/or pinto beans, you will only use a portion. Use the remainder in salads or freeze for up to 6 months for later use.
For gluten-free, use gluten-free pasta.

INGREDIENTS

3¼ cups low-sodium vegetable broth, divided into ¼ cup + 3 cups

1 cup diced onion (about ½ medium)

1 cup diced celery (about 2 stalks)

1 cup diced carrot (about 2 medium)

1 tbsp Bragg soy seasoning or tamari

1½ tsp minced garlic (about 3 cloves)

1 tsp dried mushroom powder

½ tsp Spike all-purpose seasoning or Old Bay seasoning

½ tsp salt

½ tsp dried marjoram or oregano

¼ tsp dried thyme

¼ tsp ground allspice

freshly ground black pepper, to taste

2 cups diced Roma tomato (3–4 medium) + a small amount for garnish

1 cup trimmed and chopped fresh or frozen green beans

1 cup cooked, drained, and rinsed red kidney beans

1 cup cooked, drained, and rinsed pinto beans

2 tbsp tomato paste

1 tbsp minced rosemary

1 bay leaf

2 cups water

1 cup uncooked small bow-tie or spiral whole-grain pasta

½ cup fresh or frozen corn kernels

½ cup frozen or canned lima beans

1 tbsp minced sage leaves

1 tbsp minced basil leaves

2 tbsp minced parsley leaves, divided into 1 tbsp + 1 tbsp for garnish

DIRECTIONS

1. In a large soup pot, add ¼ cup low-sodium vegetable broth on medium-high heat. Once hot, add 1 cup diced onion and sauté until translucent and beginning to darken (about 5 minutes). Let the broth cook off so onions can brown, but add a little water if they begin to stick. If they become too dry, onions may burn.

2. Add 1 cup each diced celery and carrot, 1 tbsp Bragg seasoning, 1½ tsp minced garlic, 1 tsp dried mushroom powder, ½ tsp each Spike seasoning, salt, and dried marjoram, ¼ tsp each dried thyme and ground allspice, and freshly ground black pepper. Stir to combine, cover with a lid, and cook for about 5 minutes or until veggies start to soften. Stir occasionally and add a little water if they begin to stick.

3. Add 2 cups diced tomato, 1 cup chopped green beans, 1 cup each cooked kidney and pinto beans, 2 tbsp tomato paste, 1 tbsp minced rosemary, and 1 bay leaf. Stir until well combined before adding 3 cups low-sodium vegetable broth and 2 cups water. Increase heat and bring to a boil. Reduce to medium-low, cover, and simmer for an additional 5–10 minutes.

4. Add 1 cup uncooked pasta and ½ cup each corn kernels and lima beans. Cook an additional 6–10 minutes or until pasta is al dente. Add 1 tbsp each minced sage, basil, and parsley leaves. Let sit for 5 minutes before serving.

5. Remove the bay leaf, ladle the soup into bowls, and serve with a sprinkle of parsley and a few slices of diced tomato.

NUTRITION: PER 1½-CUP SERVING: Calories 207; Carbs 42g; Fat 1g; Protein 10g; Sodium 338mg; Sugar 9g

Just Veggies

Rosemary Beets	119
Sautéed Greens	121
Green Bean and Squash Curry with Cucumber Raita	123
Grilled Zucchini and Leeks with Walnuts	125

Protein Powered Side Dishes

Marinated Edamame	127
Lemon and Garlic Oyster Mushrooms with Black-Eyed Peas	129
Roasted Tofu	131

Special Spuds

Gold Rush Potato Nuggets	133
Spicy Chili Unfries with Chipotle Aioli	135

Extras

Chipotle Cornbread	137
Garlic Parsley Bread	139
Herbed Biscuits	141

Rosemary Beets

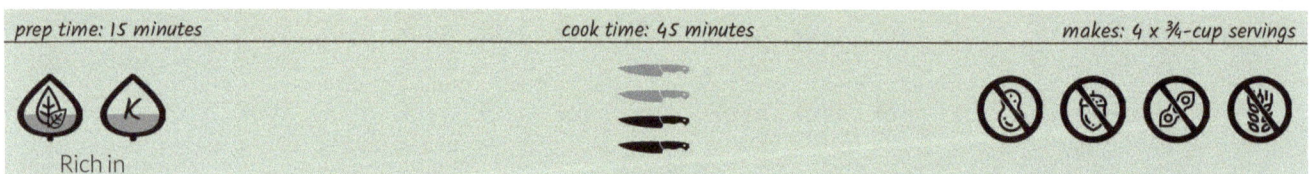

prep time: 15 minutes | cook time: 45 minutes | makes: 4 x ¾-cup servings

Rich in

Rosemary Beets are a big favourite of Carrot Rick, not only 'cause they're colourful and full of flavour, but 'cause they're rich in antioxidants, folic acid, potassium, and fibre. Plus, they taste amazing. The sharp, earthy notes from the rosemary and dried mustard match perfectly with the sweetness of the beets, creating a savoury treat. Strawberry Sal presents these beets on a bed of tender beet leaves along with a sprinkling of fresh rosemary when she wants to impress with a pretty dish. Another option is to pair them up with Sautéed Greens (page 121), especially when you buy your beets with their greens attached. We find that vegan butter adds a better flavour than olive oil, but feel free to use the one that fits your needs or what you happen to have on hand.

INGREDIENTS

3 medium beets + water to cook

1 tbsp apple cider vinegar

½ tsp salt

1 tbsp vegan butter

1 tbsp minced rosemary + a few whole leaves for garnish

1 tsp dry mustard

freshly ground black pepper, to taste

DIRECTIONS

1. Wash 3 medium beets but leave them whole and unpeeled, retaining at least 1 inch of roots and stalk. This reduces the amount of flavour, colour, and juices that escape into the water as they cook. In a medium saucepan, add whole beets, enough water to cover the beets by more than 1 inch, 1 tbsp apple cider vinegar, and ½ tsp salt. Cover with a lid and bring to a boil. Reduce to medium-low and simmer until tender (20–35 minutes depending on the size of your beets). Add more water if needed to keep beets submerged.

2. Once beets are cooked and tender, immerse immediately in cold water. Let them sit for a few minutes. Once cool to the touch, remove the skins, and cut off the tops and tails. The skin should just slide off. Next, slice each beet into ¼-inch-thick round slices.

3. Place frying pan on medium-high heat and add 1 tbsp vegan butter. Once hot, add 1 tbsp minced rosemary, 1 tsp dry mustard, and freshly ground black pepper. Stir to combine before adding beet rounds. Brown each side for about 5 minutes. Add a sprinkling of fresh rosemary as a garnish before serving.

NUTRITION: *PER ¾-CUP SERVING: Calories 74; Carbs 10g; Fat 3g; Protein 2g; Sodium 396mg; Sugar 7g*

SIDES - JUST VEGGIES

Sautéed Greens

prep time: 15 minutes   cook time: 20 minutes   makes: 4 x ¼-cup servings

Rich in

Cooking up beet leaves is a mighty fine way to enjoy the bounty of the earth. These tender shoots are delicious and nutritious, especially when sautéed to perfection. Plus, this is one swell way to sneak some greens into your diet. All you need do is buy your beets at the farmers market or local grocery store with the greens attached and in good condition. That way, you can either serve the greens up on their own or along with Rosemary Beets (page 119). These two together make a mighty fine pairing of nutritious side dishes. When sautéing the greens, the combination of horseradish and rosemary really makes the flavour of the leaves sing. This recipe works well with a variety of greens; we have also used it successfully with kale and bok choy. For us, the flavour of vegan butter is preferable over olive oil in this recipe, but feel free to use what you like best.

For a soy-free version, use soy-free vegan Worcestershire sauce.

INGREDIENTS

2 tbsp vegan butter

1 cup diced onion (about ½ medium)

3–4 bunches of beet greens + a few ribbons for garnish

1 tbsp horseradish sauce

1 tbsp chopped rosemary

2 tsp Bestcestershire Sauce (vegan Worcestershire sauce)

1 tsp dry mustard

¼ tsp Spike all-purpose seasoning or Old Bay seasoning

DIRECTIONS

1. Place large frying pan on medium-high heat and add 2 tbsp vegan butter. Once hot, add 1 cup diced onion and sauté until translucent and beginning to darken (about 5 minutes). Add a little water if onions start to stick and there is no liquid left in the pan.

2. While onion cooks, wash and dry 3–4 bunches of greens. Remove any thick stems and cut into ribbons (about 4 cups), keeping a few aside for garnish.

3. When onions are ready, add 1 tbsp each horseradish sauce and chopped rosemary, 2 tsp Bestcestershire Sauce, 1 tsp dry mustard, and ¼ tsp Spike seasoning. Stir until well combined before addingabout 4 cups ribboned greens. The greens will initially take up a lot of space but stir often as they wilt and shrink. Continue to cook until wilted and tender (10–15 minutes). Serve immediately with a garnish of fresh beet green ribbons.

NUTRITION: PER ¼-CUP SERVING: *Calories 93; Carbs 7g; Fat 8g; Protein 1g; Sodium 219mg; Sugar 2g*

SIDES - JUST VEGGIES

Green Bean and Squash Curry with Cucumber Raita

Green Bean and Squash Curry: prep time: 25 minutes	cook time: 50 minutes	makes: 4 x 2-cup servings
Cucumber Raita: prep time: 15 minutes	cook time: 1 minute	makes: 4 x ¼-cup servings

Rich in

Potato Pat will often serve up this curry as a tempting side dish 'cause it's sure to delight anyone interested in eatin' healthy morsels. The spicy green beans and squash make a fabulous side dish when paired with vegan Cucumber Raita and Tempting Toor Dal Tadka (Page 199). However, in a pinch, this dish can also stand alone, especially when paired with a tasty flatbread like garlic naan or whole-wheat roti. Butternut squash delivers deep, rich flavour and satisfying texture. Coconut milk adds a lovely, creamy mouthfeel. The green beans and yellow potatoes are above-board the perfect complement to the overall taste. No matter how you enjoy it, this dish feels like a warm hug from mum after a long day!

Prepare the Cucumber Raita a day in advance to speed up the process. Use long English cucumbers for the best effect, as they have smaller seeds and do not need deseeding.
If you cannot find French or long green beans, use regular green beans (page 19). Fresh or frozen green beans work well.

INGREDIENTS

CUCUMBER RAITA (makes 1 cup)

- ¾ cup raw cashews, soaked in water for at least 4 hours
- ¼ cup unsweetened cashew milk
- 1 tbsp lemon juice (about ½ lemon)
- 1 tbsp coconut oil
- ¼ tsp salt
- pinch of ground nutmeg
- ½ large English cucumber or field cucumber
- 2 tbsp grated onion
- 1 tbsp grated carrot + a small amount for garnish
- ½ tsp minced garlic (about 1 clove)
- ½ tsp ground cumin
- freshly ground black pepper, to taste
- ⅛ tsp cumin seeds for garnish

GREEN BEAN AND SQUASH CURRY (makes 8 cups)

- 2 tbsp olive oil
- 1 cup diced onion (about ½ medium)
- 1 medium jalapeño pepper, cut into rounds
- ½ tsp cumin seeds
- ½ tsp black mustard seeds
- ½ tsp fenugreek seeds
- 1 tsp minced garlic (about 2 cloves)
- 1 tsp finely grated ginger root
- 1 tsp garam masala
- ½ tsp turmeric
- ½ tsp ground coriander seeds
- ⅛ tsp ground cloves
- 1 tbsp water
- 2 cups diced butternut squash in small cubes (about 1 small squash)
- 1 cup diced yellow potato in small cubes (about 1 medium-small potato)
- 1 tsp salt
- 4 cups cut French or long green beans in 1-inch pieces
- 1 tsp sugar
- 1 cup coconut milk
- chopped cilantro for garnish

DIRECTIONS

1. Prepare **Cucumber Raita**:

   a. Drain and rinse the soaked cashews. Place them in a food processor along with ¼ cup cashew milk, 1 tbsp each lemon juice and coconut oil, ¼ tsp salt, and pinch of ground nutmeg. Process until smooth and creamy (3–5 minutes), scraping down sides as needed with a rubber spatula.

   b. Peel and grate half an English cucumber (about ½ cup). If you use half a field cucumber, peel and deseed before grating. Wrap grated cucumber in a dry, clean towel or cheesecloth and squeeze out excess water.

   c. In a medium bowl, mix processed cashew mixture, grated and drained cucumber, 2 tbsp grated onion, 1 tbsp grated carrot, ½ tsp each minced garlic and ground cumin, and freshly ground black pepper. Stir until everything is well combined and the mixture is smooth. Refrigerate for a few hours before serving to allow flavours to meld together.

   d. Dry toast ⅛ tsp cumin seeds in a small frying pan on medium heat. Shake pan continuously to keep cumin seeds moving until they darken slightly and emit a pleasant earthy aroma (about 1 minute).

   e. Serve Cucumber Raita with curry. Garnish with a sprinkling of grated carrot and toasted cumin seeds.

2. Prepare **Green Bean and Squash Curry**:

   a. Place medium saucepan on medium-high–medium heat and add 2 tbsp olive oil. Once hot, add 1 cup diced onion and sauté until translucent and beginning to darken (about 5 minutes). Add a little water if onions start to stick.

   b. Add jalapeño pepper rounds and ½ tsp each cumin seeds, black mustard seeds, and fenugreek seeds. Cook for several minutes until seeds pop.

   c. In a mortar or a small wooden bowl, add 1 tsp each minced garlic, finely grated ginger root, and garam masala, ½ tsp each turmeric and ground coriander seeds, and ⅛ tsp ground cloves. Smash to a pulp with a pestle before adding 1 tbsp water. Stir until mixture forms a paste.

   d. Add curry paste to onions and cook for 1–2 minutes. Add 2 cups diced butternut squash, 1 cup diced potato, and 1 tsp salt. Cook until vegetables start to soften (about 10 minutes). Stir often, and add a little water if vegetables begin to stick.

   e. Add 4 cups cut green beans and 1 tsp sugar. Stir until well combined, and cover the pot with a lid.

   f. Cook on medium heat for 20–30 minutes, stirring about every 10 minutes. Cook until vegetables are soft and tender. Add a little water if vegetables start to stick.

   g. Add 1 cup coconut milk to the cooked vegetables and stir until a lovely gravy forms.

   h. Serve hot with Cucumber Raita and a sprinkling of fresh chopped cilantro.

NUTRITION: CURRY ONLY - PER 2-CUP SERVING: Calories 333; Carbs 37g; Fat 19g; Protein 9g; Sodium 628mg; Sugar 8g;
CUCUMBER RAITA - PER ¼-CUP SERVING: Calories 248; Carbs 14g; Fat 19g; Protein 8g; Sodium 117mg; Sugar 4g

SIDES - JUST VEGGIES

Grilled Zucchini and Leeks with Walnuts

prep time: 25 minutes + time to soak walnuts   cook time: 20 minutes   makes: 4 x 1-cup servings

Rich in

You may think grills are only good for cooking meat, but this ain't so. Grilling adds depth and increases the flavour of your veggies, making them taste down-right a-maz-ing. So, we decided to give zucchini and leeks a turn on the grill, and wow! Do they taste blazing good! You don't want to miss out on this simple pleasure, so throw some coals on the firepit and get to grilling. Y'all can add a little protein if you're so determined — just toss in a cup of cooked red kidney or fava beans.

Soaking walnuts before roasting them removes bitterness, creating a more mellow and buttery nut flavour.
Zest the lemon before cutting and juicing.
For soy-free, replace Bragg soy seasoning or tamari with coconut aminos (soy-free seasoning) (page 15) and use soy-free vegan Worcestershire sauce.

INGREDIENTS

SPECIAL ROASTED WALNUTS
(makes ½ cup)

- ½ cup raw walnuts + water for soaking
- 2 tbsp lemon juice (about 1 lemon)
- 2 tbsp olive oil
- 1 tbsp lemon zest (about 1 lemon)
- 1 tsp minced garlic (about 2 cloves)
- ¼ tsp salt
- freshly ground black pepper, to taste

OTHER INGREDIENTS

- 2 tbsp grapeseed oil
- 1 tbsp balsamic vinegar
- 2 tsp Bragg soy seasoning or tamari
- 1 tsp Bestcestershire Sauce (vegan Worcestershire sauce)
- ½ tsp Spike all-purpose seasoning or Old Bay seasoning
- freshly ground black pepper, to taste
- 2 medium leeks
- 2 medium zucchini
- ¼ cup chopped parsley leaves + a few leaves for garnish
- 2 tbsp chopped mint leaves
- ½ tsp balsamic vinegar reduction for garnish
- lemon zest for garnish

DIRECTIONS

1. Prepare *Special Roasted Walnuts*:

   a. Soak ½ cup walnuts in water for 30 minutes. Preheat oven to 350°F.

   b. Drain and rinse the soaked walnuts. Place in a small roasting pan and cook for 5 minutes or until they start to brown. Remove from the oven.

   c. In a small dish, toss roasted walnuts with 2 tbsp each lemon juice and olive oil, 1 tbsp lemon zest, 1 tsp minced garlic, ¼ tsp salt, and ground black pepper. Toss until walnuts are well coated.

2. Heat grill to medium-high heat. If you do not have a grill, you can use a broiler at 500°F, but it does not provide the same deep flavour (although it is still wonderfully satisfying).

3. In a small bowl, mix 2 tbsp grapeseed oil, 1 tbsp balsamic vinegar, 2 tsp Bragg seasoning, 1 tsp Bestcestershire Sauce, ½ tsp Spike seasoning, and freshly ground black pepper. Stir until well combined.

4. Leave 2 medium leeks whole and cut 2 medium zucchini in half lengthwise. Brush leeks and zucchini with prepared grapeseed oil mixture. Grill vegetables, turning often, until tender and charred in spots (5–7 minutes per side). Do not overcook. The vegetables are better left firm rather than too soft.

5. Cut off and discard any unwanted, over-grilled portion of the vegetables. Cut grilled leeks into discs and chop grilled zucchini into chunks. Place in a serving dish. Add walnut mixture, ¼ cup chopped parsley leaves, and 2 tbsp chopped mint leaves. Stir until well combined. Place in a serving dish and sprinkle on a few slices of lemon zest, a couple of parsley leaves, and a drizzle of balsamic vinegar reduction. Serve hot as a tasty side dish.

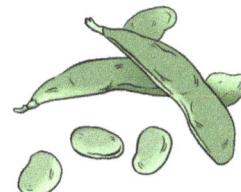

NUTRITION: *PER 1-CUP SERVING:* Calories 268; Carbs 13g; Fat 23g; Protein 4g; Sodium 335mg; Sugar 4g

Marinated Edamame

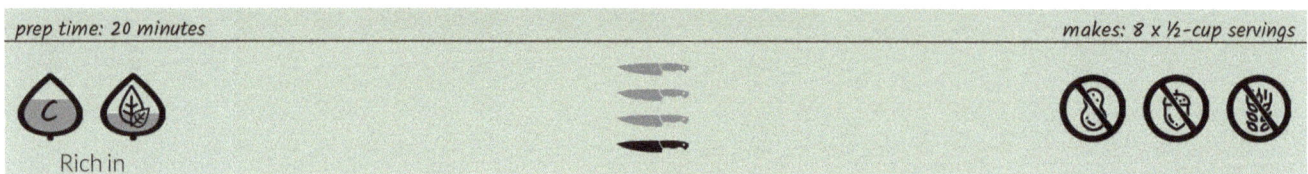

prep time: 20 minutes makes: 8 x ½-cup servings

Rich in

When you have a yearning for some extra protein, Marinated Edamame is sure-fired to satisfy. Pomegranate and edamame are not usually served together, but this doesn't stop us (we are, after all, the Veggie OUTLAWS). Strawberry Sal loves the pretty contrast of red against green, and Carrot Rick is quick to point to the high nutritional value of the seeds. Cashew Sue likes to serve this tidbit up at get-togethers during Christmastime, and not just 'cause it's easy to make. This side dish tastes great, and the festive colours add to the holiday mood. If you don't have or don't want to use pomegranate seeds, the dish still works great. That's 'cause marinated edamame is lip-smacking good, no matter how it's served. In any event, the black sesame seeds add a subtle nutty flavour, a slight crunch, and more nutrients, plus they look fantastic.

Increase the edamame to 4 cups if you are not using pomegranate seeds.

INGREDIENTS

3½ cups frozen shelled edamame beans + boiling water for soaking

1 lemon

2 garlic cloves

½ cup pomegranate seeds (optional) + a few for garnish

1 tbsp toasted sesame oil

1 tbsp black sesame seeds + small amount for garnish

1 tsp salt

freshly ground black pepper, to taste

DIRECTIONS

1. Cover 3½ cups frozen shelled edamame beans in boiling water and let sit for 10 minutes. Drain and rinse. While the edamame soaks, zest the lemon peel until you have 2 tsp of zest. Then cut and juice the lemon. Next, peel and mince 2 garlic cloves. You should have about 2 tbsp lemon juice, 2 tsp lemon zest, and 1 tsp minced garlic.

2. Mix 3½ cups drained and rinsed edamame, ½ cup pomegranate seeds, 2 tbsp lemon juice, 1 tbsp each toasted sesame oil and black sesame seeds, 2 tsp lemon zest, 1 tsp each salt and minced garlic, and freshly ground black pepper. Stir until well combined. Serve immediately or let sit for up to 1 hour to intensify the flavours.

3. To serve, place in a pretty dish and garnish with a couple of pomegranate seeds and a sprinkling of black sesame seeds.

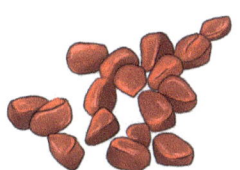

NUTRITION: PER ½-CUP SERVING (with pomegranate seeds): Calories 121; Carbs 12g; Fat 5g; Protein 7g; Sodium 317mg; Sugar 3g

Lemon and Garlic Oyster Mushrooms with Black-Eyed Peas

prep time: 15 minutes   cook time: 40 minutes   makes: 4 x 1⅓-cup servings

Rich in

Seeing as how we're simple folk, you won't find any royalty around here, except maybe in the produce section at the market. 'Cause, that's where you'll find the king of mushrooms, the oyster mushroom. Keep an eye open for the king trumpet (which, as the largest oyster mushroom, trumps them all). The smaller oyster mushrooms with long, thin stems may not be related to the king. But they taste fantastic, making them the prince of mushrooms (at least, that's the rumour in Livewood). Either king or prince works royally since both have a lovely meaty texture and plenty of umami. If using the larger version, cut the stems into round, scallop-sized pieces. Despite which ones you have on hand, go forth knowing these noble fungi are versatile, filling, and super tasty. All you need do for tender and succulent meat with a deliciously rich flavour is pan-fry, then steam them in a lemon-garlic sauce. For a meal fit for a king (or queen or your favourite person), pair the tender mushrooms with the earthy, nutty flavour of black-eyed peas.

Zest the lemon before cutting and juicing.

INGREDIENTS

4 cups oyster mushroom

1 tsp cumin seeds

2 tbsp vegan butter

1 cup diced onion (about ½ medium)

1½ tsp minced garlic (about 3 cloves)

1 tsp Spike all-purpose seasoning or Old Bay seasoning

½ tsp dried mushroom powder

freshly ground black pepper, to taste

¼ cup water

2 tbsp lemon juice (about 1 lemon)

2 cups cooked, drained, and rinsed black-eyed peas

2 tbsp minced parsley leaves + a few leaves for garnish

lemon zest for garnish

DIRECTIONS

1. Prepare 4 cups oyster mushroom. If using smaller oyster mushrooms, pull them apart into chunks or slice them into whatever size you desire. If using large trumpet oyster mushrooms, cut the stems into round, scallop-sized pieces.

2. Dry toast 1 tsp cumin seeds in a small frying pan on medium heat. Shake the pan continuously to keep cumin seeds moving until they darken slightly and emit a pleasant earthy aroma (about 1 minute).

3. Place a large frying pan on medium-high heat and add 2 tbsp vegan butter. Once hot, add 1 cup diced onion and sauté until translucent and beginning to darken (about 5 minutes).

4. Add 1½ tsp minced garlic, 1 tsp Spike seasoning, ½ tsp dried mushroom powder, and freshly ground black pepper. Cook for 1–2 minutes to let the flavours meld into the onions before adding prepared oyster mushrooms.

5. Cook until mushrooms brown and start to become tender (10–15 minutes). Add 1 tsp toasted cumin seeds.

6. Add ¼ cup water and 2 tbsp lemon juice, cover, and steam for 15–20 minutes or until the stems are tender.

7. Add 2 cups cooked black-eyed peas and 2 tbsp minced parsley. Simmer until heated through.

8. Serve immediately garnished with a couple of parsley leaves and a sprinkling of lemon zest.

NUTRITION: PER 1⅓-CUP SERVING: *Calories 205; Carbs 26g; Fat 7g; Protein 10g; Sodium 532mg; Sugar 5g*

Roasted Tofu

prep time: 15 minutes   cook time: 20 minutes   makes: 4 x ½-cup servings

Rich in Ca

Roasted Tofu comes together with a snap of the fingers and, like magic, disappears just as quickly ('cause they're just that good). These outstanding tofu chips have many uses. Not only do they make a bang-up addition to any meal, especially when you're looking for a little extra protein, but they're a star in stir-fries. Potato Pat loves them as a splendiferous appetizer, especially when served with a dipping sauce. Try Chipotle Aioli (page 135), Snappy Peanut Sauce (page 193), or Garlic-Ginger Dipping Sauce (page 164). Put out all three and see which one you like best.

INGREDIENTS

12-oz package extra-firm tofu

1 tbsp grapeseed oil + ¼ tsp for greasing the pan

1 tbsp Bragg soy seasoning or tamari

1 tbsp balsamic vinegar

1 tbsp minced basil leaves

1½ tsp minced garlic (about 3 cloves)

1 tsp Bestcestershire Sauce (vegan Worcestershire sauce)

½ tsp Spike all-purpose seasoning or Old Bay seasoning

freshly ground black pepper, to taste

DIRECTIONS

1. Cut a 12-oz package extra-firm tofu into ⅛- x 1-inch rectangle chips and place them in a medium bowl.
2. In a small dish, mix 1 tbsp each grapeseed oil, Bragg seasoning, balsamic vinegar, and minced basil leaves, 1½ tsp minced garlic, 1 tsp Bestcestershire Sauce, ½ tsp Spike seasoning, and freshly ground black pepper. Mix until well combined and spread over tofu chips. Toss until each piece is well coated. Marinate for 15–30 minutes.
3. Preheat oven to 400°F. Spray a baking sheet with oil or spread with a thin layer of oil (¼ tsp oil).
4. Toss, and then arrange the marinated tofu in a single layer on the prepared baking sheet and cook for 15–20 minutes. Stir at the 10-minute mark.
5. Serve immediately.

NUTRITION: PER ½-CUP SERVING: *Calories 149; Carbs 3g; Fat 11g; Protein 13g; Sodium 329mg; Sugar 1g*

Gold Rush Potato Nuggets

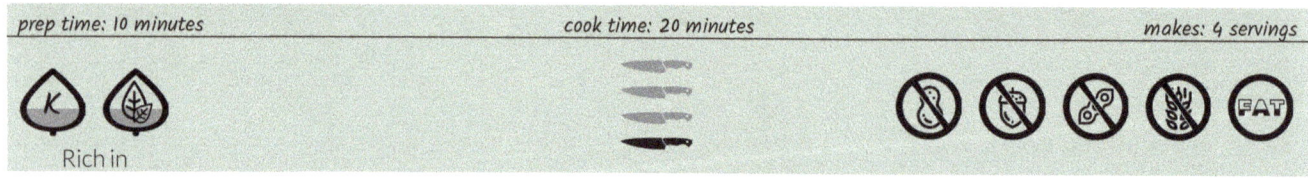

prep time: 10 minutes　　　cook time: 20 minutes　　　makes: 4 servings

Rich in

If you're in pursuit of a tater that's low in fat and tastes better than anything you could dream of, then look no further. You'll strike it rich with these Gold Rush Potato Nuggets. Plus, it doesn't take hard work, only a slight twist of the wrist. Roast these little treasures with pre-cooked baby or new nugget potatoes for the best result. Cashew Sue boils up a big pot of small new potatoes and serves them hot with vegan butter. Then, the next day she'll squish the leftovers and roast them, transforming them into delightful nuggets of delicious flavour. The result is a tasty treat that is enjoyable all on its own, or with a splash of ketchup, or (Potato Pat's favourite) Chipotle Aioli (page 135). Enjoy these potatoes with veggie dogs, plant-based burgers, or a veggie sandwich.

Using Red, yellow, or purple potatoes adds a fun element and is pleasing to both the eye and the belly.

INGREDIENTS

30 previously boiled baby nugget potatoes (about 2½ lbs)

1 tsp grapeseed oil, divided into 2 x ½ tsp

½ tsp Spike all-purpose seasoning or Old Bay seasoning, divided into 2 x ¼ tsp

1 tsp minced rosemary

DIRECTIONS

1. Preheat oven to 425°F.
2. On a large baking sheet, gently flatten 30 pre-cooked baby potatoes with a potato masher. Squish them down but do not pulverize them. Once flattened, turn each one over so the masher marks face down.
3. Spray grapeseed oil evenly over potatoes or use a pastry brush to spread a thin layer of oil over them (½ tsp oil). Sprinkle ¼ tsp Spike seasoning evenly over the tops.
4. Turn each potato so the masher marks face up. This is important because it helps the potatoes to become crunchier.
5. Spray grapeseed oil evenly over potatoes or use a pastry brush to spread a thin layer of oil over them (½ tsp oil). Sprinkle ¼ tsp Spike seasoning and 1 tsp minced rosemary evenly over potatoes. Bake for 15–20 minutes or until the potatoes become brown and crispy. Serve immediately.

NUTRITION: *PER SERVING: Calories 100; Carbs 27g; Fat 1g; Protein 5g; Sodium 80mg; Sugar 2g*

Spicy Chili Unfries with Chipotle Aioli

Chili Unfries: prep time: 15 minutes + time to soak potatoes *cook time: 30 minutes* *makes: 4 x 1-cup servings*
Aioli: prep time: 10 minutes *makes: 4 x ¼-cup servings*

Rich in

When you've got a terrible longing for fries but are looking for something healthier, these potatoes'll do the trick every time. These unfries are a cut above traditional fries. For starters, they're crunchy on the outside and creamy on the inside. Next, they can be as spicy or as mild as you like. And finally, they're baked and not fried, making them a healthier choice. Serve the unfries right out of the oven with Chipotle Aioli (a fancy way of saying vegan mayonnaise). This yummy sauce can also be used on burgers, sandwiches, or as a dip. For a milder aioli, use 1 tsp powdered chipotle pepper. For something with more kick, use more chipotle peppers, with or without the seeds. Both the unfries and the dipping sauce are quick and simple recipes that'll disappear like lightning once they hit the table.

Double or triple Chipotle Aioli recipe. Refrigerate for a week or freeze in ½ cup servings for up to 6 months. It is handy to prepare the roasted garlic in advance, but if you do not have time, replace it with minced garlic.

INGREDIENTS

CHIPOTLE AIOLI (makes 1 cup)

- ½ cup cashews, soaked in water for at least 4 hours
- 3 tbsp lime juice (2–3 limes)
- 3+ tbsp cashew milk
- 2 tbsp olive oil
- 1 chipotle pepper, chopped with seeds removed (from chipotle peppers canned in adobo sauce), or 1 tsp powdered chipotle pepper (or to taste)
- ½ tsp salt
- ½ tsp dried oregano or marjoram leaves
- 3–5 roasted garlic cloves (page 139 or 1 garlic clove, minced

SPICY CHILI UNFRIES

- 2⅓ tbsp grapeseed oil, divided into 2 tbsp + 1 tsp
- 4 medium russet potatoes
- ¼ tsp salt
- 4 cups boiling water
- ¼–1 tsp chili powder, to taste
- ¼ tsp Spike all-purpose seasoning or Old Bay seasoning
- ¼ tsp smoked paprika

DIRECTIONS

1. Prepare **Chipotle Aioli**:

   a. Drain and rinse the soaked cashews. Place in a food processor or blender along with 3 tbsp each lime juice and cashew milk, 2 tbsp olive oil, 1 chopped chipotle pepper, ½ tsp each salt and dried oregano, and 3–5 roasted garlic cloves. Process until smooth and creamy (3–5 minutes), scraping down sides as needed with a rubber spatula.

   b. If the aioli is too thick, add more milk, 1 tbsp at a time (to ensure it does not become too runny), and process until it reaches the desired texture.

2. Prepare **Spicy Chili Unfries**:

   a. Preheat oven to 450°F. Spray a large baking sheet with oil or, using a pastry brush, spread a thin layer of oil on the sheet (1 tsp oil).

   b. Peel and cut 4 medium russet potatoes lengthwise into slices (about 4 cups). Place slices in a narrow dish, sprinkle with ¼ tsp salt, and cover with 4 cups boiling water. Let the potatoes soak for 10 minutes. This process helps the fries to develop a crunchy outside and a soft creamy inside.

   c. Drain potatoes, pat dry, and place in a dry dish. Add 2 tbsp grapeseed oil and sprinkle with ¼–1 tsp chili powder (we like to use 1 tsp) and ¼ tsp each Spike seasoning and smoked paprika. Using your fingers, toss the potatoes. Then spread them evenly on the prepared baking sheet in a single layer.

   d. Bake for 20–30 minutes. Check fries after 10–15 minutes, and if they have started to brown, flip them with a spatula. Continue baking until the fries are golden.

   e. Serve immediately with the Chipotle Aioli.

NUTRITION: CHILI UNFRIES ONLY - PER 1-CUP SERVING: *Calories 190; Carbs 27g; Fat 8g; Protein 3g; Sodium 197mg; Sugar 1g;*
CHIPOTLE AIOLI - PER 1¼-CUP SERVING: *Calories 158; Carbs 9g; Fat 13g; Protein 3g; Sodium 336mg; Sugar 2g*

Chipotle Cornbread

prep time: 20 minutes   cook time: 30 minutes   makes: 10 x ¾" slices

Rich in: Ca, (leaf)

This cornbread is so good that it's hard to have just one slice, but who says you can only have one? When you've got a hungry crew hovering over your shoulder looking for some good eats, place this bread on the table, and let everyone dig in. It makes a great snack and is out of sight with Seriously the Best Chili con Veggies (page 175). For a bit of heat and a lot of flavour, Strawberry Sal adds finely chopped chipotle peppers in adobo sauce. Saucy Peanut likes to add finely chopped canned jalapeño peppers (but then it's no longer Chipotle Cornbread, but rather Jalapeño Cornbread). If you don't like heat, just omit the peppers. You can also try using a tasty shredded vegan cheese in place of the peppers. Chipotle Cornbread has only 2 grams of fat per serving, allowing you to slather on vegan butter without any guilt. Slice and refrigerate or freeze any leftover bread, then just warm it in the toaster before serving.

Make sure you use cornmeal and not corn flour. Cornmeal has a coarser texture that is needed in this recipe. For nut-free, replace cashew milk with vegan nut-free milk of your choice.

INGREDIENTS

¼ tsp grapeseed for greasing the pan
2 tbsp ground flax seeds
⅓ cup water
Milk Mixture (makes 1 cup)
   ⅔ cup oat milk
   ¼ cup cashew milk
   4 tsp coconut milk
1 tbsp lemon juice (about ½ lemon)
1 cup cornmeal
1 cup whole-wheat flour
2 tsp baking powder
½ tsp baking soda
¼ tsp salt
¼ cup unsweetened applesauce
¼ cup packed brown sugar
½ cup frozen corn kernels + a few for topping
½ cup chopped canned chipotle peppers in adobo sauce + a few for topping

DIRECTIONS

1. Preheat oven to 400°F. Spray a 5- x 8-inch loaf pan with oil or, using a pastry brush, spread a thin layer of oil in the pan (¼ tsp oil).
2. In a medium bowl, mix 2 tbsp ground flax seeds with ⅓ cup water and let thicken for at least 5 minutes.
3. In a small bowl, add 1 cup Milk Mixture (⅔ cup oat milk, ¼ cup cashew milk, and 4 tsp coconut milk) and 1 tbsp lemon juice. Stir and let thicken for at least 5 minutes. The lemon juice will cause milk to thicken slightly.
4. In a separate large bowl, sift 1 cup each cornmeal and whole-wheat flour, 2 tsp baking powder, ½ tsp baking soda, and ¼ tsp salt.
5. Pour thickened Milk Mixture into thickened flax seed mixture and add ¼ cup each applesauce and brown sugar. Using an electric hand mixer, blend on high for 3–5 minutes, creating bubbles.
6. Make a well in the centre of the dry ingredients, slowly add wet ingredients, and stir until just blended. Be careful not to overmix. Fold in ½ cup each frozen corn and chopped canned chipotle peppers in adobo sauce.
7. Spread batter evenly in the prepared loaf pan and add a few corn kernels or chilpotle pepper bits to the top. Bake until the loaf is golden brown, batter has pulled away slightly from edges, top bounces back when tapped, and a toothpick inserted in the centre comes out clean (about 20–30 minutes). Let it set for 15 minutes before removing it from the pan.
8. Serve immediately while still warm.

NUTRITION: PER ¾" SLICE: *Calories 142; Carbs 27g; Fat 2g; Protein 4g; Sodium 244mg; Sugar 6g*

SIDES - EXTRAS

Garlic Parsley Bread

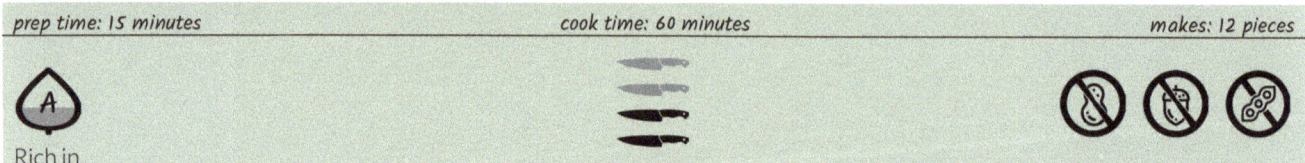

prep time: 15 minutes   cook time: 60 minutes   makes: 12 pieces

Rich in A

This bread is to die for, and fights may break out over the last piece. But, if the savoury aroma of roasting garlic and parsley doesn't give it away, just keep a-walking and a-whistling when it's all gone. 'Cause if anyone finds out there was Garlic Parsley Bread, and they missed out, they're sure to pitch a fit. This warm mouthwatering treat is, without a doubt, a winner. Especially when served as an appetizer, with pasta, or alongside a bowl of soup. Cashew Sue is famous for pairing this bread with our Mediterranean Pasta (page 151). The secret to this recipe is roasting the garlic first and using lots of vegan butter. Of course, you could cut down on the amount of fat, but we don't recommend it; just go for it and enjoy! By good rights, this truly is comfort food at its best.

Prepare the roasted garlic a day or two ahead of time to speed up the process when you're cold and hungry, and you don't want to waste any time getting your hands on some warm and satisfying Garlic Parsley Bread. You can always roast extra, peel the leftover roasted cloves, and freeze them individually on a small plate for about 30 minutes before transferring them to a small container, freeze for up to 6 months. That way, you can pull out one or two roasted cloves as needed.
For soy-free, use soy-free vegan butter.

INGREDIENTS

ROASTED BULB OF GARLIC
1 whole garlic bulb
¼ cup low-sodium vegetable broth
1 tsp olive oil
1 large sprig of parsley leaves

OTHER INGREDIENTS
1 loaf of whole-wheat baguette
2–3 sprigs of parsley leaves
½ cup vegan butter
¼ tsp onion powder
¼ tsp Spike all-purpose seasoning or Old Bay seasoning

DIRECTIONS

1. Prepare *Roasted Bulb of Garlic*:

    a. Preheat oven to 350°F.

    b. Remove the outer skin from the whole garlic bulb and cut ¼–½ inch off the tip of the bulb, exposing the ends of the individual cloves within.

    c. Place in a small baking dish (like a ramekin). Cover with ¼ cup low-sodium vegetable broth, 1 tsp olive oil, and a sprig of parsley leaves.

    d. Loosely cover the top with aluminum foil (do not seal the baking dish, or the garlic will steam instead of bake). Cook for 35–40 minutes or until garlic is tender when pressed with a fork. Remove from the oven and let cool. Leave the oven on.

2. While garlic cools, remove stems from 2–3 parsley sprigs and chop the leaves (about 1 tbsp).

3. In a small bowl, combine ½ cup vegan butter, 1 tbsp chopped parsley, ¼ tsp each onion powder and Spike seasoning, and squeeze all the cloves from the roasted garlic into the vegan butter (discard the garlic skins). Cream the butter, parsley, seasonings, and roasted garlic together to make a nice spread.

4. Cut baguette in half and evenly spread the mixture onto the cut sides.

5. Fit pieces back together, wrap loaf in aluminum foil, and place on a baking sheet. Bake for about 20 minutes or until bread is crispy on the outside and the butter has melted inside.

6. Slice into individual pieces and serve immediately.

NUTRITION: *PER PIECE: Calories 120; Carbs 8g; Fat 8g; Protein 2g; Sodium 179mg; Sugar 0g*

Herbed Biscuits

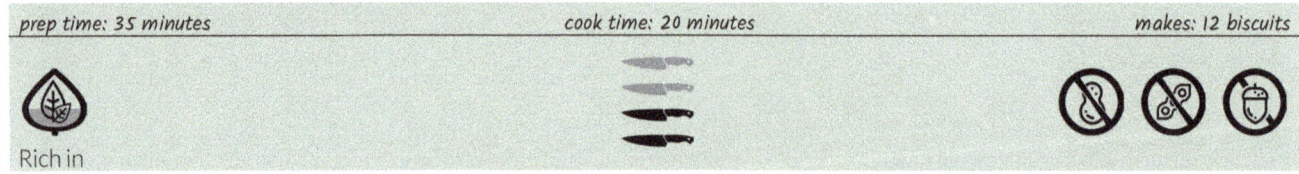

prep time: 35 minutes   cook time: 20 minutes   makes: 12 biscuits

Rich in

As any dough wrangler will tell you, there's an art to biscuit making. One secret is refrigerating the uncooked, shaped biscuits for 10–15 minutes before popping them in the oven. Another trick is not overhandling the dough — it's best to use a soft touch when adding the ingredients. These biscuits are amazing as is, flavourful, tender, and flaky. But if you're in the mood or want to change things up, you can make them plain, without the herbs, or add a little of whatever you're craving — try blueberries and rosemary, or cinnamon and raisins, or even small chunks of tasty vegan cheese. No matter what flavourings you add (or don't), you're in for a real treat with these addictive biscuits. Be forewarned; you'll want to have plenty close to hand. Just slather on some vegan butter while they're still hot, and you'll see why.

We use a combination of 1½ cups whole-wheat pastry flour and ¾ cup all-purpose flour for the best balance of health and texture. Since whole-wheat flour has less gluten, using more of it means your biscuits will not rise as much. That's why we use whole-wheat pastry flour, which is more finely ground than regular whole-wheat flour and produces a lighter, softer biscuit.
To knead the dough, place it on a floured surface, and using the heels of both hands simultaneously, push down and away. Next, fold the dough in half, turn it in a half-circle, and repeat.
For nut-free, replace cashew milk with vegan nut-free milk of your choice.

INGREDIENTS

1 tsp grapeseed oil, divided into 2 x ½ tsp

1 lemon

Milk Mixture (makes 1 cup)
  ⅔ cup oat milk
  ¼ cup cashew milk
  4 tsp coconut milk

1 tbsp apple cider vinegar

1½ tbsp black mustard seeds or caraway seeds

12 medium sage leaves

1½ cups whole-wheat pastry flour

¾ cup all-purpose flour + small amount for kneading the dough

1 tbsp baking powder

2 tsp sugar

¾ tsp salt

½ tsp baking soda

¼ tsp dry mustard

½ cup semi-solid coconut oil (page 17)

freshly ground rock salt

DIRECTIONS

1. Preheat oven to 450°F. Place parchment paper on a baking sheet or spread a thin layer of grapeseed oil (½ tsp) on the baking sheet.

2. Zest a lemon and divide zest into 1 tbsp and 1½ tsp. Juice 1 tbsp lemon juice from the zested lemon.

3. In a liquid measuring cup, add 1 cup Milk Mixture (⅔ cup oat milk, ¼ cup cashew milk, and 4 tsp coconut milk) and 1 tbsp each lemon juice and apple cider vinegar. Stir and let thicken for at least 5 minutes.

4. Dry toast 1½ tbsp black mustard seeds in a small frying pan on medium heat. Shake the pan continuously to keep seeds moving until they darken slightly and emit a pleasant aroma (3–5 minutes). Divide into 1 tbsp and 1½ tsp.

5. Mince 12 medium sage leaves (about 1½ tbsp). Then divide into two-thirds and one-third (about 1 tbsp and 1½ tsp).

6. In a large bowl, sift 1½ cups whole-wheat pastry flour, ¾ cup all-purpose flour, 1 tbsp baking powder, 2 tsp sugar, ¾ tsp salt, ½ tsp baking soda, and ¼ tsp dry mustard. Stir until well combined.

7. Scoop ½ cup semi-solid coconut oil, 1 tbsp at a time, into flour mixture and using a pastry cutter, or a couple of butter knives, cutting in opposite directions, or a balloon whisk, cut the oil into the flour until mixture starts to look like crumbs. This should take 3–5 minutes. Repeatedly press the cutter straight down into the dough firmly without twisting. This will help your biscuits to rise. Do not overmix, or dough may become tough.

8. Add 1 tbsp each lemon zest, toasted seeds, and chopped sage to the flour mixture. Stir briefly to combine.

9. Slowly pour in ⅔ cup thickened milk, mixing continuously with a fork until no dry patches remain. If the dough is still too dry, slowly pour in more thickened milk, 2 tbsp at a time, until no dry patches remain and the dough leaves the sides of the bowl and forms into a rough ball. Depending on your flour, you may not need all the milk mixture. Too much milk makes dough sticky, and not enough makes dry biscuits. If the dough is still too dry after adding all the milk, slowly add cold water 1 tbsp at a time. If the dough feels too sticky, add a little more flour. Do not overhandle the dough, or it may become tough.

10. Scrape dough onto a lightly floured surface and knead 4–6 times.

11. Shape and flatten the dough by hand into a 1-inch-thick rectangle. Cut biscuits with a 2-inch biscuit cutter. Place on prepared baking sheet (1 inch apart for crispy sides). Spray the top of each biscuit, or use a pastry brush to spread a thin layer of oil on top of each one (½ tsp oil). Sprinkle finely ground rock salt, 1½ tsp each toasted seeds, lemon zest, and chopped sage evenly over the tops of the biscuits.

12. Refrigerate for 10–15 minutes before baking. This step lets the gluten relax (important when using whole-wheat flour) and chills the oil, giving the muffins more time to rise.

13. Bake until golden brown (10–15 minutes). Remove immediately from the baking sheet and place on a wire rack for at least 10 minutes before serving.

NUTRITION: *PER BISCUIT: Calories 190; Carbs 19g; Fat 11g; Protein 3g; Sodium 332mg; Sugar 1g*

PASTA and RISOTTO

Macaroni

Friendly Mac 'n' Cheez	145
Grandma's Macaroni, Creamy Style	147

Seasonal Pasta

Pasta Primavera with Rhubarb Tomato Sauce	149
Mediterranean Pasta	151
Creamy Artichoke Hearts with Spaghetti Squash	153

Risotto

Pumpkin Lentil Risotto	155

Friendly Mac 'n' Cheez

prep time: 40 minutes   cook time: 75 minutes   makes: 4 x 2-cup servings

Rich in: A, C, (leaf), Fe, K, Ca

We love mac 'n' cheese, so we pulled up our bootstraps, put on our thinking caps, and created a delicious vegan option. Joining forces, Carrot Rick brought in roasted squash (pointing out the health benefits), and Cashew Sue added nuts, insisting on extra creaminess. Our Friendly Mac 'n' Cheez brings everyone together. It's so good it'll have cheese-loving mac 'n' cheese aficionados asking for seconds. When we served this version to three young'uns who all love oozy, gooey, cheesy mac 'n' cheese, they said, and we quote: "This is amazing" and "This Mac 'n' Cheez is delicious, holy moly." We recommend you keep your fork handy 'cause you may need it to fight off your dinner companions.

Prepare the roasted squash and garlic as well as the Cashew Creme Cheez the day before to speed up the process when you cook the macaroni.
We recommend roasting the whole squash and refrigerating or freezing any extra for up to 6 months.

INGREDIENTS

CASHEW CHEEZ (makes 3 cups)

½ large butternut squash + water to cook

½ head of Roasted Bulb of Garlic (page 139)

¾ cup raw cashews, soaked in water for at least 4 hours

3 tbsp pine nuts, soaked in water for at least 4 hours

Milk Mixture (makes 1 cup)

⅔ cup oat milk

¼ cup cashew milk

4 tsp coconut milk

3½ tbsp nutritional yeast

1½ tbsp apple cider vinegar

1½ tbsp coconut oil

2 tsp lemon juice (from ½ lemon)

1½ tsp arrowroot powder

1 tsp salt

¼ tsp ground allspice

freshly ground black pepper, to taste

pinch of ground nutmeg

SIMPLE BREADCRUMB TOPPING (makes 2 cups)

2 slices stale whole-wheat bread

½ cup sliced green onion (about 4 medium)

2 tbsp vegan butter

OTHER INGREDIENTS

3 cups dry whole-wheat elbow macaroni (12-oz package) (makes 6 cups cooked)

1 tbsp olive oil

20 cherry tomatoes or 1 large tomato

½ tsp paprika

DIRECTIONS

1. Prepare **Cashew Cheez**:

    a. Preheat oven to 375°F.

    b. Discard any seeds that fall out of the cut butternut squash, but leave any seeds that are still inside. Place a small amount of water in the bottom of a shallow baking dish, add butternut squash skin side up, and bake for 30–40 minutes or until squash can be easily pierced with a fork. Let the squash cool before removing and discarding the outer skin and the remaining seeds. This is easier to do once the flesh is soft. Set aside 2 cups cooked butternut squash and refrigerate any extra to use later.

    c. Peel and discard the skins from the cloves within ½ head of Roasted Bulb of Garlic (6–8 cloves).

    d. Drain and rinse the soaked cashews and pine nuts. Place in a food processor or blender along with 1 cup Milk Mixture (⅔ cup oat milk, ¼ cup cashew milk, and 4 tsp coconut milk), 3½ tbsp nutritional yeast, 1½ tbsp each apple cider vinegar and coconut oil, 2 tsp lemon juice, 1½ tsp arrowroot powder, 1 tsp salt, ¼ tsp ground allspice, freshly ground black pepper, and a pinch of ground nutmeg. Process until smooth and creamy (3–5 minutes), scraping down sides as needed with a rubber spatula.

    e. Add 2 cups cooked butternut squash and the peeled, roasted garlic cloves. Blend until smooth and creamy (3–5 minutes), scraping sides as needed with a rubber spatula.

2. Prepare **Simple Breadcrumb Topping**: Slightly toast 2 slices stale bread. Chop and place in a food processor and pulse until crumbly. If not using a food processor, chop or crumble toasted bread (about 1½ cups) into a small bowl. Add ½ cup sliced green onion and 2 tbsp vegan butter. If in a food processor, pulse a few times until well combined, or if in a small bowl, mix with a spoon until blended.

3. Preheat oven to 375°F.

4. Cook 3 cups dry macaroni until pasta is al dente (follow package directions). Once cooked, drain and place the noodles (about 6 cups) in a large bowl with 1 tbsp olive oil.

5. Slice 20 cherry tomatoes into halves (or 1 large tomato into rounds). Separate out 8 halves (or the end pieces of the large tomato) and dice them into smaller pieces.

6. Add Cashew Cheez and the diced tomatoes (not the halves or the rounds) to the cooked pasta. Stir until well combined. Transfer to a medium casserole dish or Dutch oven (about 3.5 quart) and spread until even. Top with Simple Breadcrumb Topping and the tomato halves (or slices). Sprinkle on ½ tsp paprika. Bake covered for 20–30 minutes or until the casserole is bubbling. Remove the cover and cook for 5 minutes longer to let the topping crisp up. Remove from the oven and let set for 5 minutes before serving.

NUTRITION: PER 2-CUP SERVING: Calories 760; Carbs 101g; Fat 33g; Protein 22g; Sodium 756mg; Sugar 15g

Grandma's Macaroni, Creamy Style

prep time: 50 minutes   cook time: 70 minutes   makes: 6 x 2-cup servings

Rich in: A, K, (leaf), C, Ca, Fe

This macaroni dish tastes like love and comfort because it has everything needed to make you feel all warm and cozy inside. Besides, it reminds us of Grandma. She made it for us when we were just little veggieroos, and we loved it. So we countrified her recipe and added vegan sausage, mushrooms, and our special Cashew Cheez. A good trick is to make the Breadcrumb Mixture, the Farmesan, the Fake'n Bacon, and the Cashew Cheez a day or two in advance. Then all you need do is boil the pasta, fry up the sausage and mushroom mixture, and quickly toss everything together before baking. Serve this mouth-watering dish with a few colourful veggies, a glass of red wine, and a little extra Farmesan, and you're hunky-dory.

Make double or triple the amount of Fake'n Bacon, then freeze leftovers for up to 9 months for future use.
For soy-free, replace Bragg soy seasoning or tamari with coconut aminos (soy-free seasoning) (page 15) and use soy-free vegan Worcestershire sauce and soy-free vegan sausages.

INGREDIENTS

FAKE'N BACON *(makes ¼ cup)*

- ¼ tsp olive oil for greasing the pan
- ¼ cup unsweetened coconut chips or flakes (not shredded coconut)
- 1½ tsp Bragg soy seasoning or tamari (or soy sauce)
- 1½ tsp maple syrup
- ½ tsp liquid smoke
- ¼ tsp Bestcestershire Sauce (vegan Worcestershire sauce)
- ¼ tsp smoked paprika

BREADCRUMB TOPPING *(makes 3 cups)*

- 3 slices stale whole-wheat bread
- ⅓ cup sliced green onion (about 3 medium)
- ⅓ cup Farmesan (page 89)
- ¼ cup minced basil leaves
- 1 tbsp nutritional yeast
- ⅓ cup vegan butter
- ¼ cup Fake'n Bacon (see above)

OTHER INGREDIENTS

- 3 cups dry whole-wheat elbow macaroni (12-oz package) (makes 6 cups cooked)
- 1 tbsp olive oil
- ¼ cup low-sodium vegetable broth
- 1 cup chopped onion (about ½ medium)
- 12 medium mushrooms
- 2 vegan Italian-style sausages
- 1 tbsp Bragg soy seasoning or tamari
- 1 tsp Bestcestershire Sauce (vegan Worcestershire sauce)
- 1 tsp Spike all-purpose seasoning or Old Bay seasoning
- 3 cups creamy vegan tomato soup (page 18)
- 3 cups Cashew Cheez (page 145)

DIRECTIONS

1. Prepare **Fake'n Bacon**:

   a. Preheat oven to 300°F. Spray a rimmed baking sheet with oil or, using a pastry brush, spread a thin layer of oil on the sheet (¼ tsp oil).

   b. Put ¼ cup unsweetened coconut chips in a dish. In a separate dish, mix 1½ tsp each Bragg seasoning and maple syrup, ½ tsp liquid smoke, and ¼ tsp each Bestcestershire Sauce and smoked paprika. Pour liquid mixture over coconut chips and toss until evenly coated.

   c. Spread in a single layer on prepared baking sheet. Bake for 7 minutes, stir, and flip chips. Turn heat off and leave chips in the cooling oven for 10 minutes to crisp up. Remove from the oven.

2. Prepare **Breadcrumb Topping**:

   a. Slightly toast 3 slices stale bread. Chop and place in a food processor and pulse until crumbly. If not using a food processor, chop or crumble toasted bread (about 2½ cups) into a small bowl.

   b. Add ⅓ cup each sliced green onion and Farmesan, ¼ cup minced basil leaves, and 1 tbsp nutritional yeast. If in a food processor, pulse a few times until well combined, or if in a small bowl, mix with a spoon. Add ⅓ cup vegan butter and either pulse in a food processor or mix until well combined. Stir in ¼ cup Fake'n Bacon, but do not process or break up the Fake'n Bacon chips.

3. Preheat oven to 350°F.

4. Cook 3 cups dry whole-wheat elbow macaroni until pasta is almost al dente (follow package directions). Drain and rinse pasta (about 6 cups cooked). Place cooked pasta in a large bowl and add 1 tbsp olive oil. Stir until pasta is well coated.

5. While pasta cooks, place large a frying pan on medium-high heat and add ¼ cup low-sodium vegetable broth. Once hot, add 1 cup chopped onion and sauté until translucent and beginning to darken (about 5 minutes). Let the broth cook off so onions can brown, but add a little water if they start to stick. If they become too dry, onions may burn.

6. Chop 12 medium mushrooms (about 3 cups) and cut 2 vegan Italian-style sausages into ½-inch semi-circles (about 1½ cups). Add to the onions along with 1 tbsp Bragg seasoning and 1 tsp each Bestcestershire Sauce and Spike seasoning. Cook until mushrooms and sausages are brown and tender (about 10 minutes). Add a little water if the ingredients begin to stick.

7. Stir 3 cups creamy vegan tomato soup and the sausage and mushroom mixture into the cooked pasta. Pour into a medium casserole dish (about 3.5-quart). Cover with 3 cups Cashew Cheez and top with Breadcrumb Mixture.

8. Cover with a lid and bake for 30 minutes or until bubbling. Remove lid and cook for 5 minutes or until topping is slightly browned. Remove from the oven and let set for 5 minutes before serving.

NUTRITION: *PER 2-CUP SERVING: Calories 819; Carbs 88g; Fat 41g; Protein 30g; Sodium 1,395mg; Sugar 14g*

Pasta Primavera with Rhubarb Tomato Sauce

prep time: 35 minutes   cook time: 55 minutes   makes: 6 x 2-cup servings

Rich in

Sometimes when you're hungry, it's just gotta be pasta. Since rhubarb is a tart plant, many a folk'll pair it with some sweet fruit. Which, without a doubt, is a swell idea. 'Cause who doesn't like strawberry rhubarb pie or stewed rhubarb — check out our Rhubarb and Strawberry Treat (page 237). Although those are the ole standards, we wanted to do something different. Carrot Rick and Strawberry Sal put their heads together and did a little experimentation. They cooked up tomatoes, herbs, and white wine, tossed in some rhubarb and, of course, pasta (plus a few other goodies), and eureka! A dang good dish was born. We like to serve it with our tasty Vegan Caesar Salad (page 89) and fresh sourdough bread.

If you don't have enough fresh tomatoes on hand, use a combination of fresh and canned: 2 cups fresh tomatoes and 3 cups canned low-sodium diced tomatoes (28-oz can). If you don't have any cherry tomatoes on hand, use 1 cup of diced fresh tomatoes.

INGREDIENTS

¾ cup raw walnuts

RHUBARB TOMATO SAUCE

  2 tbsp olive oil, divided into 2 x 1tbsp

  1 cup diced onion (about ½ medium)

  1 tbsp minced garlic (about 6 cloves)

  5 cups diced fresh tomato (6–7 medium)

  1 cup white wine

  ½ tsp salt, divided into 2 x ¼ tsp

  1 cup chopped fresh rhubarb (about 2 small stalks)

  ½ cup diced green onion (about 4 medium)

  1 tbsp dried chili flakes

  ½ tsp sugar

  1 cinnamon stick

  1 cup cherry tomato halves

  2 tbsp chopped basil leaves

  2 tbsp + 2 tsp chopped parsley leaves, divided into 2 tbsp + 2 tsp for garnish

  1 tbsp chopped thyme leaves

  1 tbsp chopped oregano leaves

  ⅛ tsp ground cinnamon

  freshly ground black pepper, to taste

OTHER INGREDIENTS

3 cups dry whole-wheat fusilli or penne pasta (about 12-oz dry) (about 6 cups cooked)

1 tsp olive oil

1 cup water

1 cup sliced cauliflower

½ cup sliced fennel bulb (about ½ medium)

½ cup snow or snap peas

Farmesan (page 89) (optional)

DIRECTIONS

1. Preheat oven to 375°F.
2. Place ¾ cup raw walnuts in a small roasting pan and cook for 5–7 minutes or until brown. Remove from the oven and let cool.
3. Prepare **Rhubarb Tomato Sauce**:

    a. Place large saucepan on medium-high heat and add 1 tbsp olive oil. Once hot, add 1 cup diced onion and sauté until translucent and beginning to darken (about 5 minutes). Add a little water if onions start to stick.

    b. Add 1 tbsp minced garlic and cook until garlic softens (1–2 minutes). Do not let garlic become brown, or it may become bitter. Add a little water if the mixture begins to stick.

    c. Add 5 cups diced fresh tomato, 1 cup white wine, and ¼ tsp salt. Cook until tomatoes are tender (10–15 minutes).

    d. While tomatoes cook, place a different saucepan on medium heat and add 1 tbsp olive oil. Once hot, add 1 cup chopped fresh rhubarb, ½ cup diced green onion, 1 tbsp dried chili flakes, ½ tsp sugar, and a cinnamon stick. Stir until well combined, cover with a lid, and reduce to medium-low. Cook until rhubarb is tender (about 5 minutes). Remove from the stovetop and discard the cinnamon stick.

    e. When tomato mixture is ready, remove from stovetop and process with an immersion blender, a food processor, or a blender until smooth. Return blended tomato mixture to saucepan. Add 1 cup cherry tomato halves, 2 tbsp each chopped basil and parsley leaves, 1 tbsp each chopped thyme and oregano leaves, ¼ tsp salt, ⅛ tsp ground cinnamon, freshly ground black pepper, and rhubarb mixture. Continue cooking until heated through (about 5 minutes). Cover and keep warm.

4. Cook 3 cups dry fusilli pasta according to package directions (about 6 cups cooked). Drain when pasta is al dente, add 1 tsp olive oil, and toss until pasta is well coated in oil.
5. While pasta cooks, heat 1 cup water in the bottom of a steamer pot. Add 1 cup sliced cauliflower and ½ cup sliced fennel bulb. Steam until cauliflower starts to soften (about 5 minutes), then add ½ cup snow peas. Cook for 1 minute. Do not overcook the veggies, as they are much nicer when they still have a little crunch. Remove from the stovetop and drain water. Cover with lid and set aside until pasta is cooked.
6. Place on individual plates in this order: 1 cup pasta, ⅓ cup steamed vegetables, 2 tbsp roasted walnuts, and ¾ cup pasta sauce. Top with Farmesan and a sprinkle of parsley.

NUTRITION: *PER 2-CUP SERVING (without Farmesan):* *Calories 437; Carbs 58g; Fat 17g; Protein 12g; Sodium 218mg; Sugar 8g*

Mediterranean Pasta

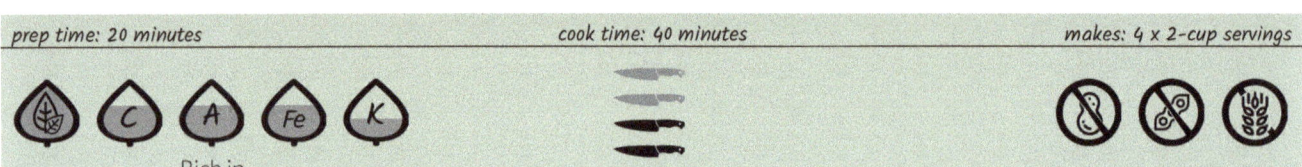

prep time: 20 minutes   cook time: 40 minutes   makes: 4 x 2-cup servings

Rich in

When you make this pasta, you'll feel the warmth of the Mediterranean, and not just 'cause this dish is made with olives, tomatoes, and capers. Your body will tingle with delight from all the health benefits while smacking your lips after each bite. The best part is that you don't have to be in the Mediterranean, 'cause despite where your homestead is, this versatile pasta is a sure winner. You can make this tasty dish in so many different ways it'll make your head spin. One option is to try it with or without the Farmesan (our vegan version of parmesan cheese). Or you can make it fat-free by leaving out the pine nuts and replacing the olive oil with vegetable broth. Make it low-fat by keeping the pine nuts but opting for vegetable broth instead of oil. Try substituting sun-dried tomatoes or artichokes for the olives. Use gluten-free pasta, legume-based pasta, or just good ole regular pasta. All versions are super satisfying, especially when served with Garlic Parsley Bread (page 139) and a green salad. If you decide to use Farmesan, make it a day or two ahead of time to speed up the process and consider doubling or tripling the amount. Then store in the freezer for future use.

For gluten-free, use gluten-free pasta.

INGREDIENTS

3 cups dry whole-wheat fusilli or penne pasta (about 12-oz dry, makes about 6 cups cooked)

1–1½ cups pasta water (saved after cooking the pasta)

¼ cup olive oil, divided into 3 tbsp + 1 tbsp

2 cups diced onion (about 1 medium)

½ cup pine nuts

4 cups sliced mushroom (about 16 medium)

1½ tsp minced garlic (about 3 cloves)

1 tsp Spike all-purpose seasoning or Old Bay seasoning

½ cup pitted and sliced Kalamata olives (cut into thirds lengthwise)

¼ cup lemon juice (about 2 lemons)

1 tbsp capers

4 cups cherry tomato halves or chopped fresh tomatoes

2 tbsp minced basil leaves + a few sprigs for garnish

1 tbsp minced oregano leaves

1 tbsp minced parsley leaves

Farmesan (page 89)

DIRECTIONS

1. Cook 3 cups dry fusilli pasta according to package directions (about 6 cups cooked). Drain when pasta is al dente, making sure to set aside at least 1½ cups of the pasta cooking water. Rinse pasta and return it to the empty cooking pot. Add 3 tbsp olive oil, stir until pasta is well coated, cover with a lid, and set aside.

2. While pasta cooks, place large frying pan on medium heat and add 1 tbsp olive oil. Once hot, add 2 cups diced onion and sauté until translucent and beginning to darken (about 5 minutes). Add a little water if onions start to stick. Add ½ cup pine nuts and cook until nuts darken (an additional 5 minutes). Add 4 cups sliced mushroom, 1½ tsp minced garlic, and 1 tsp Spike seasoning. Stir until well combined and cook until mushrooms are brown (about 10 minutes). Add a little water if the ingredients begin to stick.

3. Add ½ cup pitted and sliced Kalamata olives, ¼ cup lemon juice, and 1 tbsp capers. Stir until well combined and cook for 3–5 minutes.

4. Add the mushroom and olive mixture to the cooked pasta, along with 4 cups cherry tomato halves, 2 tbsp minced basil, and 1 tbsp each minced oregano and parsley leaves. Toss until well combined. Add hot pasta water, ¼ cup at a time, to the pasta mixture, stirring after each addition, until pasta is creamy but not too runny. Cover and set aside for 5 minutes to let flavours meld.

5. Divide into 4 serving bowls and sprinkle each with Farmesan and a couple of small basil leaves for garnish.

NUTRITION: *PER 2-CUP SERVING (without Farmesan): Calories 698; Carbs 117g; Fat 31g; Protein 45g; Sodium 405mg; Sugar 10g*

Creamy Artichoke Hearts with Spaghetti Squash

prep time: 35 minutes   cook time: 60 minutes   makes: 4 x 2-cup servings

Rich in

This creamy, flavourful sauce is splendid with whole-grain penne. But Carrot Rick started thinking — hmmm, what if we replaced the pasta with spaghetti squash? Well, Cashew Sue was up to the task, and surprise, surprise… the spaghetti squash version tasted better. We challenge you to try both options because this is a "pasta" dish you won't want to miss, despite how you choose to enjoy it. So sprinkle with Farmesan, serve hot with a salad and Garlic Parsley Bread (page 139), and watch your hungry gang wolf it down.

For the cooked chickpeas, you can either cook up some dried beans in advance or just open a can. Then, drain and save the chickpea water from the can for later use as aquafaba, aka: egg white substitute (page 14).
For gluten-free, use spaghetti squash or gluten-free pasta and use gluten-free flour for the thickener.

INGREDIENTS

1 large spaghetti squash (or 6 cups cooked whole-grain pasta)

1 cup raw walnuts + a few for garnish

½ medium onion

3 garlic cloves

6–8 cooked artichoke hearts

¼ cup artichoke water (saved from the canned artichoke hearts)

1½ cups pitted olives (combination of Kalamata and black California olives) + a few for garnish

1 cup cooked chickpeas

4 sprigs of oregano leaves

12–14 basil leaves + a few for garnish

3 tbsp olive oil

3 tbsp whole-wheat flour

1 cup low-sodium vegetable broth

Milk Mixture (makes 1 cup)

  ⅔ cup oat milk

  ¼ cup cashew milk

  4 tsp coconut milk

½ tsp salt

freshly ground black pepper, to taste

Farmesan (page 89) (optional)

DIRECTIONS

1. Preheat oven to 400°F.
2. Cut spaghetti squash in half lengthwise, remove seeds, and place cut side down on a rimmed baking dish. Bake for 30–35 minutes or until squash is al dente but slightly tender when pierced with a fork. (This recipe works better with somewhat firm squash rather than overly soft squash.) Remove cooked squash from heat and let cool. When cool to the touch, separate squash strands with a fork (about 6 cups).
3. Roast 1 cup raw walnuts (plus a couple extra for garnish), cook them at the same time as the spaghetti squash. Roast walnuts for 5–6 minutes or until the nuts darken. Remove from the oven. Set aside a few pieces for garnish.
4. While squash cooks, prepare the rest of the ingredients. Dice ½ medium onion (about 1 cup) and peel and mince 3 garlic cloves (about 1½ tsp). Drain and thinly slice 6–8 cooked artichoke hearts (about 1 cup), saving ¼ cup artichoke water. Slice a mixture of 1½ cups pitted olives (combination of Kalamata and black California olives) into circles (about 1 cup). Measure 1 cup cooked chickpeas. Mince 4 sprigs of oregano leaves (about 2 tbsp) and chop 12–14 basil leaves (about 2 tbsp). Set aside a small amount of the sliced olives and chopped basil for garnish.
5. Place a large saucepan on medium-high heat and add 3 tbsp olive oil. Once hot, add about 1 cup diced onion and sauté until translucent and beginning to darken (about 5 minutes). Add about 1½ tsp minced garlic and cook for 1–2 minutes or until garlic begins to soften. Do not let garlic become brown, or it may become bitter.
6. Slowly sift in 3 tbsp whole-wheat flour and whisk continuously until all flour is completely absorbed, ensuring no lumps appear. Cook for a few minutes or until the mixture starts to bubble.
7. Slowly add ¼ cup artichoke water while whisking continuously until the mixture is smooth. Slowly whisk in 1 cup low-sodium vegetable broth and 1 cup Milk Mixture (⅔ cup oat milk, ¼ cup cashew milk, and 4 tsp coconut milk) until mixture is smooth.
8. Add about 1 cup each sliced artichoke hearts, sliced black olive mixture, cooked chickpeas, and roasted walnuts, ½ tsp salt, and freshly ground black pepper. Stir until well combined and bring mixture to a slow boil. Cook for an additional 5 minutes or until sauce thickens.
9. Add 6 cups squash strands and about 2 tbsp each minced oregano and chopped basil. Stir well, heat through, and serve immediately. Garnish each serving with a couple of olives, some walnut bits, and a few basil leaves. If desired, you can also sprinkle on some Farmesan.

NUTRITION: *PER 2-CUP SERVING: Calories 540; Carbs 46g; Fat 37g; Protein 13g; Sodium 952mg; Sugar 12g*

Pumpkin Lentil Risotto

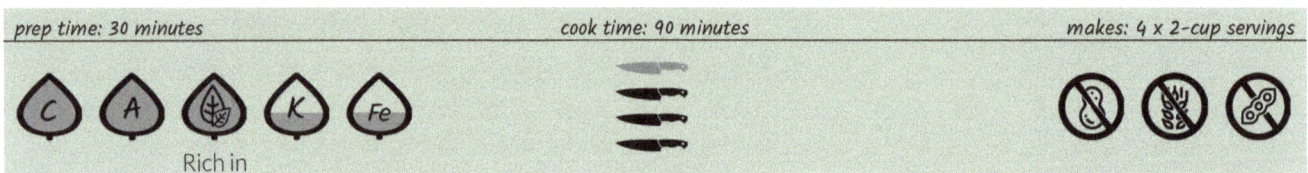

prep time: 30 minutes   cook time: 90 minutes   makes: 4 x 2-cup servings

Rich in: C, A, (leaf), K, Fe

This risotto is tasty, healthy, and ooh, so creamy. When you round up whole-grain rice, roasted pumpkin, and lentils, cook them just right, then add some cashew creme, you'll find a whole-grain risotto that really works. The crowning stroke is adding the lentils, which adds both extra protein and extra creaminess. This dish is a real winner, and come hell or high water, you're gonna want to make it. However, given that fresh pumpkins are only available for a few months in the fall, butternut squash makes a great substitute. Serve up this risotto with a crisp green salad, and your kinfolk'll be banging on your door, hankering for a bite of this yummy dinner.

We recommend cooking the pumpkin in advance (page 21).
For soy-free, replace Bragg soy seasoning or tamari with coconut aminos (soy-free seasoning) (page 15).

INGREDIENTS

3 tbsp olive oil, divided into 1 tbsp + 2 tbsp

1 cup diced onion (about ½ medium)

1 tbsp Bragg soy seasoning or tamari

1 tbsp minced garlic (about 6 cloves)

1 tbsp dried mushroom powder

1 tsp grated ginger root

1 tsp ground nutmeg

½ tsp ground cinnamon

½ tsp salt

4 cups chopped mushroom (about 16 medium)

1 cup diced orange or red bell pepper (about 1 medium) + a few slices for garnish

1½ cups raw short-grain brown rice, washed and rinsed

¾ cup white wine

2¼ cups mushroom broth + additional ¼ cup, if needed

CASHEW CREME (makes 1 cup), divided into ¾ cup + ¼ cup for topping (optional)

  1 cup raw cashews, soaked in water for at least 4 hours

  ¼ cup cashew milk

  1 tbsp nutritional yeast

  ¼ tsp salt

OTHER INGREDIENTS

1½ cups cooked brown lentils

2 cups roasted pumpkin, divided into 1 cup purée + 1 cup chunks (page 21)

1 tbsp minced sage leaves, divided into 2 tsp + 1 tsp whole and minced leaves for garnish

DIRECTIONS

1. Place a large saucepan on medium heat and add 1 tbsp olive oil. Once hot, add 1 cup diced onion and sauté until translucent and beginning to darken (about 5 minutes). Add a little water if onions start to stick.

2. Add 1 tbsp each Bragg seasoning, minced garlic, and dried mushroom powder, 1 tsp each grated ginger root and ground nutmeg, and ½ tsp each ground cinnamon and salt. Stir until well combined and cook for 1–2 minutes to let the flavours seal into onions.

3. Add 4 cups chopped mushroom and 1 cup diced orange bell pepper. Cook until mushrooms soften (about 10 minutes). Add a little water if the ingredients start to stick.

4. Add 2 tbsp olive oil and 1½ cups washed and rinsed raw short-grain brown rice. Pan-fry until rice changes colour and becomes somewhat translucent (10–12 minutes). Stir often to avoid sticking. Add a little water if mixture begins to stick.

5. Add ¾ cup white wine, stirring often. Let it bubble up, and once bubbles have subsided and wine has cooked in (about 5 minutes), add 2¼ cups mushroom broth, bring to a boil, lower heat, cover, and simmer for 30–40 minutes or until rice is soft.

6. Prepare **Cashew Creme:** (Prepare while rice cooks.)

    a. Drain and rinse the soaked cashews. Put them in a food processor or blender along with ¼ cup cashew milk, 1 tbsp nutritional yeast, and ¼ tsp salt.

    b. Process until smooth and creamy (3–5 minutes), scraping down sides as needed with a rubber spatula. Set aside ¼ cup of Cashew Creme for garnish.

7. To the cooked rice, add 1½ cups cooked brown lentils, 1 cup each pumpkin purée and cooked pumpkin chunks, ¾ cup Cashew Creme, and 2 tsp minced sage. Stir ingredients until well combined. Add an additional ¼ cup mushroom broth if the mixture is too thick. Cover with a lid, and simmer for 10–15 minutes on low until heated through. Serve immediately.

8. Garnish each serving with a couple of orange bell pepper slices and a mixture of minced and whole sage leaves. Serve the remaining ¼ cup Cashew Creme on the side as an option for additional creaminess.

NUTRITION: *PER 2-CUP SERVING (without Cashew Creme optional topping):* *Calories 650; Carbs 89g; Fat 23g; Protein 23g; Sodium 931mg; Sugar 9g*

MEALS

On the Lighter Side

 Avocado and Sun-Dried Tomato Toast   159
 Desperado Pizza with Dipping Sauce   161

Wrap It Up!

 Crunchy Lettuce Wraps   164
 Rainbow Rice Wraps   167

One-Dish Meals

 Versatile Pot Pie   169
 Shepherdless Pie   172
 Seriously the Best Chili con Veggies   175
 Big Bowl, Yummy Style   178

Avocado and Sun-Dried Tomato Toast

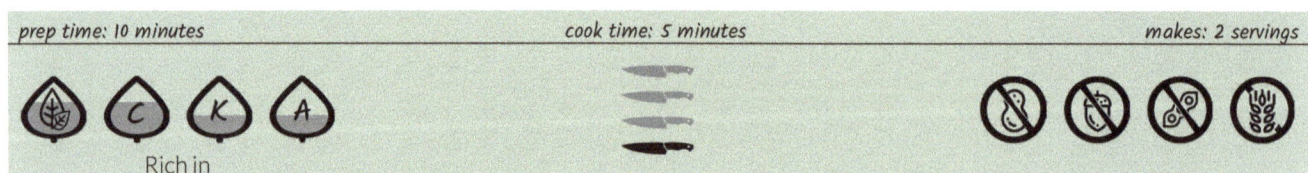

prep time: 10 minutes   cook time: 5 minutes   makes: 2 servings

Rich in

There's no need for toiling over a hot flame when you're hungry and in a hurry. 'Cause when you're fixin' for a fast meal, this one's delightfully simple to make. Strawberry Sal loves to serve Avocado and Sun-Dried Tomato Toast open-faced. This way, the sandwich is just the right size to fit your mouth, plus you'll savour the taste for twice as long! Carrot Rick is a big fan of making his own spread, which always tastes the best, plus that way, you're guaranteed to feed your body with healthy, whole foods. Some good options are Herb Hummus (page 55), Sun-dried Tomato Pesto (page 197), or Chipotle Aioli (page 135). If you have a mind to, you can mix and match the spreads, which is a sure-fire way to indulge your taste buds. Carrot Rick strongly recommends using organic tomatoes, which taste better than conventional and have way more nutrients and way less pesticides.

For gluten-free, use gluten-free bread.

INGREDIENTS

4 slices whole-wheat sourdough bread

2 tbsp Herb Hummus (page 55) or use your favourite sandwich spread, divided into 4 x 1½ tsp

1 avocado, sliced

1 tomato, sliced

4 tsp julienne-cut sun-dried tomato, packed in oil, divided into 4 x 1 tsp

10 Kalamata olives, pitted and sliced (about 4 tsp)

Spike all-purpose seasoning or Old Bay seasoning

American saffron

freshly ground black pepper, to taste

balsamic reduction (page 14)

DIRECTIONS

1. Toast 4 slices of whole-wheat sourdough bread.
2. Load 1½ tsp Herb Hummus (or spread of your choice) on each slice. Then add, in this order, avocado slices, sliced tomatoes, and 1 tsp each julienned sun-dried tomato and sliced Kalamata olives. Sprinkle with Spike seasoning, American saffron, and freshly ground black pepper. Drizzle with balsamic reduction.
3. Serve each person 2 slices and enjoy!

NUTRITION: PER SERVING: *Calories 497; Carbs 69g; Fat 20g; Protein 14g; Sodium 505mg; Sugar 3g*

Desperado Pizza with Dipping Sauce

prep time: 45 minutes   cook time: 65 minutes   makes: 2 x 9" pizzas (6 servings)

Rich in

When you're desperate for a slice of pizza, this one fits the bill. It'll please any outlaw as well as all your inlaws, 'cause this pizza breaks all the laws. So when people ask, "Yes, yes, yes, but what do you use instead of cheese?" The answer is caramelized onion sauce, flavourful toppings, and dipping sauce. After all, a good pizza is defined by the sauce, the toppings, and the crust, and this pie has 'em all. The crust is thin, crispy, and easy to assemble, and the best part, since there's no need for yeast, there's no fussin' about. The onion sauce makes a delicious base, but if you're looking for variety, try Sun-Dried Tomato Pesto (page 197), a marinara sauce, or whatever sauce captures your imagination. For the toppings, you can pop on artichoke hearts, olives, fresh or sundried tomato, basil, mushrooms, peppers, or whatever pleases your fancy. For a tasty twist, you can substitute in roasted red peppers. Another option is to throw on some Farmesan (page 89) or balsamic reduction (page 14) for garnish. The final touch is the dipping sauce, which takes no time to put together, but is mandatory. So have fun, and break free of the cheese!

This recipe makes a lovely light pizza crust. Using whole-wheat flour instead of all-purpose will result in a denser and more bread-like crust. However, if you're short on time, use a ready-made store-bought pizza crust.
Consider making the onion sauce in advance, so when you're desperate for pizza, you just need to make the dough and throw on the toppings.

INGREDIENTS

CARAMELIZED ONION SAUCE
(makes ¾ cup)
- 2 large onions
- 2 tbsp olive oil
- 2 tbsp balsamic vinegar
- ½ tsp sugar
- ⅛ tsp salt
- ¼ cup low-sodium vegetable broth
- ¼ tsp freshly ground black pepper

PIZZA DIPPING SAUCE *(makes 1¾ cups)*
- 1 cup tomato pasta sauce
- 2 tbsp pitted and chopped Kalamata olives (about 5)
- 2 tbsp chopped cooked or canned artichokes
- 2 tbsp water
- 1 tbsp chopped sun-dried tomato, packed in oil
- 1 tbsp minced basil leaves
- 1 tbsp minced oregano or marjoram leaves
- 1 tsp balsamic vinegar
- ⅛ tsp ground allspice
- ⅛ tsp Spike all-purpose seasoning or Old Bay seasoning
- freshly ground black pepper, to taste

EASY PIZZA CRUST *(no yeast)*
- ¼ cup grapeseed oil + ½ tsp for greasing the pan + 1 tsp for oiling your fingers
- 2¼ cups all-purpose flour + small amount for kneading the dough
- 1 tbsp baking powder
- 1 tbsp minced thyme leaves
- 1 tbsp minced parsley leaves
- 1 tbsp minced oregano leaves
- ½ tsp salt
- freshly ground black pepper, to taste
- 1 cup water, divided into ¾ cup + ¼ cup

DIRECTIONS

1. Prepare **Caramelized Onion Sauce**:

    a. Slice 2 large onions into rings (about 6 cups).

    b. Place large frying pan on medium-high heat and add 2 tbsp olive oil. Once hot, add sliced onion, spreading evenly across the bottom of the pan, coating onions in oil. Reduce to medium and sauté, stirring occasionally (about every 7 minutes), until onions become brown and translucent (20–30 minutes). If you stir too often, onions will not have time to brown, but if you wait too long, they may burn.

    c. Sprinkle 2 tbsp balsamic vinegar, ½ tsp sugar, and ⅛ tsp salt evenly over onions and stir until well combined. Continue to cook for an additional 15 minutes or until onions become light brown and caramelized. Add a little water if onions begin to stick.

    d. In a food processor or blender, add ¼ cup low-sodium vegetable broth, the caramelized onions, and ¼ tsp ground black pepper. Process for 5–10 minutes, scraping down sides as needed with a rubber spatula. Continue to process until the mixture is smooth and creamy.

2. Prepare **Pizza Dipping Sauce**:

    a. In a small saucepan, mix 1 cup tomato pasta sauce, 2 tbsp each pitted and chopped Kalamata olives, chopped artichoke hearts, and water, 1 tbsp each chopped sun-dried tomato, minced basil, and minced oregano, 1 tsp balsamic vinegar, ⅛ tsp each ground allspice and Spike seasoning, and freshly ground black pepper.

    b. Heat until mixture starts a slow boil, stir, and cook for 1–2 minutes before removing from heat. Serve warm as a dipping sauce for pizza.

3. Prepare **Easy Pizza Crust**:

    a. Spray two 9-inch pizza pans (or use a baking sheet to make one large, non-circular pizza) with grapeseed oil or, using a pastry brush, spread a thin layer of oil on the sheet (½ tsp oil).

    b. In a large bowl, sift 2¼ cups all-purpose flour, 1 tbsp each baking powder, minced thyme, minced parsley, and minced oregano leaves, ½ tsp salt, and freshly ground black pepper. Combine with a fork until everything is well mixed.

    c. In a small measuring cup, add ¾ cup water and ¼ cup grapeseed oil. Stir until well combined.

    d. Make a well in the middle of the dry ingredients, pour in the water and oil mixture, and combine using a fork until no dry patches remain. The dough should hold together but not be too.

INGREDIENTS, con't

TOPPINGS

- ¼ cup pitted and sliced Kalamata olives (about 10), divided into 2 x 2 tbsp
- ¼ cup chopped cooked or canned artichoke hearts, (1–2 whole hearts), divided into 2 x 2 tbsp
- ¼ cup chopped red bell pepper, divided into 2 x 2 tbsp
- ¼ cup sliced mushroom, divided into 2 x 2 tbsp (about 2 medium)
- 2 tbsp chopped sun-dried tomato, packed in oil, divided into 2 x 1 tbsp
- 2 tbsp minced basil leaves, divided into 2 x 1 tbsp

DIRECTIONS, con't

   e. crumbly. If the pastry is still too dry, slowly add up to ¼ cup water, 1 tbsp at a time, checking the consistency of the dough after each addition. Finish mixing the dough with your fingertips until it forms into a ball.

   f. Knead the dough for about 2 minutes on a lightly floured surface. (To knead the dough, place it on a floured surface, and using the heels of both hands simultaneously, push down and away. Next, fold the dough in half, turn it in a half-circle, and repeat.)

   g. Using oiled fingertips and the base of your palms, press and stretch the dough evenly into the shape of the oiled pizza pans. Press extra dough towards the edges and create a lip of dough around the rim.

4. Preheat oven to 400°F.

5. Top each pizza crust with 6 tbsp Caramelized Onion Sauce, 2 tbsp each pitted and sliced Kalamata olives, chopped artichoke hearts, chopped red bell pepper, and sliced mushroom, and 1 tbsp each chopped sun-dried tomato and minced basil. Cook until the dough browns (about 15 minutes).

6. Remove from the the oven and let sit for about 5 minutes. Slice and serve with Pizza Dipping Sauce and enjoy!

NUTRITION: PER ⅓ PIZZA SERVING: *Calories 363; Carbs 49g; Fat 15g; Protein 6g; Sodium 744mg; Sugar 8g*

Crunchy Lettuce Wraps

prep time: 40 minutes   cook time: 30 minutes   makes: 4 x 4-wrap servings

Rich in: A, 🌿, C, Ca, Fe, K

There'll be no need for persuading when you put Crunchy Lettuce Wraps on the table 'cause your crew'll be reaching for more after just one taste. But, for the best results, you'll want to be sure you have everything you need close at hand. First, use a whole head of butter lettuce, selecting large leaves and keeping them intact. Next, prepare a savoury, crunchy, Asian-Style chickpea filling and use hoisin sauce generously. We suggest you make your own hoisin sauce since it's spectacular, but the store-bought version works if you're feeling lazy or are in a hurry. Finally, dip and dunk your wrap in our Garlic-Ginger Dipping Sauce. But be quick when there's only one last wrap left, or you'll miss out.

> Make the sauces and rice ahead of time to speed up the process. We also suggest you double or triple the Hoisin and Garlic-Ginger Dipping Sauce recipes and freeze the extra for up to 6 months to use later.
> For soy-free, replace Bragg soy seasoning or tamari with coconut aminos (soy-free seasoning) (page 15) and use soy-free vegan Worcestershire sauce.
> Cook up some dried chickpeas in advance or simply open a 19-oz can (which is 2 cups of drained beans). Drain and save the chickpea water from the can for later use as aquafaba, aka: egg white substitute (page 14). Alternatively, you can replace chickpeas with crumbled tofu or vegan ground meat.

MEALS - WRAP IT UP!

INGREDIENTS

VEGGIE OUTLAWS HOISIN SAUCE *(makes 1 cup), divided into 2 x ½ cup*

- ⅓ cup diced sweet potatoes + water to cook
- ½ cup saved sweet potato water
- 2 tbsp raw sesame seeds
- 2 tbsp maple syrup
- 1 tbsp tamari or Bragg soy seasoning
- 1 tbsp rice wine vinegar
- 1½ tsp toasted sesame oil
- 1 tsp molasses
- ½ tsp minced garlic (about 1 clove)
- ½ tsp Sriracha sauce or chili garlic sauce
- ¼ tsp five-spice powder
- ¼ tsp ground chili pepper

GARLIC-GINGER DIPPING SAUCE *(makes 1 cup)*

- ⅔ cup water
- ¼ cup lemon juice (about 2 lemons)
- 2 tbsp tamari or Bragg soy seasoning
- 1 tbsp toasted sesame oil
- 1 tbsp minced garlic (about 6 cloves)
- 2 tsp sugar
- 1½ tsp grated ginger root
- 1 tsp Sriracha sauce or chili garlic sauce

DIRECTIONS

1. Prepare *Veggie OUTLAWS Hoisin Sauce*:

    a. Put ⅓ cup diced sweet potatoes in a small pan and cover with water. Bring to a boil and cook until potatoes are tender (about 10 minutes). Remove from water (makes about ¼ cup cooked), save ½ cup potato water, and put cooked potatoes in a small bowl to cool.

    b. While potatoes cook, dry toast 2 tbsp sesame seeds in a small frying pan on medium heat. Shake the pan continuously to keep seeds moving until they darken slightly and emit a pleasant nutty aroma (about 1 minute). Remove from heat, let cool, and place toasted sesame seeds in a spice or coffee grinder. Grind into a sesame paste.

    c. In a small food processor or blender, add cooked sweet potatoes, ½ cup sweet potato water, sesame paste, 2 tbsp maple syrup, 1 tbsp each tamari and rice wine vinegar, 1½ tsp toasted sesame oil, 1 tsp molasses, ½ tsp each minced garlic and Sriracha sauce, and ¼ tsp each five-spice powder and ground chili pepper. Process until smooth and creamy (2–3 minutes), scraping down the sides as needed with a rubber spatula. Divide into 2 x ½ cup portions and set aside.

2. Prepare *Garlic-Ginger Dipping Sauce*:

    a. In a small saucepan, add ⅔ cup water, ¼ cup lemon juice, 2 tbsp tamari, 1 tbsp each toasted sesame oil and minced garlic, 2 tsp sugar, 1½ tsp grated ginger root, and 1 tsp Sriracha sauce. Bring to a boil, cook for 1–2 minutes, remove from heat, and cover with a lid.

    b. Heat just before serving and strain into 4 x ¼ cup serving dishes.

INGREDIENTS, con't

CRUNCHY ASIAN-STYLE CHICKPEAS (makes 3 cups)

2 cups cooked chickpeas

1 tbsp toasted sesame oil

1 cup diced onion (about ½ medium)

½ cup Veggie OUTLAWS Hoisin Sauce (see above)

2 tbsp tamari or Bragg soy seasoning

2 tbsp rice wine vinegar

1½ tbsp grated ginger root

2 tsp Bestcestershire Sauce (vegan Worcestershire sauce)

1½ tsp minced garlic (about 3 cloves)

1 tsp minced lime leaves (about 2 leaves)

1 tsp Sriracha sauce or chili garlic sauce

1 cup drained and chopped water chestnuts

OTHER INGREDIENTS

16 whole and relatively large butter lettuce leaves

1 cup shredded carrot (2–3 medium)

1 cup sliced red bell pepper (about 1 medium)

1 cup bean sprouts

1 cup warm cooked brown jasmine rice

2 tbsp minced pickled ginger

DIRECTIONS, con't

3. Prepare **Crunchy Asian-Style Chickpeas**:

    a. Lightly squash 2 cups cooked chickpeas with a potato masher but avoid over mashing. You want them to be big enough to sink your teeth into but not so big they are still completely round.

    b. Place medium frying pan on medium-high heat and add 1 tbsp toasted sesame oil. Once hot, add 1 cup diced onion and sauté until translucent and beginning to darken (about 5 minutes). Add a little water if onions start to stick.

    c. Add ½ cup Veggie OUTLAWS Hoisin Sauce, 2 tbsp each tamari and rice wine vinegar, 1½ tbsp grated ginger root, 2 tsp Bestcestershire Sauce, 1½ tsp minced garlic, and 1 tsp each minced lime leaves and Sriracha sauce. Stir until well combined and cook for 1–2 minutes to let flavours seal into onions. Add 2 cups lightly squashed chickpeas and 1 cup chopped water chestnuts. Cook until heated through (about 5 minutes). Serve hot.

4. Rinse 16 whole and relatively large butter lettuce leaves, pat dry, and place on a serving plate. Be careful not to tear them.

5. On a large serving platter, arrange bowls of hot Crunchy Asian-Style Chickpeas, 1 cup shredded carrot, 1 cup sliced bell pepper, 1 cup bean sprouts, and 1 cup warm cooked brown jasmine rice.

6. To serve, set out the platter with the fillings, the plate of lettuce leaves, ½ cup Veggie OUTLAWS Hoisin Sauce, and 2 tbsp minced pickled ginger in the middle of the table. Give each person a ¼-cup bowl of warm Garlic-Ginger Dipping Sauce. Invite them to place a lettuce leaf on their plate and spoon on a portion of rice, sprouts, chickpeas, a scoop of hoisin sauce, and the remaining veggies. Wrap the lettuce around the filling like a burrito, dip it into the sauce, and enjoy! Repeat with the remaining lettuce leaves.

NUTRITION: PER SERVING: *Calories 476; Carbs 66g; Fat 43g; Protein 17g; Sodium 1,556mg; Sugar 21g*

Rainbow Rice Wraps

prep time: 20 minutes   makes: 4 x 4-wrap servings

Rich in A, C

These little beauties are both a feast for the eyes and a feast for the belly that'll satisfy you, right down to your toes. Here you'll find beautiful rice wraps filled with bright veggies naturally displaying the colours of the rainbow. Not only are they pretty, but, like a rainbow, there's a treasure to be found at the end. Discover a trove of vitamins, antioxidants, and other nutrients that your body craves. For a fun meal, place all the ingredients on a platter, put it on the table alongside a dish of warm water, then soften each wrap as needed. That way, you and your kinfolk can build each roll just the way you like. Another option is to add Roasted Tofu (page 131). These superb tofu chips are fun to sneak into the wrap or serve on the side with extra Snappy Peanut Sauce. (Another good reason to double the peanut sauce recipe.) You and your posse can prepare the rolls any way you like, then cut them in half or leave them whole, and that's a wrap!

The recipe for Snappy Peanut Sauce makes 1 cup. It's a good idea to double the Snappy Peanut Sauce recipe to use as a dip for Roasted Tofu. Refrigerate any leftover sauce in an airtight container and use it within 5 days or freeze it for future use.

INGREDIENTS

2 cups bean sprouts

1½ cups spinach leaves or another type of greens, like kale, mustard greens, or arugula

a bunch of Thai basil and/or cilantro leaves (about ¾ cup)

1 large carrot

1 medium daikon radish

1 small raw beet

1 small orange or yellow bell pepper

½ cup raw peanuts

16 pieces of 8-inch round rice paper (14-oz package) + warm water for soaking

½ cup Snappy Peanut Sauce (page 193)

DIRECTIONS

1. Prepare the veggies. Wash and drain 2 cups bean sprouts, 1½ cups spinach leaves, and a bunch of Thai basil or cilantro leaves (or a combination of both). Peel a large carrot, a medium daikon radish, and a small beet. Then shave into ribbons using a vegetable peeler (about ¾ cup each). Remove seeds and pulp from a small orange bell pepper and thinly slice. Place all the prepared veggies on a serving platter along with ½ cup raw peanuts.

2. Prepare rice paper. Place a 12-inch-diameter flat-bottomed bowl on the table and fill it halfway with warm water. Next to it, place a clean serving plate. Soak a single piece of rice paper in warm water for 5 seconds, so it is malleable but not soggy. (If the rice paper is in the water for too long, it will be unusable. If this happens, toss it and grab a new one.) Assemble each roll separately as soon as the rice wrap softens. Replace water in the bowl with more warm water when it cools.

3. Place the softened wrap on a plate or other clean, flat surface. Spread 1–3 sprigs of Thai basil or cilantro leaves in a line 3 inches above the bottom of the wrap, keeping clear of both edges by about 1 inch. Cover the herbs with a large spinach leaf, 2 smaller leaves, or equivalent. Then layer on vegetable ribbons. Use strips of carrot, radish, beet, and bell pepper. Drizzle 1½ tsp Snappy Peanut Sauce on vegetables. Cover with ⅓ cup bean sprouts and a sprinkling of raw peanuts.

4. Tuck the bottom of the wrap over the filling, roll the sides around it, and repeat until you make 16 rolls. Either place them on a platter or let everyone build their own wraps.

NUTRITION: PER 4-WRAP SERVING: *Calories 307; Carbs 48g; Fat 14g; Protein 4g; Sodium 757mg; Sugar 9g*

Versatile Pot Pie

prep time: 50 minutes   cook time: 80 minutes   makes: 6 servings

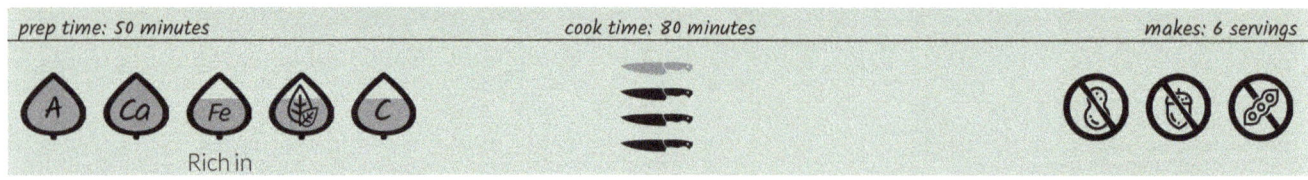

Rich in

This veggie pot pie is versatile. You can vary the veggies, the protein source, and the topping. So, mix it up and shake up some good eats every time. Keep in mind that the pie experience you create depends on which herb and topping you're fixin' to use. If you've got a craving for a savoury pie, add the rosemary, but go for the tarragon if you're wanting a more sweetly robust pie. Just be sure to use the same herb in both the filling and the crust. Have fun mixing and matching with the crust. The olive crust creates a fruity-salty flavour, whereas the sun-dried tomato crust creates a more sweetly-tart flavour. Plus, you can have fun and let your imagination run wild while creating entertaining and unique shapes with the pastry for the top of your pie. We challenge you to be versatile and make a different pie every time.

For soy-free, replace Bragg soy seasoning or tamari with coconut aminos (soy-free seasoning) (page 15), use soy-free vegan Worcestershire sauce, and use chickpeas for your vegan protein.

169

INGREDIENTS

SAVOURY PIE FILLING

¼ cup low-sodium vegetable or mushroom broth

1 cup diced onion (about ½ medium)

2 tbsp Bragg soy seasoning or tamari

1 tbsp minced garlic (about 6 cloves)

1 tbsp dried mushroom powder

2 tsp Bestcestershire Sauce (vegan Worcestershire sauce)

¼ tsp Spike all-purpose seasoning or Old Bay seasoning

1½ cups vegan protein of your choice: use crumbled tofu (½ of 12-oz package extra-firm tofu), chickpeas (13.5-oz can, drained), or other vegan meat

2 cups sliced mushroom (about 8 medium)

2 cups broccoli florets or veggie of your choice

1 cup sliced carrot (about 2 medium)

1 tbsp minced rosemary or tarragon leaves

1 tbsp minced parsley leaves

1 tbsp minced oregano or marjoram leaves

BROTH

3 tbsp vegan butter

3 tbsp all-purpose flour

¼ cup white wine

1½ cups mushroom broth

1½ tsp dried mushroom powder

½ tsp mustard powder

1 bay leaf

freshly ground black pepper, to taste

DIRECTIONS

1. Prepare *Savoury Pie Filling*:

    a. Place Dutch oven or large saucepan on medium-high heat and add ¼ cup low-sodium vegetable broth. Once hot, add 1 cup diced onion and sauté until translucent and beginning to darken (about 5 minutes). Add a little water if onions start to stick, but let the broth cook off so onions can brown. If they become too dry, the onions may burn.

    b. Add 2 tbsp Bragg seasoning, 1 tbsp each minced garlic and dried mushroom powder, 2 tsp Bestcestershire Sauce, and ¼ tsp Spike seasoning. Mix until well combined and cook for about 1–2 minutes to seal flavours into the onions. Add a little water if the ingredients start to stick.

    c. Add 1½ cups vegan protein like crumbled extra-firm tofu, chickpeas, or other vegan meat. Stir until well combined. Cook until protein starts to brown (5–7 minutes). Add a little water if the ingredients begin to stick.

    d. Add 2 cups each sliced mushroom and broccoli florets (or veggie of your choice) and 1 cup sliced carrot. Stir until well combined. Cook until mushrooms start to brown and veggies begin to soften (about 5 minutes). Add a little water if the ingredients start to stick.

    e. Add 1 tbsp each minced rosemary, parsley, and oregano. You can vary the herbs you use depending on the flavour combination you are seeking. Cover and set aside.

2. Prepare *Broth*:

    a. Place saucepan on medium heat and add 3 tbsp vegan butter. Once hot and liquified, reduce to medium-low. Slowly sift in 3 tbsp all-purpose flour, whisking continuously to ensure no lumps appear. Continue to whisk until all the flour is completely absorbed and the mixture is smooth. Cook for a few minutes until the mixture starts to bubble.

    b. Add ¼ cup white wine, whisking continuously. The mixture may bubble up but continue to whisk until the bubbles subside.

    c. Slowly add 1½ cups mushroom broth, ¼ cup at a time, whisking continuously. Once the mixture is smooth, add 1½ tsp dried mushroom powder, ½ tsp dry mustard powder, 1 bay leaf, and freshly ground black pepper. Whisk until well combined. Stirring continuously, bring to a low boil, and cook until the mixture thickens (about 3 minutes). Remove from heat.

3. Remove the bay leaf before pouring the broth over the cooked vegetables in the Dutch oven. If you don't have a Dutch oven, transfer the cooked vegetables to a deep casserole dish and pour the broth over them.

4. Preheat oven to 375°F.

INGREDIENTS, con't

NICELY SPICED PIE CRUST

⅓ cup Kalamata olives or oil-packed sun-dried tomato + a few for garnish

1¼ cups whole-wheat pastry flour + small amount for rolling the dough

1 tsp baking powder

1 tsp salt

1 tbsp minced rosemary, tarragon, parsley, marjoram, or oregano leaves + a few for garnish

⅓ cup cold water + more if needed

1 tsp white wine vinegar

¼ cup semi-solid coconut oil (page 17)

DIRECTIONS, con't

5. Prepare *Nicely Spiced Pie Crust*:

    a. Coarsely chop ⅓ cup pitted Kalamata olives or oil-packed sun-dried tomato.

    b. In a medium bowl, sift 1¼ cups whole-wheat pastry flour and 1 tsp each baking powder and salt. Add 1 tbsp minced herbs. Stir a few times to ensure ingredients are well mixed.

    c. In a small dish, mix ⅓ cup cold water with 1 tsp white wine vinegar.

    d. Add ¼ cup semi-solid coconut oil to the flour mixture, 1 tbsp at a time. Using a pastry cutter (or 2 butter knives, cutting in opposite directions, or a balloon whisk), press straight down, repeating in different spots. Cut the oil into the flour mixture until it looks like crumbs. Do not overdo it, or the dough may become tough.

    e. Slowly pour the cold-water mixture over the flour mixture, 1 tbsp at a time, mixing continuously with a fork until no dry patches remain and the dough starts to form into a ball. If you reach this stage before using all the water, do not add more water. If the pastry is too dry after adding all the water, slowly add more cold water, 1 tbsp at a time. If the dough feels too sticky, add a little more flour. Try not to overhandle the dough, or it may become tough.

    f. Once the dough starts to form into a ball, add ⅓ cup chopped olives or sundried tomato. Continue to work the dough until chopped olives or sundried tomatoes are incorporated and the dough forms into a ball.

    g. Immediately roll out the dough using 2 sheets of parchment paper. Place one sheet on the counter and lightly sprinkle flour over it. Place the ball of dough on top and sprinkle lightly with flour. Place the second sheet of parchment paper over the dough. Using a pastry roller, roll out the dough until it is ¼-inch thick and one inch larger all the way around than your Dutch oven or baking dish. (To get an even thickness, rotate the dough after each roll.) Gently peel off the top piece of parchment paper.

6. Place the lid of your Dutch oven or baking dish over your rolled-out dough, and using a bread knife, cut the dough 1 inch larger than the size of the baking dish. Carefully place the dough on top of the filling in your baking dish, bunching up any excess around the edges. Remove the bottom piece of parchment paper. Gather up the leftover dough, place it between 2 sheets of parchment paper, and roll to a ⅛-inch thickness. Use cookie cutters to cut out fun shapes. Place them on top of your pot pie.

7. Bake for 35–40 minutes. When done, the pie should be golden brown and bubbling. Remove from oven and let set for at least 10 minutes before garnishing with a few olives or sundried tomatoes and a sprinkle of fresh herbs. Dig in and enjoy!

NUTRITION: PER SERVING: Calories 447; Carbs 45g; Fat 24g; Protein 13g; Sodium 1,525mg; Sugar 4g

Shepherdless Pie

Shepherdless Pie: prep time: 35 minutes + time to marinate
Quick and Creamy Mushroom Gravy: prep time: 10 minutes
cook time: 65 minutes
cook time: 20 minutes
makes: 6 x 1⅔-cup servings
makes: 6 x ½-cup servings

       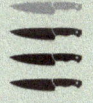

Rich in

Down in our little corner of Livewood, we serve our version of shepherd's pie. Since we make it without meat (or shepherds), we decided to call it Shepherdless pie — as no shepherds are needed. If you weren't already aware, Shepherd's pie is a traditional English meat pie topped with mashed potatoes. We stepped up and improved upon the ole standard. Instead of ground meat, we added savoury lentils and marinated crumbled tofu, but we kept the mashed potatoes (which Potato Pat claims are the crowning glory of the dish). The Quick and Creamy Mushroom Gravy makes the pie sing and adds to the overall feeling of comfort and warmth, but it is optional. Cashew Sue likes to prepare this dish a day or two in advance, refrigerate it, and then pop it in the oven when hungry folk stop over for a visit. While the pie bakes, she cooks up the gravy for a quick and easy meal that hits the spot every time.

For nut-free, replace cashew milk with vegan nut-free milk of your choice.
For soy-free, replace Bragg soy seasoning or tamari with coconut aminos (soy-free seasoning) (page 15), use soy-free vegan Worcestershire sauce, and use lightly smashed chickpeas for your vegan protein.
For gluten-free, use gluten-free flour for the thickener.

INGREDIENTS

MASHED POTATOES (makes 4 cups) for topping

- 6 medium russet potatoes + water for boiling
- ½ tsp salt, divided into 2 x ¼ tsp
- ⅓ cup oat milk
- 2 tbsp vegan butter
- ⅛ tsp white pepper

OTHER INGREDIENTS

- 2 cups extra-firm tofu (12-oz package), or lightly squashed cooked chickpeas, or vegan meat of your choice
- 3 tbsp minced sage leaves, divided into 2 tbsp + 1 tbsp
- 1 tbsp Bragg soy seasoning or tamari
- 1 tbsp minced garlic (about 6 cloves)
- 1 tbsp Bestcestershire Sauce (vegan Worcestershire sauce), divided into 2 x 1½ tsp
- 1¼ tsp Spike all-purpose seasoning or Old Bay seasoning, divided into 2 x ½ tsp + ¼ tsp to sprinkle on top
- ¼ cup low-sodium vegetable broth
- 1 cup chopped onion (about ½ medium)
- 1 tbsp dried mushroom powder
- ½ tsp paprika, divided into 2 x ¼ tsp
- ¼ tsp ground allspice
- freshly ground black pepper, to taste
- 1 cup diced celery with leaves (about 2 stalks)
- ½ cup diced carrot (about 1 medium)
- 2 cups fresh or frozen green peas
- 2 cups cooked, drained, and rinsed brown lentils
- 1 tbsp minced parsley leaves
- 1 tbsp minced thyme leaves + small amount to sprinkle on top
- 2 tbsp red wine (medium-bodied, like a merlot)
- 1–2 cups saved potato water (see above)

DIRECTIONS

1. Prepare **Mashed Potatoes** for topping: Peel and dice 6 medium russet potatoes (about 5 cups). Place in a large pot and cover with water mixed with ¼ tsp salt. Cover with a lid and bring to a boil. Continue to cook on medium-high heat until tender (10–15 minutes). When potatoes are soft, drain water, but retain 2 cups of potato water. Mash potatoes with ⅓ cup oat milk, 2 tbsp vegan butter, ¼ tsp salt, and ⅛ tsp white pepper until smooth (makes 4 cups).

2. While potatoes cook, place in a medium bowl, 2 cups crumbled extra-firm tofu, 2 tbsp minced sage leaves, 1 tbsp each Bragg seasoning and minced garlic, 1½ tsp Bestcestershire Sauce, and ½ tsp Spike seasoning. Toss tofu in seasoning and marinate for at least 15 minutes, stirring occasionally.

3. Preheat oven to 425°F.

4. Place a large Dutch oven or large saucepan on medium-high heat and add ¼ cup low-sodium vegetable broth. Once hot, add 1 cup chopped onion and sauté until translucent and beginning to darken (about 5 minutes). Add a little water if onions start to stick, but let the broth cook off so onions can brown. If they become too dry, the onions may burn.

5. Add 1 tbsp each minced sage leaves and dried mushroom powder, 1½ tsp Bestcestershire Sauce, ½ tsp Spike seasoning, and ¼ tsp each paprika and ground allspice, and freshly ground black pepper. Cook for 1–2 minutes to seal flavours into the onions. Add a little water if the ingredients begin to stick.

6. Add the marinated tofu and cook until tofu browns (about 5 minutes). Add 1 cup diced celery and ½ cup diced carrot and cook until carrots begin to soften (about 5 minutes). Add a little water if the ingredients start to stick.

7. Add 2 cups each fresh or frozen green peas and cooked brown lentils and 1 tbsp each minced parsley and thyme leaves. Stir until well combined and slowly pour in 2 tbsp red wine and then 1–2 cups potato water, ½ cup at a time, until the mixture is moist and creamy but not soupy.

8. If using a Dutch oven, bake the Shepherdless Pie right in the Dutch oven. Otherwise, transfer the mixture to a large baking dish oven.

9. Layer the mashed potatoes on top. Then smooth and shape the topping to make the pie look pretty. Sprinkle on ¼ tsp each paprika and Spike seasoning. Bake uncovered for 35 minutes or until the potatoes brown and the mixture bubbles. Remove from the oven and let set it for at least 5 minutes.

10. Slice pie into wedges, add a sprinkle of minced herbs, and serve with Quick and Creamy Mushroom Gravy.

INGREDIENTS, con't

QUICK AND CREAMY MUSHROOM GRAVY *(makes 3 cups) (optional)*

¼ cup olive oil, divided into 1 tbsp + 3 tbsp

1 cup diced onion (about ½ medium)

⅓ cup dried mushroom powder

2 tbsp Bragg soy seasoning or tamari

1 tsp paprika

¼ tsp Spike all-purpose seasoning or Old Bay seasoning

¼ tsp ground allspice

freshly ground black pepper, to taste

¼ cup all-purpose flour

⅓ cup red wine (medium-bodied, like a merlot)

2 cups mushroom broth

Milk Mixture (makes ¾ cup)

½ cup oat milk

3 tbsp cashew milk

1 tbsp coconut milk

1½ tsp minced thyme leaves

DIRECTIONS, con't

11. Prepare **Quick and Creamy Mushroom Gravy**: (Make while Shepherdless Pie bakes.)

    a. Place saucepan on medium-high heat and add 1 tbsp olive oil. Once hot, add 1 cup diced onion and sauté until translucent and beginning to darken (about 5 minutes).

    b. Add ⅓ cup dried mushroom powder, 2 tbsp Bragg seasoning, 1 tsp paprika, ¼ tsp each Spike seasoning and ground allspice, and freshly ground black pepper. Stir until well combined and cook for 1–2 minutes. Add a little water if the ingredients start to stick.

    c. Add the remaining 3 tbsp olive oil and cook for 1–2 minutes before reducing the heat to medium-low. Slowly sift in ¼ cup all-purpose flour, whisking continuously until all the flour is completely absorbed, ensuring no lumps appear. Cook for a few minutes until the mixture heats up and flour bubbles and thickens, stirring often.

    d. Slowly pour in ⅓ cup red wine, whisking continuously. The mixture may become gummy but continue to whisk until the wine is completely absorbed. Slowly pour in 2 cups mushroom broth, ½ cup at a time, whisking continuously. Once all the broth has been added, and the mixture is smooth (without any lumps). Then slowly pour in ¾ cup Milk Mixture (½ cup oat milk, 3 tbsp cashew milk, and 1 tbsp coconut milk), whisking continuously until smooth. Bring to a slow boil and cook until the gravy thickens (about 5 minutes). Add 1½ tsp minced thyme leaves. Serve hot with pie.

NUTRITION: **SHEPHERDLESS PIE ONLY** (no gravy) - *PER SERVING:* Calories 423; Carbs 66g; Fat 8g; Protein 18g; Sodium 507mg; Sugar 6g; **QUICK AND CREAMY MUSHROOM GRAVY** - *PER ½-CUP SERVING:* Calories 151; Carbs 12g; Fat 10g; Protein 2g; Sodium 570mg; Sugar 2g

MEALS - ONE-DISH MEALS

Seriously the Best Chili con Veggies

Chili con Veggies: prep time: 20 minutes	cook time: 55 minutes	makes: 4 x 2-cup servings
Boxcar Green Chile Sauce: prep time: 20 minutes	cook time: 45 minutes	makes: 8 x ¼-cup servings

Rich in

Chili con veggies means chili with vegetables and is a fun way to present vegan chili. Typically, chili is a spicy dish of meat, chili peppers, beans, tomatoes, and seasonings. Our recipe improves on the original because it replaces the meat with veggies and provides the opportunity for an extra burst of chilis. Not only do chilis taste great, but they're brimming with nutrients. We highly recommend you take the time to make up Boxcar Green Chile Sauce because it adds a level of authenticity. Plus, when added to the veggie chili, it creates a dish that is out of this world. The best part is that you can stir in as much or as little Boxcar Green Chile Sauce into each bowl according to taste. This is seriously the best vegetarian chili, and the secret — besides all the awesome ingredients — is using canned diced tomatoes with the liquid drained off. Trust us, you and your compadres will be amazed and pleased with the result. Easy Guacamole (page 183) and Chipotle Cornbread (page 137) also make great additions to this dish.

You can use poblano or Anaheim chili peppers if you can't find Hatch chiles, but these are milder. If you want more heat you can add one or two jalapeno peppers. If you prefer a milder sauce use a green bell pepper plus one other chili pepper of your choice. Refrigerate leftover Boxcar Green Chile Sauce for up to a week or freeze and use at a later date. Or double the recipe and freeze in ½-cup containers for up to 6 months. Then, serve it with Let's Flex Tacos (page 183), Portobello Mushroom Fajitas (page185), or ... use your imagination.

For soy-free, replace Bragg soy seasoning or tamari with coconut aminos (soy-free seasoning) (page 15) and use soy-free vegan Worcestershire sauce.

Use gluten-free flour as a thickener for gluten-free option.

See details for Boxcar Green Chile Sauce on the next page. Omit Boxcar Green Chile Sauce for low-fat option.

INGREDIENTS

SERIOUSLY THE BEST CHILI CON VEGGIES:

- ¼ cup low-sodium vegetable broth
- 1 cup diced onion (about ½ medium)
- 1 tsp cumin seeds
- 2 tbsp Bragg soy seasoning or tamari
- 1 tbsp minced garlic (about 6 cloves)
- 1 tbsp ground cumin
- 2 tsp Bestcestershire Sauce (vegan Worcestershire sauce)
- 1 tsp ground Ancho chili pepper (page 13)
- ½ tsp smoked paprika
- 2 cups sliced mushroom (about 8 medium)
- 1 cup diced zucchini (about 1 medium)
- 1 cup diced green bell pepper (about 1 medium)
- 1 cup diced celery (about 2 stalks)
- 1 cup diced carrot (about 2 medium)
- 28-oz can low-sodium diced tomatoes
- ¼ cup tomato paste
- 1½ cups cooked red kidney beans
- 1½ cups cooked pinto beans or canned chili-style beans (page17)
- 2 tbsp chopped cilantro leaves
- ½ tsp salt
- Fresh Tomato Salsa (optional) (page 51)

DIRECTIONS

1. Prepare **Seriously the Best Chili con Veggies**:

    a. Place a large soup pot on medium-high heat and add ¼ cup low-sodium vegetable broth. Once hot, add 1 cup diced onion and 1 tsp cumin seeds. Sauté until onion is translucent and beginning to darken and cumin seeds start to brown (about 5 minutes). Add a little water if onions begin to stick, but let the broth cook off so onions can brown. If they become too dry, the onions may burn.

    b. To the cooked onions, add 2 tbsp Bragg seasoning, 1 tbsp each minced garlic and ground cumin, 2 tsp Bestcestershire Sauce, 1 tsp ground Ancho chili pepper, and ½ tsp smoked paprika. Stir until well combined and cook for 1–2 minutes to seal flavours into the onions. Add a little water if the ingredients start to stick.

    c. Add 2 cups sliced mushroom and cook until they begin to brown (5–10 minutes). Next, add 1 cup each diced zucchini, green bell pepper, celery, and carrot. Cook for an additional 10–15 minutes or until the veggies soften. Add a little water if the ingredients begin to stick.

    d. While the vegetables cook, drain the liquid from a 28-oz can of low-sodium canned tomatoes and retain about 2 cups of canned diced tomatoes. (Keep the excess liquid to add to soups or make a fresh vegan cocktail like a Caesar or Bloody Mary.) Add drained canned tomatoes and ¼ cup tomato paste to the veggies. Stir and cook for a few minutes to let the flavours meld.

    e. Add 1½ cups each cooked red kidney beans and pinto beans, 2 tbsp chopped cilantro, and ½ tsp salt. Simmer until the flavours intensify, and the chili is heated through (about 20 minutes).

    f. Divide among bowls and serve hot. Place Boxcar Green Chile Sauce (details on the next page), Fresh Tomato Salsa, and any other preferred toppings on the side. Then everyone can garnish their bowl according to taste.

INGREDIENTS, con't

BOXCAR GREEN CHILE SAUCE
(optional)

- ¼ tsp grapeseed oil for greasing the pan
- 4–5 Hatch green chiles (about 3 cups)
- 3 tbsp olive oil, divided into 2 tbsp + 1 tbsp
- 1 cup diced onion (about ½ medium)
- 2 tbsp minced garlic (about 1 bulb)
- 1 tsp ground cumin
- ⅛ tsp black pepper
- 2 tbsp whole-wheat flour
- 1 cup low-sodium vegetable broth
- 2 tbsp white wine vinegar
- 1 tbsp chopped oregano leaves
- 1 tsp salt

DIRECTIONS, con't

2. Prepare **Boxcar Green Chile Sauce**:

    a. Preheat oven to 450°F. Spray roasting pan with oil or, using a pastry brush, spread a thin layer of oil on pan (¼ tsp oil).

    b. Wash 4–5 Hatch green chiles and place in roasting pan. Roast for 10–15 minutes, then flip. Cook for an additional 10 minutes or until peppers brown and collapse.

    c. Immediately remove peppers from the oven, place them in a glass dish, and cover to let peppers "steam" for about 15 minutes.

    d. While peppers "steam," place saucepan on medium heat and add 2 tbsp olive oil. Once hot, add 1 cup diced onion and sauté until translucent and beginning to darken (about 5 minutes). Add a little water if onions start to stick.

    e. Add 2 tbsp minced garlic and cook until garlic starts to soften (1–2 minutes). Do not let the garlic brown, or it may become bitter.

    f. Add 1 tbsp olive oil, 1 tsp ground cumin, and ⅛ tsp black pepper. Stir and cook for 1–2 minutes. When hot, slowly sift in 2 tbsp whole-wheat flour, whisking continuously to ensure no lumps appear, and cook for 3–4 minutes or until the mixture darkens. Remove from stovetop.

    g. Remove skin, seeds, and stems from roasted peppers, and chop pepper flesh (about 1 cup). Stir into onion mixture and add 1 cup low-sodium vegetable broth, 2 tbsp white wine vinegar, 1 tbsp chopped oregano leaves, and 1 tsp salt. Cook for at least 15 minutes or until the mixture thickens, stirring often. Add water or broth if sauce becomes too thick.

    h. Using an immersion blender, a small food processor, or blender, blend with several pulses but do not over-mix. The sauce is best with a slightly chunky consistency.

NUTRITION: CHILI ONLY (no toppings or chile sauce) - PER 2-CUP SERVING: *Calories 306; Carbs 56g; Fat 1g; Protein 19g; Sodium 1,216mg; Sugar 13g;* **BOXCAR GREEN CHILE SAUCE** - PER ¼-CUP SERVING: *Calories 80; Carbs 8g; Fat 5g; Protein 1g; Sodium 316mg; Sugar 2g*

Big Bowl, Yummy Style

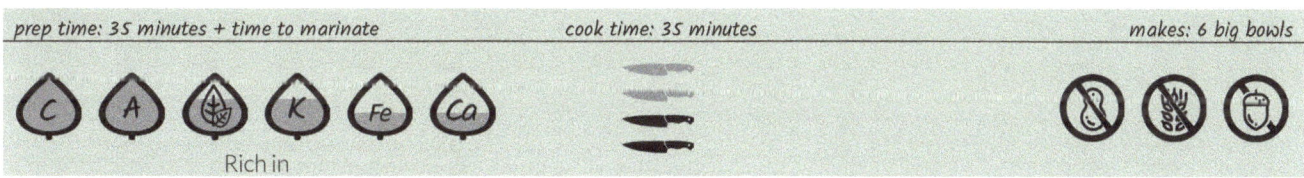

prep time: 35 minutes + time to marinate   cook time: 35 minutes   makes: 6 big bowls

Rich in: C, A, (leaf), K, Fe, Ca

The bountiful blesssings of the earth abounds, stirring us to tinker and rustle up all manner of toothsome grub. It's clear as day, ain't nothing gonna steer us away from fashioning our version of a Big Bowl. Keep in mind there are many types of Big Bowl, most influenced by the Buddha bowl concept. These bowls are typically a vegetarian meal prepared in a — you guessed it — big bowl and usually include whole grains, vegetables, and plant protein. Our Big Bowl is not to be missed. Not only is it yummy, colourful, and filling, but it's also packed full of nutrient-rich foods. The tahini dressing perfectly complements all the incredible flavours, making this dish Yummy Style. We recommend you marinate the veggies overnight. Then, when you roast them, the flavours have had a chance to settle into the veggies. Plus, it speeds up the process when you want to serve this meal to your hungry gang. If you don't eat all 6 bowls in one serving, you can refrigerate any leftovers and have them cold the next day for lunch. Yummy!

For nut-free, omit the walnuts.

MEALS - ONE-DISH MEALS

INGREDIENTS

ROASTED TOFU AND VEGGIES
(makes 8 cups)

- 1 tbsp grapeseed oil + ¼ tsp for greasing the pan
- 2 tbsp Bragg soy seasoning or tamari
- 2 tbsp chopped basil or oregano leaves
- 1 tbsp balsamic vinegar
- 2 tsp Bestcestershire Sauce (vegan Worcestershire sauce)
- 1½ tsp minced garlic (about 3 cloves)
- ½ tsp Spike all-purpose seasoning or Old Bay seasoning
- ½ tsp American saffron
- 3 large portobello mushrooms, sliced into strips (about 6 cups)
- 2 medium zucchinis, chopped (about 2 cups)
- 12-oz package medium-firm tofu, cut into ¼-inch slices (about 2 cups)
- 1 medium red bell pepper, with seeds and pulp removed, sliced into strips (about 1 cup)
- 2 medium carrots, chopped (about 1 cup)
- 1 small fennel bulb, thinly sliced (about 1 cup)
- 1 cup sliced fresh green beans
- ½ cup sliced red onion
- ¼ cup pumpkin seeds
- ¼ cup walnuts

DIRECTIONS

1. Prepare **Roasted Tofu and Veggies**:

    a. Preheat oven to 400°F. Spray rimmed baking sheet with oil or, using a pastry brush, spread a thin layer of oil on the sheet (¼ tsp oil).

    b. In a small bowl, mix 2 tbsp each Bragg seasoning and chopped basil leaves, 1 tbsp each grapeseed oil and balsamic vinegar, 2 tsp Bestcestershire Sauce, 1½ tsp minced garlic, and ½ tsp each Spike seasoning and American saffron. Stir until well combined.

    c. In a large bowl, add about 6 cups sliced portobello mushroom, about 2 cups each chopped zucchini and sliced tofu, about 1 cup each sliced red bell pepper, chopped carrot, sliced fennel bulb, and sliced green beans, ½ cup sliced red onion, and ¼ cup each pumpkin seeds and walnuts.

    d. Pour marinade over vegetables, toss until well coated, and let sit for at least 15 minutes to allow the flavours to soak into the vegetables.

    e. Place marinated vegetables on the prepared baking sheet and roast for 30–35 minutes, turning at the 15-minute mark. Cook until tender.

INGREDIENTS, con't

TAHINI DRESSING (makes 1½ cups)

½ cup tahini

½ cup hot water

1 tbsp white miso paste

¼ cup olive oil

¼ cup balsamic vinegar

4 tsp Sriracha sauce or chili garlic sauce

1 tbsp raw blue agave nectar or maple syrup

2 tsp Dijon mustard

1 tsp nutritional yeast

1 tsp Bragg soy seasoning or tamari

¼ tsp American saffron

OTHER INGREDIENTS

½ cup frozen shelled edamame beans + a few for garnish + boiling water for soaking

½ cup frozen sweet corn kernels + boiling water for soaking

1½ cups warm, cooked rainbow quinoa or short-grain brown rice

¾ cup mixed bean sprouts (see page 22)

½ cup baby or chopped kale

1 avocado, with pit removed and cut into 8 strips or 1–2 cooked beets, chopped

12 cherry tomatoes, cut into halves

⅓ cup minced parsley leaves

DIRECTIONS, con't

2. Prepare **Tahini Dressing**: In a bowl, add ½ cup each tahini and hot water and 1 tbsp white miso paste. Whisk until well combined and creamy. Next, add ¼ cup each olive oil and balsamic vinegar, 4 tsp Sriracha sauce, 1 tbsp agave nectar, 2 tsp Dijon mustard, 1 tsp each nutritional yeast and Bragg seasoning, and ¼ tsp American saffron. Mix until well combined.

3. In separate bowls, place ½ cup each frozen shelled edamame beans and frozen corn kernels. Cover each with boiling water and let sit for a minimum of 10 minutes. Drain and rinse.

4. Arrange 6 big bowls in a row. In each bowl, add ½ cup warm cooked quinoa, topped with 2 tbsp dressing. Then add 1⅓ cups hot roasted vegetable mixture, 2 tbsp mixed bean sprouts, 4 tsp each baby kale, edamame beans, and corn kernels, and 2 avocado strips or 2 tbsp chopped beets. The beets add nice colour to the dish, and if you have both avocado and beets, feel free to add both.

5. Top each serving with 4 tomato halves, 2 tbsp dressing, 2 tsp minced parsley, and a few edamame beans. Drizzle any remaining dressing over the top and serve immediately.

NUTRITION: PER BOWL: Calories 580; Carbs 53g; Fat 36g; Protein 19g; Sodium 741mg; Sugar 16g

MAINS

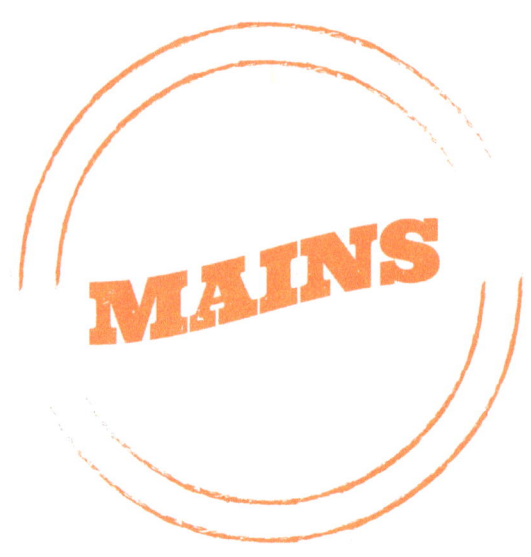

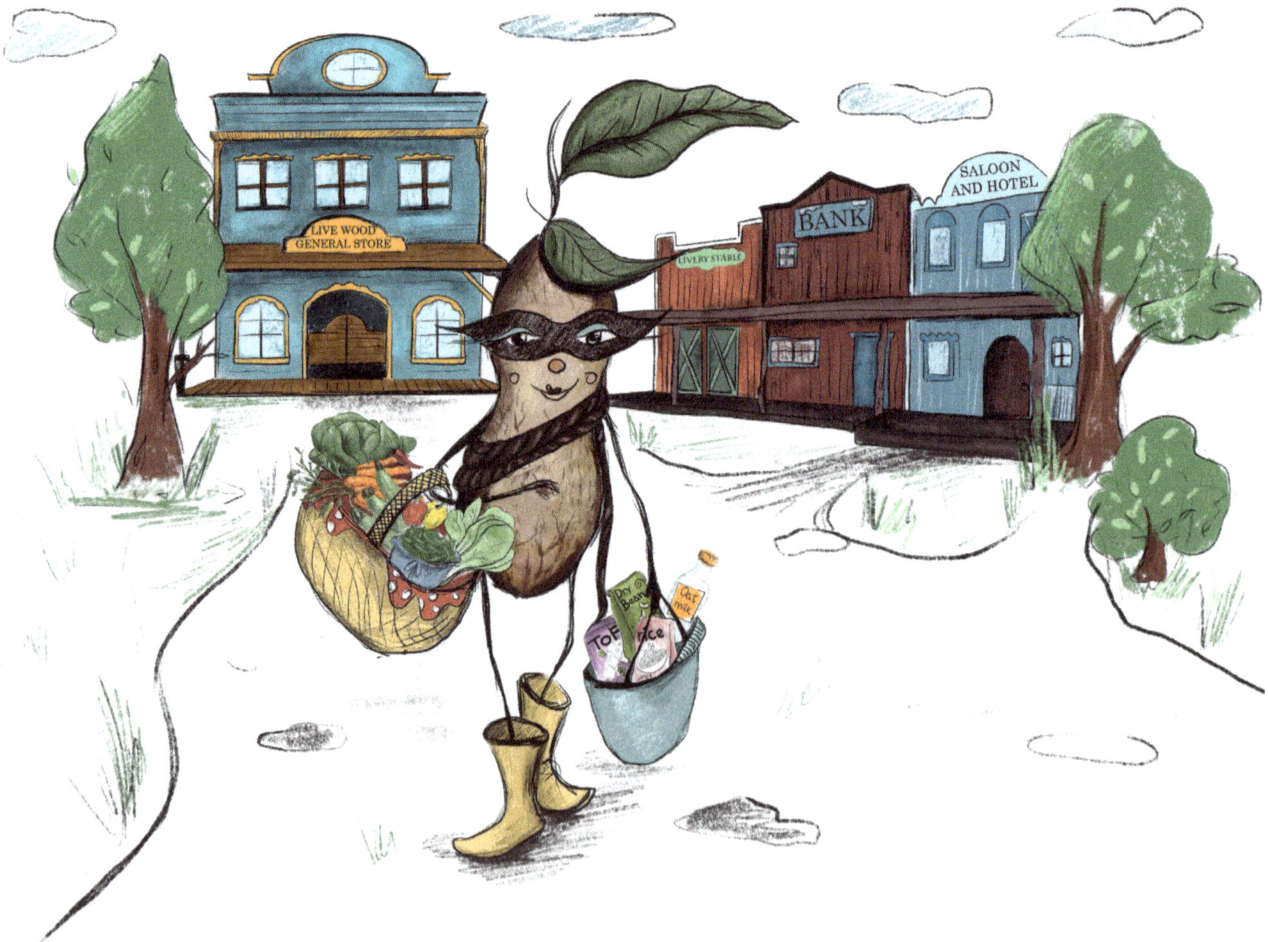

LIVE WOOD
GENERAL STORE
LIVERY STABLE
BANK
SALOON
AND HOTEL
Dry Beans
Oat milk

With Rice

Let's Flex Tacos	183
Portobello Mushroom Fajitas with Chili-Lime Sauce	185
Saloon Gumbo with Cajun Rice and Tofu	188
Cabbage Roll Casserole	191

Stir-Fries

Peanutty Tofu Stir-Fry	193
Fast Teriyaki Stir-Fry	195

Must Haves

Millet and Spinach Patties with Sun-Dried Tomato Pesto	197
Tempting Toor Dal Tadka with Tangy Tomato Chutney	199

Let's Flex Tacos

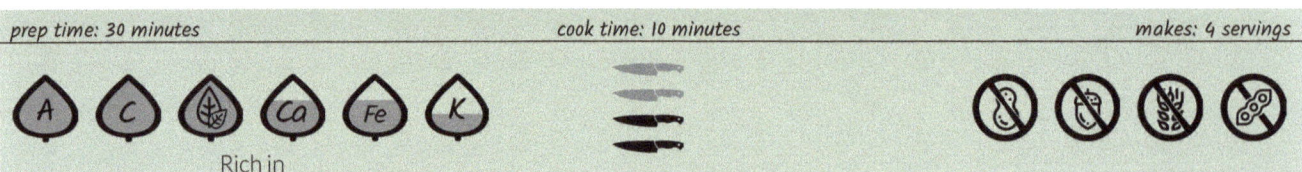

prep time: 30 minutes   cook time: 10 minutes   makes: 4 servings

Rich in

Tacos without any kind of cheese or dairy? Yup! Here they are, and they're fantastic. The brown rice adds weight to the meal and provides a nice texture. These can be served several ways, depending on what you're craving. They hit the spot, whether piled in hard taco shells or heaped on soft tortillas. For a lower-fat option, serve the filling on its own as a taco salad. If you want to experiment, replace the chili beans with vegan meat of your choice. Just use the same spices, and you'll have a filling that's sure to delight. Consider including Chili-Lime Sauce (page 185) or Boxcar Green Chile Sauce (page 175) as both make excellent additions to this meal. So let's flex our imagination and run wild with the possibilities.

For soy-free, replace Bragg soy seasoning or tamari with coconut aminos (soy-free seasoning) (page 15) and use soy-free vegan Worcestershire sauce.
The recipe for Fresh Tomato Salsa makes 2 cups. Make it up and divide it into ½ cup for the Easy Guacamole and 1½ cups to serve with the tacos as a tasty addition.

INGREDIENTS

EASY GUACAMOLE (makes 1 cup)

- 1 slightly soft avocado
- ½ cup Fresh Tomato Salsa (page 51) or chopped fresh tomatoes
- 2 tbsp chopped cilantro
- 1 tbsp lime juice (about 1 lime)
- ½ tsp ground cumin
- ¼ tsp cayenne pepper
- ¼ tsp salt
- ⅛ tsp garlic powder
- ⅛ tsp onion powder

TACO FILLING (makes 3 cups)

- ¼ cup low-sodium vegetable broth
- 1 cup diced onion (about ½ medium)
- 1 tbsp Bragg soy seasoning or tamari
- 2 tsp minced garlic (about 6 cloves)
- 1 tsp Bestcestershire Sauce (vegan Worcestershire sauce)
- ½ tsp paprika
- ½ tsp ground cumin
- ¼ tsp ground Ancho chili pepper (page 13)
- ¼ tsp dried oregano
- ⅛ tsp cayenne pepper
- ⅛ tsp dried red pepper flakes
- 2 x 13.5-oz cans chili-style beans (page 17), or 3 cups mixed pinto and red kidney beans, ground soy, or vegan meat of your choice

OTHER INGREDIENTS

- 2 cups cooked, warm brown rice
- 2 cups shredded romaine lettuce (about ½ head)
- 1 large fresh tomato, diced (about 1 cup)
- 1 medium orange, red, or yellow bell pepper, sliced with pulp and seeds removed (about 1 cup)
- 1½ cups Fresh Tomato Salsa (page 51)
- ½ cup Cilantro-Lime Dressing (page 79)
- 12 taco shells or corn and wheat flour tortillas

DIRECTIONS

1. Prepare *Easy Guacamole*:

    a. Cut avocado in half and remove the pit. Scoop out the avocado flesh from both halves and place it in a bowl. Using a fork, mash the avocado until smooth and creamy (about ⅔ cup).

    b. Add ½ cup Fresh Tomato Salsa, 2 tbsp chopped cilantro, 1 tbsp lime juice, ½ tsp ground cumin, ¼ tsp each cayenne pepper and salt, and ⅛ tsp each garlic powder and onion powder. Stir until well combined and refrigerate for at least 30 minutes to enhance the flavour.

2. Prepare *Taco Filling*:

    a. Place large nonstick frying pan on medium-high heat and add ¼ cup low-sodium vegetable broth. Once hot, add 1 cup diced onion and sauté until translucent and beginning to darken (about 5 minutes). Add a little water if onions start to stick, but let the broth cook off so onions can brown. If they become too dry, the onions may burn.

    b. Add 1 tbsp Bragg seasoning, 2 tsp minced garlic, 1 tsp Bestcestershire Sauce, ½ tsp each paprika and ground cumin, ¼ tsp each ground Ancho chili pepper and dried oregano, and ⅛ tsp each cayenne pepper and dried red pepper flakes. Combine and cook for 1–2 minutes to let the flavours seal into the onions. Add a little water if the ingredients begin to stick.

    c. Add 3 cups chili-style beans (we use Heinz canned beans and include the liquid). Stir until liquid is absorbed and beans are heated through. Serve Hot.

3. Serve family-style. Place on the table bowls filled with Taco Filling, warm brown rice, shredded lettuce, fresh diced tomato, diced bell peppers, Easy Guacamole, Fresh Tomato Salsa, Cilantro-Lime Dressing, and 12 tacos shells or tortillas.

4. Invite everyone to scoop the fillings into a taco shell or tortilla, alternating beans, rice, lettuce, tomatoes, and red bell peppers. Top with Cilantro-Lime Dressing, Easy Guacamole, and Fresh Tomato Salsa.

NUTRITION: *PER SERVING* (without shells or tortillas): *Calories 549; Carbs 72g; Fat 23g; Protein 18g; Sodium 1,608mg; Sugar 15g*

Portobello Mushroom Fajitas with Chili-Lime Sauce

Fajitas: prep time: 35 minutes + time to marinate
Chili-Lime Sauce: prep time: 20 minutes

cook time: 55 minutes
cook time: 35 minutes

makes: 4 x 3-fajita servings
makes: 4 x ½-cup servings

Rich in

Not only do these fajitas taste fantastic, but they're fun to eat. Set out serving dishes filled with Fajita Rice, Roasted Veggies, Fresh Tomato Salsa, Easy Guacamole, Chili-Lime Sauce, heated tortillas, and fresh veggies. Then sit back and let your posse dig in. Everyone can build their idea of the perfect fajita. No matter how they make it, they're gonna have a satisfying trip down tasty lane. Here're a few hints for sure-fire success. First, take the time to make the Chili-Lime Sauce, 'cause it's not to be missed. Next, add the black beans, which provide a nice texture and a little protein. Finally, roast the veggies and black beans to enjoy the wonderful deep flavour. As a couple of steps require dark beer for flavouring, you get to enjoy a sip or two of beer as your reward for cooking.

Make the Chili-Lime Sauce the day before to help speed up the process. Consider doubling the recipe and freeze the extra for up to 6 months. That way, you always have some on hand to use with tacos, as a dipping sauce, or in Seriously the Best Chili con Veggies (page 175). The Boxcar Green Chile Sauce (page 175) is also great with this meal, but it is hotter and is not gluten-free. You can vary the hotness level of your Chili-Lime Sauce. Add more jalapeño peppers, or use a serrano pepper if you like it spicier. Another option is to leave in the seeds, which increases the heat.
For gluten-free, replace wheat tortillas with 100% corn tortillas.

INGREDIENTS

CHILI-LIME SAUCE (makes 1½ cups)

- ¼ tsp grapeseed oil for greasing the pan
- 3–4 different chili peppers — we use jalapeño, poblano, and Anaheim pepper
- ¼ cup + 2 tbsp low-sodium vegetable broth, divided into ¼ cup + 2 tbsp
- 1 cup diced onion (about ½ medium)
- 1 cup fresh diced tomato
- 2 tbsp chopped oregano or marjoram leaves
- 1 tbsp ground cumin
- 1 tsp Spike all-purpose seasoning or Old Bay seasoning
- 3 tbsp dark beer (like Guinness)
- 2 tbsp lime juice (3–4 limes)

ROASTED VEGGIES WITH BLACK BEANS (makes 2 cups)

- ½ cup dark beer (like Guinness)
- 1½ tbsp lime juice (1–1½ limes)
- 1 tbsp grapeseed oil + ¼ tsp for greasing the pan
- 1½ tsp minced garlic (about 3 cloves)
- 1 tsp chili powder
- 1 tsp ground cumin
- ½ tsp salt
- ¼ tsp cayenne pepper
- 3 portobello mushroom caps
- 1 red, orange, or yellow bell pepper
- ½ sweet onion
- 1½ cups cooked black beans, drained and rinsed

DIRECTIONS

1. Prepare **Chili-Lime Sauce**:

    a. Preheat oven to 450°F. Spray roasting pan with oil or, using a pastry brush, spread a thin layer of oil on pan (¼ tsp oil).

    b. Wash 3–4 chili peppers and place on the roasting pan. Roast for 10 minutes, then flip peppers. Continue to cook for an additional 5–10 minutes or until the peppers start to brown and collapse.

    c. Immediately remove peppers from the oven, place them in a glass dish, and cover to let them "steam" for about 15 minutes. This helps to loosen the skins.

    d. While the peppers "steam," place frying pan on medium-high heat and add ¼ cup low-sodium vegetable broth. Once hot, add 1 cup diced onion and sauté until translucent and starting to brown (about 5 minutes). Add a little water if onions begin to stick, but let the broth cook off so onions can brown. If they become too dry, the onions may burn.

    e. Add 1 cup diced tomato, 2 tbsp chopped oregano leaves, 1 tbsp ground cumin, and 1 tsp Spike seasoning. Cook for about 10 minutes or until the mixture is heated through and the tomatoes are soft and tender. Add a little water if ingredients start to stick.

    f. Remove skins, seeds, and stems from roasted peppers. You should have about 1 cup roasted pepper meat.

    g. In a food processor or blender, add roasted pepper meat, cooked onion and tomato mixture, 3 tbsp dark beer, and 2 tbsp each low-sodium vegetable broth and lime juice. Process until smooth (2–3 minutes), scraping down sides as needed with a rubber spatula.

2. Prepare **Roasted Veggies with Black Beans**:

    a. In a small dish, mix ½ cup dark beer, 1½ tbsp lime juice, 1 tbsp oil, 1½ tsp minced garlic, 1 tsp each chili pepper and ground cumin, ½ tsp salt, and ¼ tsp cayenne pepper.

    b. Discard the stems from 3 portobello mushroom caps. Slice the caps into strips. Remove the seeds and pulp from a bell pepper, and cut into strips. Slice ½ sweet onion into wedges.

    c. In a large bowl, mix sliced mushroom caps, bell peppers, and onion with 1½ cups cooked, drained, and rinsed black beans. Add marinade and toss until well coated. Marinate for at least 30 minutes, tossing several times. (While vegetables marinate, prepare Fajita Rice.)

    d. Preheat oven to 400°F. Spray baking sheet with an oil dispenser or, using a pastry brush, spread a thin layer of oil on the sheet (¼ tsp oil).

INGREDIENTS, con't

FAJITA RICE (makes 2 cups)

- ½ cup raw long-grain brown rice, washed and rinsed
- ¾ cup canned low-sodium diced tomatoes (about ½ of 13.5-oz can)
- 1 cup water
- 1 cup diced red bell pepper (about 1 medium)
- 1 tsp dried minced onion
- ½ tsp chili powder
- ½ tsp ground cumin
- ½ tsp salt
- 1 tbsp minced cilantro leaves

OTHER INGREDIENTS

- 12 whole-wheat corn and flour tortillas (5½-inch diameter)
- 2 cups Fresh Tomato Salsa (page 51)
- 1 cup Easy Guacamole (page 183)

DIRECTIONS, con't

    e. Spread marinated vegetables on baking sheet and bake for 25 minutes, turning at the 15-minute mark. Cook until vegetables are tender but still slightly firm. Do not overcook.

3. Prepare *Fajita Rice*: (Prepare while veggies marinate.)

    a. Place a large saucepan on high heat and add ½ cup washed and rinsed raw long-grain brown rice, ¾ cup canned diced tomatoes, 1 cup water, 1 cup diced red bell pepper, 1 tsp dried minced onion, and ½ tsp each chili powder, ground cumin, and salt. Cover with a lid and bring to a boil. Reduce to low and simmer until all the liquid has been absorbed, 25 minutes.

    b. Remove from stovetop and stir in 1 tbsp minced cilantro leaves. Fluff with a fork and cover with a lid.

4. Heat up 12 tortillas.

5. Place in separate serving dishes: Roasted Veggies with Black Beans, Fajita Rice, Fresh Tomato Salsa, Easy Guacamole, and tortillas.

6. Serve immediately with the Chili-Lime Sauce and let everyone build their own fajitas.

NUTRITION: ROASTED VEGGIES AND FAJITA RICE ONLY (no toppings) - *PER 3-FAJITA SERVING: Calories 292; Carbs 49g; Fat 5g; Protein 10g; Sodium 1,029mg; Sugar 5g;* **CHILI-LIME SAUCE** - *PER ½-CUP SERVING: Calories 87; Carbs 19g; Fat 1g; Protein 2g; Sodium 108mg; Sugar 12g*

Saloon Gumbo with Cajun Rice and Tofu

prep time: 40 minutes + time to marinate   cook time: 90 minutes   makes: 4 x 2¼-cup servings

C A Fe Ca K
Rich in

Gumbo is a thick, spicy stew popular in Louisiana that typically includes meat or shellfish. So we've switched it up and created a super yummy plant-based version. We keep in the Cajun spice but sub in roasted veggies and charred tofu for the best taste. So follow our lead and serve up Saloon Gumbo with Cajun Rice and Tofu. All you need do is sashay to the kitchen, marinate your veggies, and sling them in the oven. Turn them round and round, and cook them 'til they're tender and brown. Then sit back and watch your kinfolk gobbling them down. The tofu is spicy and tender and goes well with Saloon Gumbo. Plus, it's a fantastic go-to when you're in need of a little extra protein.

MAINS - WITH RICE

INGREDIENTS

CAJUN TOFU (makes 8 slices)

- 3 tbsp olive oil, divided into 1 tbsp + 2 tbsp
- 1 tbsp Bragg soy seasoning or tamari
- 2 tsp Bestcestershire Sauce (vegan Worcestershire sauce)
- 1½ tsp minced garlic (about 3 cloves)
- 3 tsp Cajun seasoning, divided into 3 x 1 tsp
- 12-oz package medium-firm tofu

CAJUN RICE (makes 4 cups)

- 1½ cups raw long-grain brown rice, washed and rinsed
- 2 cups water
- 1 cup canned low-sodium diced tomatoes (⅓ of 28-oz can, use other ⅔ to make the gumbo, see below)
- 1 large red bell pepper, diced with seeds and pulp removed (about 1½ cups)
- 1 tsp Cajun spice
- 1 tsp smoked paprika
- 1 tsp salt
- 1 tbsp minced thyme leaves

CAJUN ROASTED VEGGIES (makes 4 cups)

- 1 tbsp grapeseed oil + ¼ tsp for greasing the pan
- 4 cups chopped mushroom (about 16 medium)
- 2 cups sliced okra (about 20 pods)
- 1 large green bell pepper, chopped with seeds and pulp removed (about 1½ cups)
- 1 cup sliced celery (about 2 stalks)
- 1 tbsp Bragg soy seasoning or tamari
- 2 tsp Bestcestershire Sauce (vegan Worcestershire sauce)
- 1½ tsp minced garlic (about 3 cloves)
- 1 tsp Cajun spice
- ½ tsp smoked paprika

DIRECTIONS

1. Prepare **Cajun Tofu**:

   a. In a small dish, mix 1 tbsp each olive oil and Bragg seasoning, 2 tsp Bestcestershire Sauce, 1½ tsp minced garlic, and 1 tsp Cajun seasoning. Stir until well combined.

   b. Cut 12-oz package medium-firm tofu into 8 slices. (Each slice should be 1½ inches wide x 3 inches long). Place in a shallow dish and add seasoning. Marinate tofu for at least 30 minutes, turning several times. (Prepare Cajun Rice while tofu marinates.)

   c. Without adding any oil, place nonstick frying pan on medium heat for 3–5 minutes. Pan is hot when a splash of sprinkled water dances on it. (Using your fingertips, flick a little bit of water on the pan to test.) Add 2 tbsp oil and heat for 30 seconds–1 minute.

   d. Sprinkle 1 tsp Cajun spice evenly over one side of each marinated tofu slice.

   e. When oil is hot, add the tofu slices with the Cajun spice side facing down. Pour any remaining marinade over top of tofu slices and sprinkle evenly with the remaining 1 tsp Cajun spice.

   f. Cook until the first side is browned, then flip and cook the other side (about 5 minutes per side).

2. Prepare **Cajun Rice**: (Prepare while tofu marinates.)

   a. Place saucepan on medium-high heat and add 1½ cups washed and rinsed raw long-grain brown rice, 2 cups water, 1 cup canned low-sodium diced tomatoes, about 1½ cups diced red bell pepper, and 1 tsp each Cajun spice, smoked paprika, and salt. Stir until all ingredients are combined, cover with a lid, and bring to a boil. Reduce to medium-low and simmer until all liquid has been absorbed (about 25 minutes).

   b. Remove from stovetop and stir in 1 tbsp minced thyme leaves. Fluff up with a fork and cover.

3. Prepare **Cajun Roasted Veggies**: (Prepare while tofu marinates and rice cooks.)

   a. Preheat oven to 400°F. Spray large roasting dish with oil or, using a pastry brush, spread a thin layer of oil on dish (¼ tsp oil).

   b. In a medium bowl, mix 4 cups chopped mushroom, 2 cups sliced okra, about 1½ cups chopped green bell pepper, and 1 cup sliced celery. Add 1 tbsp each grapeseed oil and Bragg seasoning, 2 tsp Bestcestershire Sauce, 1½ tsp minced garlic, 1 tsp Cajun spice, and ½ tsp smoked paprika. Toss until vegetables are well coated and marinate for at least 10 minutes.

   c. Place in prepared dish and roast for 30–35 minutes or until vegetables are tender, stirring at the 15-minute mark. Do not overcook.

INGREDIENTS, con't

OTHER INGREDIENTS

1¼ cups low-sodium vegetable broth, divided into ¼ cup + 1 cup

1 cup diced onion (about ½ medium)

2 tbsp minced thyme leaves + more for garnish

1 tbsp Cajun spice

½ tsp smoked paprika

2 cups canned low-sodium diced tomatoes (⅔ of 28-oz can — remaining ⅓ of a can is used to make Cajun Rice)

1½ cups cooked, drained, and rinsed red kidney beans

½ cup red wine (medium-bodied, like a merlot)

freshly ground black pepper, to taste

dash of Tabasco sauce or other hot sauce

½ cup diced tomato (about 1 small)

DIRECTIONS, con't

4. Place a large saucepan on medium-high heat and add ¼ cup low-sodium vegetable broth. Once hot, add 1 cup diced onion and sauté until translucent and beginning to darken (about 5 minutes). Add a little water if onions start to stick, but let broth cook off so onions can brown. If they become too dry, onions may burn.

5. To the cooked onions, add 2 tbsp minced thyme leaves, 1 tbsp Cajun spice, and ½ tsp smoked paprika. Stir until well combined and cook for 1–2 minutes to let flavours seal into onions. Add a little water if the ingredients begin to stick.

6. Add roasted vegetables (about 4 cups), 2 cups canned diced tomatoes, 1½ cups cooked, rinsed, and drained kidney beans, 1 cup low-sodium vegetable broth, ½ cup red wine, freshly ground black pepper, and a dash or two of Tabasco sauce. Mix until well combined. Bring to a boil, then lower heat and let the gumbo simmer for at least 10 minutes.

7. Divide into 4 servings of 1 cup Cajun Rice and 1¼ cups Saloon Gumbo. Top each serving with 2 slices of Cajun Tofu, diced tomato, and a sprinkling of minced thyme. Serve immediately.

NUTRITION: PER 2½ -CUP SERVING: *Calories 672; Carbs 99g; Fat 19g; Protein 24g; Sodium 2,357mg; Sugar 11g*

Cabbage Roll Casserole

prep time: 35 minutes + time to marinate   cook time: 85 minutes   makes: 6 x 1²/₃-cup servings

Rich in: A, Ca, C, 🌿, Fe, K

Without a doubt, our Cabbage Roll Casserole goes above and beyond those old-fashioned cabbage rolls. Since that oldfangled version is made with beef and pork, there's really no comparison, and that's no ballyhoo. Our humble and heavenly plant-based dish is quite simply much better. Not only is it healthier and tastier, but it's much easier to throw together, especially since there's no pesky rolling involved. We like to present this meal with vegan pierogies and vegan sausages. Regardless of how it's served, this dish stands alone as wonderfully satisfying comfort food, filled with hidden treasures of deliciousness.

INGREDIENTS

CRUMBLED TOFU *(makes 2 cups)*

- 12-oz package extra-firm tofu, or 2 cups minced chickpeas, or vegan meat of your choice
- 2 tbsp minced oregano leaves or marjoram leaves
- 2 tbsp Bragg soy seasoning or tamari
- 1 tbsp minced garlic (about 6 cloves)
- 2 tsp Bestcestershire Sauce (vegan Worcestershire sauce)
- ¼ tsp Spike all-purpose seasoning or Old Bay seasoning
- ¼ cup low-sodium vegetable broth
- 1 cup diced onion (about ½ medium)

HUMBLE RICE *(makes 2 cups)*

- 1¾ cups low-sodium vegetable broth, divided into ¼ cup + 1½ cups
- 1 cup diced onion (about ½ medium)
- ⅔ cup raw long-grain brown rice, washed and rinsed
- 1½ tsp minced garlic (about 3 cloves)

OTHER INGREDIENTS

- ¼ tsp olive oil for greasing the pan
- ½ medium head of green cabbage + water for boiling
- 2 tbsp ground flax seeds
- ¼ cup water
- 1¼ cups cooked, drained, and rinsed brown or green lentils
- ½ cup grated carrot (1–1½ medium)
- ¼ cup chopped parsley leaves + a small amount for garnish
- 1 tbsp Bragg soy seasoning or tamari
- 1 tbsp minced oregano leaves or marjoram leaves
- ½ tsp ground black pepper
- ¼ tsp salt
- 3 cups creamy vegan tomato soup (page 18)

DIRECTIONS

1. Prepare **Crumbled Tofu**:

    a. Drain and crumble 12-oz package extra-firm tofu (about 2 cups) into a bowl. Add 2 tbsp each chopped oregano leaves and Bragg seasoning, 1 tbsp minced garlic, 2 tsp Bestcestershire Sauce, and ¼ tsp Spike seasoning. Mix well and marinate for at least 30 minutes. (While tofu marinates, prepare Humble Rice.)

    b. Once tofu has marinated for at least 30 minutes, place nonstick frying pan on medium-high heat and add ¼ cup low-sodium vegetable broth. Once hot, add 1 cup diced onion and sauté until translucent and beginning to darken (about 5 minutes). Add a little water if onions start to stick, but let the broth cook off so onions can brown. If they become too dry, the onions may burn.

    c. Add marinated tofu mixture to onions and cook for about 10 minutes or until tofu browns. Add a little water if the ingredients begin to stick. When done, remove from the stovetop.

2. Prepare **Humble Rice**: (Prepare while tofu marinates.)

    a. Place a medium saucepan on medium-high heat and add ¼ cup low-sodium vegetable broth. Once hot, add 1 cup diced onion and sauté until translucent and beginning to darken (about 5 minutes). Add a little water if onions start to stick, but let the broth cook off so onions can brown. If they become too dry, the onions may burn.

    b. Add 2/3 cup washed and rinsed raw long-grain brown rice and 1½ tsp minced garlic. Cook for about 5 minutes. Rice should change colour and become somewhat translucent. Stir often to avoid sticking. Add a little water if mixture begins to stick.

    c. Add 1½ cups low-sodium vegetable broth, cover, and bring to a boil. Reduce to low and simmer, stirring occasionally, until rice is tender and liquid has been absorbed (about 25 minutes). Remove from the stovetop, and gently fluff up with a fork.

3. Preheat oven to 350°F. Spray 9- x 13-inch baking pan with oil or, using a pastry brush, spread a thin layer of oil on pan (¼ tsp oil).

4. Bring a large pot of water to a boil. Cut ½ head of green cabbage into wedges and cook in boiling water for 5 minutes. Drain and then remove any tough outer pieces (makes about 6 cups).

5. In a small bowl, mix 2 tbsp ground flax seeds with ¼ cup water and let thicken for at least 5 minutes.

6. In a large bowl, combine Humble Rice, Crumbled Tofu, 1¼ cups cooked, drained, and rinsed brown lentils, ½ cup grated carrot, ¼ cup chopped parsley, 1 tbsp each Bragg seasoning and minced oregano leaves, ½ tsp ground black pepper, ¼ tsp salt, and thickened flax seed mixture. Mix until everything is well combined.

7. Line the bottom of the prepared pan with half of the boiled cabbage leaves. Spread mixture evenly over cabbage. Top with remaining cabbage leaves. Pour 3 cups creamy vegan tomato soup evenly over cabbage. Cover and bake for 25–30 minutes or until the mixture is bubbling. Remove the lid for the last 5 minutes to let it brown. Remove from the oven and let set for at least 5 minutes. Then, garnish with a little chopped parsley and serve.

NUTRITION: *PER 1⅔-CUP SERVING: Calories 244; Carbs 40g; Fat 5g; Protein 13g; Sodium 911mg; Sugar 9g*

Peanutty Tofu Stir-Fry

prep time: 25 minutes + time to marinate   cook time: 35 minutes   makes: 4 x 2-cup servings

Rich in: C, A, (leaf), Ca, K, Fe

You can throw this meal together lickety-split when you've got hungry kinfolk. Stir-frying is always a great option to help you beat the hungry blues. With tender-crisp veggies, Snappy Peanut Sauce, Tasty Tofu, and a scattering of raw peanuts, you'll deliver a dish that's sure to please. You can serve up this stir-fry with either a little or a lot of noodles (brown rice works just fine too). Potato Pat loads up the noodles, but Saucy Peanut prefers more stir-fry than rice. True to its name, Tasty Tofu makes a terrific appetizer or protein-rich side dish any time of day or night.

Double the Snappy Peanut Sauce so you have it on hand for Peanutty Tofu Stir-fry and as a dip for Rainbow Wraps (page 167) or Tasty Tofu. Refrigerate leftover sauce in an airtight container and use it within 5 days or freeze for up to 6 months for future use. For gluten-free option, avoid wheat noodles.

193

INGREDIENTS

TASTY TOFU (makes 2 cups)

12-oz package extra-firm tofu

4 tsp toasted sesame oil, divided into 1 tbsp + 1 tsp

1 tbsp tamari or Bragg soy seasoning

1 tbsp minced garlic (about 6 cloves)

2 tsp Bestcestershire Sauce (vegan Worcestershire sauce)

1 tsp dried mushroom powder

¼ tsp five-spice powder

SNAPPY PEANUT SAUCE (makes 1 cup)

¼ cup tamari or Bragg soy seasoning

¼ cup lime juice (3–4 limes)

¼ cup toasted sesame oil

¼ cup peanut butter

2 tbsp grated ginger root

1 tbsp minced garlic (about 6 cloves)

2 tsp maple syrup or raw blue agave nectar

1 tsp Sriracha sauce or chili garlic sauce

STIR-FRY VEGGIES (makes 6 cups)

1 tbsp toasted sesame oil

½ cup chopped onion (about ½ small)

1 tbsp tamari or Bragg soy seasoning

1 tbsp minced garlic (about 6 cloves)

½ tsp dried mushroom powder

¼ tsp five-spice powder

2 cups chopped mushroom (about 8 medium)

8 cups assorted chopped vegetables (carrots, cabbage, bok choy, green beans, snow peas, zucchini, or bell peppers)

OTHER INGREDIENTS

cooked noodles or rice

1 tbsp sesame oil to coat noodles (optional)

1 lime, cut into wedges

½ cup raw or roasted peanuts

DIRECTIONS

1. Prepare **Tasty Tofu**:

   a. Cut 12-oz package extra-firm tofu into ¼- x 1-inch rectangles (makes about 2 cups) and place in a small bowl. Add 1 tbsp each toasted sesame oil, tamari, and minced garlic, 2 tsp Bestcestershire Sauce, 1 tsp dried mushroom powder, and ¼ tsp five-spice powder. Toss until tofu is well coated. Marinate for about 30 minutes.

   b. After tofu has marinated (and while vegetable cook, see below), place a separate frying pan on medium-high heat and add 1 tsp toasted sesame oil. When hot, add marinated tofu. Cook for 10 minutes, stirring a few times, or until tofu becomes brown and slightly crispy. Remove from stovetop.

2. Prepare **Snappy Peanut Sauce**:

   a. In a small saucepan, add ¼ cup each tamari, lime juice, toasted sesame oil, and peanut butter, 2 tbsp grated ginger root, 1 tbsp minced garlic, 2 tsp maple syrup, and 1 tsp Sriracha sauce.

   b. Cook on medium heat for about 5 minutes, whisking until the ingredients are well combined, and the sauce is smooth and creamy. Remove from stovetop.

3. Prepare **Stir-fry Veggies**:

   a. Place wok or large frying pan on medium-high heat and add 1 tbsp toasted sesame oil. Once hot, add ½ cup chopped onion and sauté until translucent and beginning to darken (about 5 minutes). Add a little water if onions start to stick.

   b. Add 1 tbsp each tamari and minced garlic, ½ tsp dried mushroom powder, and ¼ tsp five-spice powder. Stir until well combined and cook for 1–2 minutes to let flavours seal into onions. Add 2 cups chopped mushroom and sauté until they start to brown (about 5 minutes). Add 8 cups assorted chopped vegetables and cook for 10–12 minutes or until veggies soften. Do not overcook. Stir-fry tastes best when veggies are on the firm side and slightly crunchy.

   c. Add 2 cups Tasty Tofu and 1 cup Snappy Peanut Sauce and stir until well combined.

4. If using noodles, stir in 1 tbsp toasted sesame oil just after cooking. Toss until noodles are well coated.

5. Divide noodles among 4 individual serving bowls. Scoop 2 cups of vegetable and tofu mixture into each bowl and top each bowl with a lime wedge and 2 tbsp of raw peanuts. Serve immediately.

NUTRITION: PER 2-CUP SERVING (without noodles or rice): *Calories 608; Carbs 48g; Fat 46g; Protein 21g; Sodium 1,505mg; Sugar 19g*

Fast Teriyaki Stir-Fry

prep time: 25 minutes   cook time: 30 minutes   makes: 4 x 2-cup servings

Rich in: C, A, (leaf), Ca, Fe, K

This stir-fry comes together in a snap. We reckon it's even quicker with frozen veggies. Plus, frozen pre-shelled edamame does the job as a satisfying protein hit. Keep in mind that when you make the Teriyaki Sauce and cook the rice ahead of time, it's as easy as one, two, three.
You may question the wisdom of using frozen veggies. But don't, 'cause they're often healthier than some fresh produce sold at the market, plus they're always available, no matter the season. We like to use both fresh and frozen. That way, we use up any fresh vegetables we have on hand and save time by slinging in frozen chopped veggies. If you're tuckered out, you can use store-bought teriyaki sauce as a quick stand-in, but we strongly suggest you take the time to make our sauce — it's way more flavoursome.

For nut-free option, avoid the cashews.

INGREDIENTS

TERIYAKI SAUCE (makes 1½ cups), divided into 1 cup + 4 x 2 tbsp

- ½ cup tamari or Bragg soy seasoning
- ½ cup + 2 tbsp water, divided into ½ cup + 2 tbsp
- ¼ cup raw blue agave nectar or maple syrup
- 2 tbsp rice wine vinegar
- 1 tbsp toasted sesame oil
- 1 tbsp grated ginger root
- 1½ tsp minced garlic (about 3 cloves)
- 1 tbsp arrowroot powder

STIR-FRY VEGGIES WITH EDAMAME BEANS (makes 8 cups)

- 1 tbsp toasted sesame oil
- 1 cup chopped onion (about ½ medium)
- 1 tbsp tamari or Bragg soy seasoning
- 2 cups chopped mushroom (about 8 medium)
- 8 cups assorted frozen or fresh chopped vegetables (broccoli florets, bok choy, carrots, green beans, or bell peppers)
- 1½ cups frozen shelled edamame beans
- ½ cup raw cashews
- 1 cup Teriyaki Sauce (see above)

OTHER INGREDIENTS

- cooked brown jasmine rice or buckwheat soba noodles
- 1 tbsp sesame oil to coat noodles (optional)
- ¼ cup sesame seeds, divided into 4 x 1 tbsp

DIRECTIONS

1. Prepare *Teriyaki Sauce*:

   a. In a small saucepan, mix ½ cup each tamari and water, ¼ cup agave nectar, 2 tbsp rice wine vinegar, 1 tbsp each toasted sesame oil and grated ginger root, and 1½ tsp minced garlic.

   b. Whisk all ingredients together and cook on medium-high heat for about 5 minutes or until heated through and garlic and ginger are tender.

   c. In a small dish, mix 1 tbsp arrowroot powder with 2 tbsp water. Stir until arrowroot powder is dissolved. Slowly pour arrowroot mixture into the heated ingredients, stirring continuously. Bring to a boil and cook for 2–3 minutes or until the mixture thickens. Remove from stovetop.

2. Prepare *Stir-fry Veggies with Edamame Beans*:

   a. Place large frying pan or wok on medium-high heat and add 1 tbsp toasted sesame oil. Once hot, add 1 cup chopped onion and sauté for 1–2 minutes. Add a little water if onions begin to stick.

   b. Add 1 tbsp tamari, stir, then add 2 cups chopped mushroom. Cook until mushrooms start to soften and become brown (about 5 minutes). Add a little water if the ingredients begin to stick.

   c. Add 8 cups frozen or fresh chopped vegetables, cover, and cook for about 10 minutes or until vegetables are tender.

   d. Add 1½ cups frozen shelled edamame beans, 1 cup teriyaki sauce, and ½ cup raw cashews to the cooked vegetables, stir until well combined and cook for about 5 minutes.

3. If using noodles, stir in 1 tbsp toasted sesame oil just after cooking. Toss until noodles are well coated.

4. Serve immediately. We recommend 2 cups of stir-fried vegetables per person for each serving of brown jasmine rice or buckwheat soba noodles. Top each with 2 tbsp teriyaki sauce and 1 tbsp sesame seeds.

NUTRITION: *PER 2-CUP SERVING (without noodles or rice): Calories 493; Carbs 59g; Fat 22g; Protein 20g; Sodium 1,950mg; Sugar 28g*

Millet and Spinach Patties with Sun-Dried Tomato Pesto

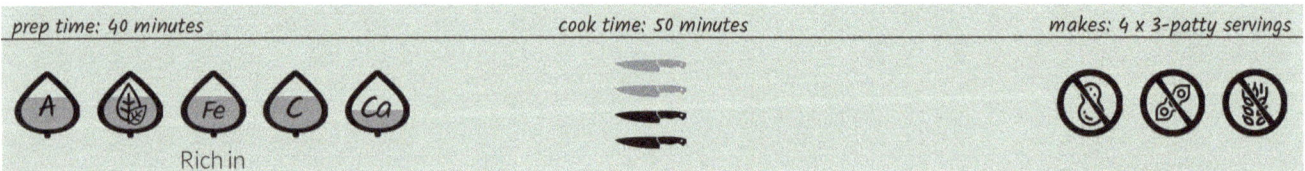

prep time: 40 minutes   cook time: 50 minutes   makes: 4 x 3-patty servings

Rich in: A, leaf, Fe, C, Ca

Potato Pat loves these patties (and it's not just for the namesake). Millet and spinach patties are de-li-cious! Plus, when you add sun-dried tomato pesto, presto — lip-smacking abounds. The outstanding combination of savoury sun-dried tomatoes with the nutty, earthy flavour of the patties is a sure winner. This is one of our favourite dinners, and it's so good there's rarely a leftover. Make extra pesto, then you can serve it over pasta for a delightful lunch. Use sun-dried tomatoes packed in olive oil and include both the tomatoes and the oil. That way, you'll get the benefit of the flavourful oil.

INGREDIENTS

SUN-DRIED TOMATO PESTO
(makes 1 cup)

½ cup tightly packed sun-dried tomato, packed in olive oil

1 cup water

½ cup raw slivered almonds

¼ cup chopped basil leaves

2 tbsp olive oil from drained sun-dried tomato

¼ tsp salt

freshly ground black pepper, to taste

1–2 tbsp olive oil, if needed

OTHER INGREDIENTS

1 cup millet

3 cups low-sodium vegetable broth

2 cups fresh spinach leaves

1 tbsp minced oregano leaves

¼ tsp salt

freshly ground black pepper, to taste

1 tbsp ground flax seeds

2 tbsp water

1 tbsp olive oil for greasing the pan, divided into 2 x 1½ tsp

DIRECTIONS

1. Prepare **Sun-Dried Tomato Pesto**: (Prepare while millet cools.)

    a. Drain and reserve oil from ½ cup tightly packed sun-dried tomato packed in olive oil.

    b. In a food processor or blender, add 1 cup water, ½ cup each tightly packed and drained sun-dried tomato and raw slivered almonds, ¼ cup chopped basil leaves, 2 tbsp olive oil from drained sun-dried tomato, ¼ tsp salt, and freshly ground black pepper.

    c. Process until smooth (5–10 minutes), scraping down sides as needed with a rubber spatula. If too thick and dry, add 1–2 tbsp olive oil.

2. Place a large pot on medium-high heat and add 1 cup millet. Toast millet on dry heat. Without adding any oil, keep swirling the pan or stir grains to keep them moving. Cook for 5–8 minutes or until grains darken slightly and emit a toasty aroma.

3. Add 3 cups low-sodium vegetable broth and bring to a boil, reduce heat, and simmer until cooked (about 25 minutes). Wash and chop 2 cups fresh spinach leaves and add to cooked millet. Add 1 tbsp minced oregano leaves, ¼ tsp salt, and freshly ground black pepper. Stir until combined and simmer for an additional 10 minutes or until all liquid has been absorbed. Remove from stovetop and let cool.

4. In a small dish, mix 1 tbsp ground flax seeds with 2 tbsp water and let thicken for at least 5 minutes.

5. Once millet has cooled, add thickened flax seed mixture and stir until well combined. Use a ⅓-cup measuring cup to form the millet and spinach mixture into 12 patties. Scoop the mixture into the measuring cup, and then use the back of a spoon to press it flat before turning it over onto a sheet of parchment paper. If needed, use the bottom of the cup to flatten each one. Repeat until 12 patties are formed.

6. Place griddle (flat grill) or frying pan on medium heat without adding any oil for about 5 minutes. You will know pan is hot when a splash of sprinkled water dances on it. (Using your fingertips, flick a little bit of water on the pan to test.) Next, spray griddle with oil or, using a pastry brush, spread a little oil (1½ tsp) on the pan and heat for 30 seconds–1 minute.

7. Once oil is hot, add patties and cook each side for about 5 minutes or until golden brown. Spray each patty with olive oil before turning to cook the other side (1½ tsp oil).

8. Top each patty with 4 tsp of Sun-Dried Tomato Pesto and serve immediately.

NUTRITION: *PER 3-PATTY SERVING: Calories 500; Carbs 55g; Fat 26g; Protein 11g; Sodium 430mg; Sugar 9g*

Tempting Toor Dal Tadka with Tangy Tomato Chutney

Tempting Toor Dal Tadka: prep time: 20 minutes	cook time: 35 minutes	makes: 4 x 1½-cup servings
Tangy Tomato Chutney: prep time: 20 minutes	cook time: 25 minutes	makes: 4 x ½-cup servings

   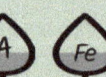    

Rich in

When you have a mind for good, soul-satisfying chow, this toor dal tadka will tempt you and your kinfolk to the table every time. We've heard tell that dal is a staple in virtually every Indian kitchen, and for good reason — which we discovered the truth of after Cashew Sue served it up for us. Our version pairs yellow lentils (toor dal) with split yellow peas. Tadka translates as tempering, aka: sautéing onion and spices in hot oil (which increases their flavour, enhancing the cooked dal). Tangy Tomato Chutney is easy to make and is a swell addition to the meal.

Bruising whole cloves of garlic releases a robust flavour. Simply use the flat side of a knife to press down on the cloves until they split. If you want a hotter sauce, use serrano peppers, which have more heat than jalapeño peppers. Another option to increase the heat level is to leave in the seeds.
You can find toor dal at your local Indian grocery or online. Although toor dal has the best flavour, you can also use channa or moong dal, but you may need to adjust the cooking times.

INGREDIENTS

1½ cups dried toor dal
½ cup dried split yellow peas
6 cups water
1–2 jalapeño peppers
2 garlic cloves
1 medium tomato
2 cilantro sprigs
1 tsp turmeric
1½ tsp salt, divided into 1 tsp + ½ tsp
½ small onion
2 tbsp olive oil
1 tsp cumin seeds
½ tsp black mustard seeds

TANGY TOMATO CHUTNEY
(makes 2 cups)

½ small onion
1 jalapeño or serrano pepper
3 large beefsteak or field tomatoes
1½ tsp olive oil
½ tsp cumin seeds
½ tsp black mustard seeds
½ tsp salt
4 cilantro sprigs

DIRECTIONS

1. Wash 1½ cups dried toor dal and ½ cup dried split yellow peas. Then place in a medium saucepan along with 6 cups water. Bring to a boil.

2. Slice 1–2 jalapeño peppers lengthwise into halves (according to taste), peel and bruise 2 garlic cloves, chop 1 medium tomato (about ¾ cup), and remove stems from 2 sprigs of cilantro, but keep a few leaves aside for garnish, and then mince the cilantro (about 1 tbsp).

3. As soon as the mixture starts to boil, add sliced jalapeño, peeled and bruised garlic cloves, and 1 tsp each turmeric and salt. Cover loosely, reduce to medium, and simmer on a low boil for about 25 minutes or until dal softens, stirring occasionally. (While dal cooks, prepare Tangy Tomato Chutney per below.)

4. Prepare the tadka: Finely chop ½ small onion (about ½ cup). Place small frying pan on medium-high heat and add 2 tbsp olive oil. Once hot, add 1 tsp cumin seeds and ½ tsp black mustard seeds. Cook until seeds brown and pop and emit a pleasant earthy aroma (about 3 minutes). Next, add about ½ cup diced onions and continue to sauté for about 5 minutes or until onions become translucent and start to brown.

5. When dal is cooked, pour tadka mixture directly into lentils and add ½ tsp salt, about ¾ cup chopped tomato, and about 1 tbsp minced cilantro. Mix until well combined, cover, and remove from stovetop.

6. Serve hot with Tangy Tomato Chutney, brown basmati rice, a few slices of red or green pepper, and a couple of cilantro leaves.

7. Prepare *Tangy Tomato Chutney*: (Prepare while dal cooks.)

    a. Dice ½ small onion (about ½ cup), remove seeds and stem from a jalapeño pepper and finely chop (about 2 tbsp), dice 3 large tomatoes (about 3 cups), and remove stems from 4 sprigs of cilantro before mincing (about 2 tbsp).

    b. Place a saucepan on medium-high heat and add 1½ tsp olive oil. Once hot, add ½ tsp each cumin and black mustard seeds, and cook until seeds brown and pop and emit an earthy aroma (2–3 minutes). Add about ½ cup diced onions and about 2 tbsp chopped jalapeño peppers. Cook until onions become translucent and start to brown (about 5 minutes). Add a little water if onions begin to stick.

    c. Add about 3 cups chopped tomato and ½ tsp salt. Cook 10-15 minutes or until tomatoes are tender.

    d. Remove from heat, add about 2 tbsp minced cilantro, and stir until well combined.

NUTRITION: **TEMPTING TOOR DAL TADKA** - *PER 1½-CUP SERVING: Calories 378; Carbs 60g; Fat 8g; Protein 24g; Sodium 882mg; Sugar 2g;* **TANGY TOMATO CHUTNEY** - *PER ½-CUP SERVING: Calories 66; Carbs 9g; Fat 3g; Protein 2g; Sodium 307mg; Sugar 5g*

HOLIDAY MEAL

Sides

Best Brussels Sprouts	203
Mashed Sweet and Russet Potatoes	205
Succulent Bread Dressing	207
Fancy Cranberry Sauce	209
Red Currant and Mushroom Gravy	211

Holiday Mains

Crunchy Nut Roast with Roasted Carrots	213
Savoury Holiday Tart	216

Great Additions

Creamy Pumpkin Pie	219
Mulled Wine	221
Nicely Spiced Cran-Apple Cider	223

Best Brussels Sprouts

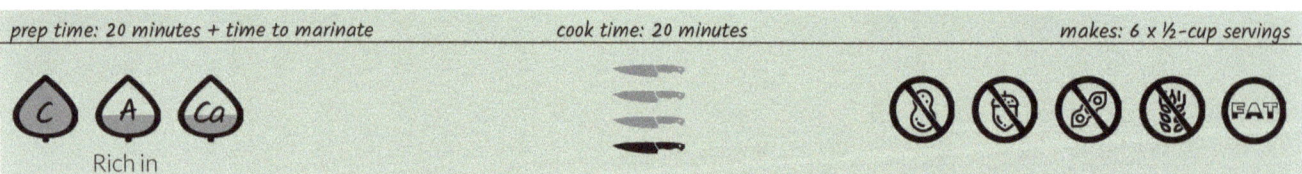

prep time: 20 minutes + time to marinate   cook time: 20 minutes   makes: 6 x ½-cup servings

Rich in

No way, no how can you have a holiday meal without these delightful little veggies. When you're fixing 'em, just cut each one in half and smother with balsamic vinegar, maple syrup, and other yummy seasonings. Then sear them in the oven for a delightful treat. Roasting the sprouts brings out a pleasant nuttiness and sweetens their flavour, while balsamic vinegar combats any bitterness. Even people who don't like Brussels sprouts will enjoy these — and for people who love 'em, watch out!

Toss the Brussels sprouts into the oven while making gravy for the holiday meal.

INGREDIENTS

4 cups Brussels sprouts
2 tbsp balsamic vinegar
2 tbsp maple syrup
1 tbsp grapeseed oil
1 tbsp orange juice
1½ tsp minced garlic (about 3 cloves)
1 tsp grated ginger root
1 tsp minced rosemary + a few leaves for garnish
½ tsp Spike all-purpose seasoning or Old Bay seasoning
½ tsp cayenne pepper
orange zest for garnish

DIRECTIONS

1. Preheat oven to 425°F.
2. Prepare Brussels sprouts. Wash 4 cups Brussels sprouts and remove yellowed or discoloured outer leaves. Cut off the stems and cut the Brussels Sprouts into halves crosswise. Place into a medium bowl.
3. In a small dish, mix 2 tbsp each balsamic vinegar and maple syrup, 1 tbsp each grapeseed oil and orange juice, 1½ tsp minced garlic, 1 tsp each grated ginger root and minced rosemary, and ½ tsp each Spike seasoning and cayenne pepper. Stir until well combined. Pour over Brussels sprouts and toss until well coated. Marinate for at least 30 minutes.
4. Spread marinated sprouts on a large baking sheet in a single layer and cook for 15–20 minutes or until they are brown and tender. (The sprouts shrink down while they cook). When they are done, remove them from the oven, garnish with orange zest and rosemary leaves, and serve immediately with a holiday meal.

NUTRITION: PER ½-CUP SERVING: Calories 70; Carbs 10g; Fat 2g; Protein 2g; Sodium 70mg; Sugar 7g

Mashed Sweet and Russet Potatoes

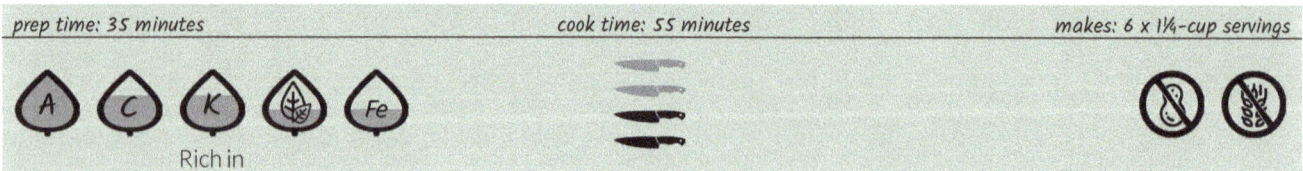

prep time: 35 minutes   cook time: 55 minutes   makes: 6 x 1¼-cup servings

Rich in: A, C, K, 🌿, Fe

When you serve up Mashed Sweet and Russet Potatoes, you're bound to find some kindred spirits who'll be clamouring to join in your feast. While plain mashed potatoes are a terrific, comforting classic, adding sweet potatoes and a few secret ingredients creates something truly splendiferous. Serve this up as a delicious side, and you'll be fondly remembered for your creamy taters. This is an excellent recipe to make during the busy holidays 'cause you can make it ahead of time and then heat it up in the oven on the big day.

Prepare several Roasted Bulbs of Garlic at the same time and use the second one for either Crunchy Nut Roast (page 213) or Savoury Holiday Tart (page 216).
Double the amount of Creamy Sauce, then use it as a topping for cooked veggies.

INGREDIENTS

CREAMY SAUCE *(makes ½ cup)*

- ½ head of Roasted Bulb of Garlic (page 139)
- ¼ cup raw cashews, soaked in water for at least 4 hours
- 1 tbsp cashew milk
- 1 tbsp white wine
- 1 tbsp coconut milk
- 1 tbsp olive oil
- 1 tbsp nutritional yeast
- 1½ tsp red miso paste
- 1 tsp dried thyme leaves
- ½ tsp white pepper

OTHER INGREDIENTS

- large pot of water
- ½ tsp salt, divided into 2 x ¼ tsp
- 3 large sweet potatoes
- 3 large russet potatoes
- 4 tsp minced parsley leaves + a small amount for garnish
- ½ tsp paprika + ¼ tsp for garnish

DIRECTIONS

1. Prepare *Creamy Sauce*:

    a. Peel cloves from ½ head of Roasted Bulb of Garlic (6–8 cloves).

    b. Drain and rinse the soaked cashews. Place in a small food processor or blender along with 1 tbsp each cashew milk, white wine, coconut milk, olive oil, and nutritional yeast, 1½ tsp red miso paste, 1 tsp dried thyme, ½ tsp white pepper, and 6–8 roasted and peeled garlic cloves.

    c. Process until smooth and creamy (3–5 minutes), scraping down sides as needed with a rubber spatula.

2. Fill a large pot with water and add ¼ tsp salt. Peel and dice 3 large sweet potatoes (about 5 cups) and 3 large russet potatoes (about 5 cups) into the salted water (the salt will stop the potatoes from oxidizing). Drain, rinse, and cover the potatoes with clean water. Add ¼ tsp salt, cover, and bring to a boil. Reduce heat and simmer for 20 minutes or until potatoes are soft.

3. Preheat oven to 375°F.

4. Drain potatoes, and using a ricer or potato masher, mash them in the pot. Add ½ cup Creamy Sauce and stir until well combined.

5. Place mashed potatoes in a 2.5-quart casserole dish. Sprinkle the top with 4 tsp minced parsley leaves and ½ tsp paprika. Cover with a lid and bake for 30 minutes or until heated through. (If refrigerating the dish before heating, add 10 minutes of cooking time.) Let set for 5 minutes. Then garnish with ¼ tsp paprika and a sprinkling of parsley leaves. Serve as a side dish for your holiday meal.

NUTRITION: PER 1¼-CUP SERVING: *Calories 279; Carbs 44g; Fat 8g; Protein 6g; Sodium 519mg; Sugar 7g*

Succulent Bread Dressing

prep time: 30 minutes   cook time: 120 minutes   makes: 6 x 1-cup servings

Rich in: Ca, Fe, C, A, K

Since rousing good food is a must for any holiday feast, this succulent dressing is not to be missed. Plus, given that it's dressing and not stuffing ('cause no poor bird was stuffed), all you need do is cook it in the oven. It's pretty, tasty, and dresses up any holiday meal. The mouth-watering flavour comes from the savoury and succulent ingredients. Enjoy it with Fancy Cranberry Sauce (page 209), Red Currant and Mushroom Gravy (page 211), and a main of your choice. You can prepare this dish ahead of time, then throw it in the oven on the big day to save time and energy. Of course, the quality of your bread affects the quality of the dressing, so try using sourdough or French bread. Drying out the bread the day before helps speed up the process.

You can use store-bought mushroom broth, but we recommend you make your own. Increase the Mushroom Broth recipe for Red Currant and Mushroom Gravy by 50%, and you will have all the broth you need for this recipe and the gravy. Zest the orange before cutting and juicing.

INGREDIENTS

- ½ loaf of whole-wheat bread
- ¼ cup ground flax seeds
- ¾ cup water
- ½ cup olive oil, divided into 2 x 2 tbsp + ¼ cup
- 2 cups diced onion (about 1 medium)
- 1 tbsp dried mushroom powder
- 1½ tsp minced garlic (about 3 cloves)
- ¼ tsp Spike all-purpose seasoning or Old Bay seasoning
- 2 cups chopped celery, including leaves (about 4 stalks)
- 1 cup raw walnuts
- 1 cup raw pine nuts
- ½ cup dried cranberries
- 1 small apple, peeled, cored, and chopped (about ½ cup)
- ¼ cup minced parsley leaves + a small amount for garnish
- 2 tbsp orange zest (about 1 orange)
- 2 tbsp minced sage leaves
- 2 tbsp minced rosemary + a few leaves for garnish
- 2 tbsp minced thyme leaves
- 2 tbsp minced oregano leaves
- ½ tsp salt
- ¼ tsp ground nutmeg
- ¼ tsp ground cloves
- ¼ tsp ground black pepper
- 2 cups Mushroom Broth (page 211), divided into 2 x 1 cup
- ⅓ cup orange juice (1–2 oranges)

DIRECTIONS

1. Preheat oven to 200°F.
2. Cut half a loaf of whole-wheat bread into bread cubes (about 6 cups), place on a large baking dish, and bake for 1 hour or until it dries out (shrinks to about 5 cups).
3. Increase oven temperature to 375°F.
4. In a small bowl, mix ¼ cup ground flax seeds with ¾ cup water and let thicken for at least 5 minutes.
5. Place a large saucepan on medium heat and add 2 tbsp olive oil. Once hot, add 2 cups diced onion and sauté until translucent and beginning to darken (about 5 minutes). Add a little water if onions start to stick.
6. Add 1 tbsp dried mushroom powder, 1½ tsp minced garlic, and ¼ tsp Spike seasoning. Stir and cook for 1–2 minutes to let flavours seal into onions before adding 2 cups chopped celery. Cook for about 5 minutes.
7. In a large bowl, mix about 5 cups dried bread cubes, cooked onion mixture, 1 cup each raw walnuts and raw pine nuts, ½ cup each dried cranberries and chopped apple, ¼ cup minced parsley leaves, 2 tbsp each orange zest and minced sage, minced rosemary, minced thyme, and minced oregano leaves, ½ tsp salt, and ¼ tsp each ground nutmeg, ground cloves, and ground black pepper. Stir and then add 1 cup Mushroom Broth, ⅓ cup orange juice, ¼ cup olive oil, and thickened flax seed. Stir until all ingredients and flavours are well combined.
8. Place mixture in a 3.5-quart casserole dish or Dutch oven. Drizzle the remaining 1 cup Mushroom Broth and 2 tbsp olive oil over the top, cover with a lid, and bake for 30 minutes. (If refrigerating the dish before heating, add 10 minutes of cooking time.) Remove lid and cook for 10–15 minutes or until the top is brown and crispy.
9. Garnish with a few rosemary leaves and a sprinkle of minced parsley. Serve as a traditional side with your holiday meal.

NUTRITION: *PER 1-CUP SERVING:* Calories 715; Carbs 55g; Fat 50g; Protein 18g; Sodium 537mg; Sugar 17g

Fancy Cranberry Sauce

prep time: 10 minutes   cook time: 20 minutes   makes: 6 x ⅓-cup servings

Rich in: Ca, Leaf, C

We may be humble folk, but that doesn't mean we don't celebrate in style. This Fancy Cranberry Sauce adds pizazz without bein' High-Falutin'. This slightly spicy and super special cranberry sauce is sure to knock your socks off. It goes great with either of our vegan holiday mains, and it spruces up the Succulent Bread Dressing (page 207). It's so good that even turkey-eating guests (if any happen to be around) will love it! If you have any leftovers, this sauce makes a fancy appetizer when served on crackers with a dab of Cashew Creme Fraîche (page 101).

INGREDIENTS

SPICE BALL

½ tsp whole allspice

½ tsp whole cloves

1 cinnamon stick, broken

cheesecloth or tea bag filter to wrap spices

OTHER INGREDIENTS

2 cups fresh cranberries

1 cup peeled and chopped pear (about 1 medium) + a few thin slivers for garnish

⅓ cup maple syrup

⅓ cup port

¼ cup dark raisins

1 tbsp lemon juice (about ½ lemon)

DIRECTIONS

1. Prepare *Spice Ball*. Place ½ tsp each whole allspice and whole cloves and 1 cinnamon stick broken into pieces in the middle of a piece of cheesecloth or inside a tea bag filter. Tie into a ball.

2. In a medium saucepan, add 2 cups fresh cranberries, 1 cup peeled and chopped pear, the spice ball, ⅓ cup each maple syrup and port, ¼ cup dark raisins, and 1 tbsp lemon juice. Bring to a low boil and simmer until pear and cranberries are soft and the liquid has reduced (15–20 minutes).

3. Discard the spice ball. Then place the sauce in a pretty serving dish, garnish with a few thin slivers of pear, and serve with your holiday meal.

NUTRITION: PER ⅓-CUP SERVING: *Calories 126; Carbs 27g; Fat 0g; Protein 0g; Sodium 7mg; Sugar 18g*

Red Currant and Mushroom Gravy

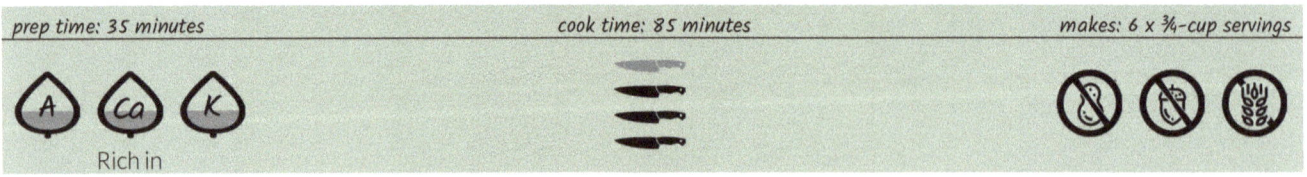

prep time: 35 minutes   cook time: 85 minutes   makes: 6 x ¾-cup servings

Rich in A, Ca, K

A gathering of friends and family around a hardy homemade meal is one of the best ways to celebrate a holiday. This festive gravy, made from mushrooms and a few tablespoons of red currant jelly, is a must for your celebratory meal. Making your own mushroom broth may take extra time, but it's so worth the effort. The savoury flavour of the broth is miles above any store-bought version. Adding in the jelly transforms the Mushroom Gravy, making it a go-to sauce for either the Savoury Holiday Tart (page 216) or the Crunchy Nut Roast (page 213). The Mushroom Gravy on its own has many uses and can be paired with Shepherdless Pie (page 172), Versatile Pot Pie (see page 169), or plain mashed potatoes. We suggest preparing the mushroom broth ahead of time. That way, the gravy comes together like greased lightning.

When preparing the mushroom broth, you can use either store-bought low-sodium mushroom broth or vegetable broth, but keep in mind the mushroom broth provides a deeper flavour than vegetable broth. Keep the strained mushrooms to use later in soups or stir-fries. Reduce the amount of salt if your broth is not low-sodium.
Bruising whole cloves of garlic releases a robust flavour. Simply use the flat side of a knife to press down on the cloves until they split. For gluten-free, use gluten-free flour as a thickener.

INGREDIENTS

MUSHROOM BROTH (makes 4 cups)

- 1 medium onion
- 2 tbsp olive oil
- 24 medium mushrooms
- 1 bulb of garlic (12–16 cloves)
- ¼ cup Bragg soy seasoning or tamari
- 1 tbsp dried mushroom powder
- 2 tsp white miso paste
- 1½ tsp Bestcestershire Sauce (vegan Worcestershire sauce)
- 1 tsp Spike all-purpose seasoning or Old Bay seasoning
- freshly ground black pepper, to taste
- 4 cups water
- 4 cups low-sodium mushroom broth or vegetable broth
- 2 sprigs of thyme

OTHER INGREDIENTS

- ¼ cup vegan butter
- ¼ cup olive oil
- 2 tbsp red currant jelly
- ½ cup whole-wheat flour

DIRECTIONS

1. Prepare **Mushroom Broth**:

    a. Chop a medium onion (about 2 cups).

    b. Place saucepan on medium-high heat and add 2 tbsp olive oil. Once hot, add chopped onion and sauté until translucent and beginning to darken (about 5 minutes). Add a little water if onion starts to stick.

    c. While onion cooks, chop 24 medium mushrooms into ½-inch pieces (about 6 cups). Peel then bruise all the cloves in a bulb of garlic (12–16 cloves).

    d. To the cooked onions, add ¼ cup Bragg seasoning, 1 tbsp dried mushroom powder, 2 tsp white miso paste, 1½ tsp Bestcestershire Sauce, and the bruised and peeled garlic cloves. Stir until well combined and cook for 1–2 minutes to let flavours seal into onions. Add about 6 cups chopped mushrooms, 1 tsp Spike seasoning, and freshly ground black pepper. Add a little water if the ingredients start to stick. Cook for about 5 minutes or until mushrooms begin to brown and the liquid has cooked off the mushrooms.

    e. Add 4 cups each water and low-sodium mushroom broth and 2 sprigs of thyme, and bring to a boil. Lower heat and simmer until reduced by half (about 1 hour).

    f. Remove from stovetop and strain out mushrooms and thyme sprigs.

2. Place a large saucepan on medium heat and add ¼ cup each vegan butter and olive oil. Once the butter is melted and the oil is hot, whisk in 2 tbsp red currant jelly until well combined.

3. Reduce heat to medium-low and slowly sift in ½ cup whole-wheat flour. Whisk continuously until all flour is completely absorbed, ensuring no lumps appear. Cook for a few minutes until the mixture starts to bubble.

4. Slowly pour in 4 cups Mushroom Broth, ½ cup at a time, whisking continuously. Once all the broth has been added and the mixture is smooth without any lumps, bring to a slow boil. Cook until the gravy thickens (about 5 minutes).

NUTRITION: PER ¾-CUP SERVING: *Calories 290; Carbs 21g; Fat 22g; Protein 5g; Sodium 579mg; Sugar 8g*

Crunchy Nut Roast with Roasted Carrots

Nut Roast: prep time: 50 minutes + time to marinate — cook time: 95 minutes — makes: 6 x 1½ x 5" servings (5 x 9" roast)
Roasted Carrots: prep time: 15 minutes + time to marinate — cook time: 35 minutes — makes: 6 x ⅔-cup servings

Rich in

Get ready for some big eatin' when you serve up Crunchy Nut Roast as the main for your holiday meal. This roast makes a dang good centrepiece for your meal and is a pleasure to share with friends or family. It's become one of our holiday traditions. Prepare the different parts of this dish over several days. Then, when the big day arrives, you can quickly pull everything together. For a spectacular spread, we like to serve Crunchy Nut Roast with Roasted Carrots along with Red Currant and Mushroom Gravy (page 211), Fancy Cranberry Sauce (page 209), Succulent Bread Dressing (page 207), Best Brussels Sprouts (page 203), and Mashed Sweet and Russet Potatoes (page 205). The Roasted Carrots add a nice touch, in both colour and flavour, but the meal works with or without them.

The cooking time can be decreased if you cook the nuts and the roasted veggies simultaneously and when you cook the roast and the roasted carrots together.
For the Creamed Cashew Base, wash and zest the orange first, then cut the orange in half and juice.

INGREDIENTS

ROASTED EGGPLANT AND MUSHROOMS (makes 1½ cups)

- 1 tbsp + ¼ tsp olive oil for greasing the pan
- 1 tbsp red miso paste
- ¼ cup warm water
- 1 tbsp balsamic vinegar
- 1 tsp Bestcestershire Sauce (vegan Worcestershire sauce)
- ½ tsp Spike all-purpose seasoning or Old Bay seasoning
- freshly ground black pepper, to taste
- 1 cup chopped onion (about ½ medium)
- 1 cup chopped portobello mushroom (about 1 medium)
- 1 cup chopped brown cremini mushroom (about 4 medium)
- 1 cup cubed eggplant (about ½ small globe eggplant)

ROASTED NUTS (makes 1¼ cups)

- ¾ cup chopped walnuts
- ½ cup pine nuts
- ½ cup sunflower seeds

CREAMY CASHEW BASE (makes 1⅔ cups)

- ½ head of Roasted Bulb of Garlic (page 139)
- 1½ cups cashews, soaked in water for at least 4 hours
- ½ cup orange juice (about 2 oranges)
- 1 tbsp orange zest (about ½ orange)
- 1 tbsp minced marjoram or oregano leaves
- 1 tbsp minced sage leaves
- 1 tbsp minced thyme leaves
- 1 tbsp minced rosemary
- 1 tbsp minced parsley leaves

DIRECTIONS

1. Prepare *Roasted Eggplant and Mushrooms*: (Cook at the same time as Roasted Nuts.)

   a. Preheat oven to 375°F. Spray a baking sheet with olive oil or, using a pastry brush, spread a thin layer of oil on the sheet (¼ tsp oil).

   b. In a small bowl, mix 1 tbsp red miso paste with ¼ cup warm water and let sit until paste softens. Stir to combine. Add 1 tbsp each olive oil and balsamic vinegar, 1 tsp Bestcestershire Sauce, ½ tsp Spike seasoning, and freshly ground black pepper. Stir until well combined.

   c. In a large bowl, add 1 cup each chopped onion, chopped portobello mushroom, chopped brown cremini mushroom, and cubed eggplant. Pour marinade over veggies and toss until well coated. Marinate for 15–30 minutes, stirring a few times.

   d. Spread marinated veggies in a single layer on prepared baking sheet. Roast for 20–30 minutes or until veggies brown and soften. Remove from oven.

2. Prepare *Roasted Nuts*: (Cook at the same time as Roasted Eggplant and Mushrooms.)

   a. In a roasting pan, place ¾ cup chopped walnuts and ½ cup each pine nuts and sunflower seeds. Roast for about 5 minutes or until nuts darken.

   b. Remove from oven.

3. Prepare *Creamy Cashew Base*: (Prepare while veggies cook.)

   a. Peel cloves from ½ head of Roasted Bulb of Garlic (6–8 cloves).

   b. Drain and rinse the soaked cashews. Put in a small food processor or blender. Add the peeled and roasted garlic cloves, ½ cup orange juice, and 1 tbsp each orange zest, minced marjoram, minced sage, minced thyme, minced rosemary, and minced parsley.

   c. Process until smooth and creamy (3–5 minutes), scraping down sides as needed with a rubber spatula.

INGREDIENTS, con't

CRUNCHY NUT ROAST RUB
(makes ⅓ cup)

½ head of Roasted Bulb of Garlic (page 139)

3 tbsp olive oil

1 tbsp minced marjoram or oregano leaves

1 tbsp minced sage leaves

1 tbsp minced thyme leaves

1 tbsp minced rosemary

1 tbsp minced parsley leaves

½ tsp salt

freshly ground black pepper, to taste

OTHER INGREDIENTS

¼ cup ground flax seeds

½ cup water

2¼ cups cooked short-grain brown rice

2 tbsp arrowroot flour

½ tsp salt

½ tsp ground black pepper

¼ cup olive oil

ROASTED CARROTS

12 medium carrots

GLAZE FOR CARROTS (makes 5 tbsp)

2 tbsp coconut oil

2 tbsp orange juice (about ½ orange)

1 tbsp maple syrup

1 tsp grated ginger root

¼ tsp paprika

¼ tsp Spike all-purpose seasoning or Old Bay seasoning

DIRECTIONS, con't

4. Prepare *Crunchy Nut Roast Rub*: (Prepare while veggies cook.)

    a. Peel cloves from the other half of a head of Roasted Bulb of Garlic (6–8 cloves).

    b. In a small bowl, add peeled roasted cloves, 3 tbsp olive oil, 1 tbsp each minced marjoram, minced sage, minced thyme, minced rosemary, and minced parsley, ½ tsp salt, and freshly ground black pepper. Press garlic cloves with a fork and mash into ingredients until everything is well combined.

5. Prepare *Crunchy Nut Roast*:

    a. Preheat oven to 375°F.

    b. In a small bowl, mix ¼ cup ground flax seeds with ½ cup water and let thicken for at least 5 minutes.

    c. In a large bowl, mix 2¼ cups cooked short-grain brown rice, Roasted Eggplant and Mushrooms mixture (about 1½ cups), and Roasted Nuts (about 1¼ cups). Stir until well combined. Add Creamy Cashew base (about 1⅔ cups), thickened flax seed mixture, 2 tbsp arrowroot flour, and ½ tsp each salt and ground black pepper. Mix with fingers until ingredients are well combined, then form mixture into a long triangular shape (similar to prime rib).

    d. In the bottom of a roasting pan, add ¼ cup olive oil and place the formed loaf in the pan. Cover with a lid and bake for 30 minutes.

    e. Remove from oven and slather Crunchy Nut Roast Rub over outside of roast. Place the marinated carrot sticks (see below) around the bottom of the pan. Leave pan uncovered and return to oven for an additional 30 minutes or until roast is firm and brown and carrots are tender.

    f. Remove from oven and let set for 10 minutes before serving.

6. Prepare *Roasted Carrots*: (Prepare during the Nut Roast's first cooking phase.)

    a. Peel and cut 12 medium carrots into ½-inch sticks (about 6 cups). Place in a medium bowl.

    b. Prepare *Glaze for Carrots*. Place small frying pan on medium heat. Add 2 tbsp each coconut oil and orange juice, 1 tbsp maple syrup, 1 tsp grated ginger root, and ¼ tsp each paprika and Spike seasoning. When hot and after ginger softens, remove from stovetop and pour glaze over carrots. Toss until carrots are well coated and marinate for 15–20 minutes.

    c. Cook with roast (after adding Crunchy Nut Roast Rub to the roast) for the last 30 minutes of cooking time (see above). Serve along with the roast.

NUTRITION: CRUNCHY NUT ROAST ONLY - *PER SERVING: Calories 776; Carbs 50g; Fat 58g; Protein 20g; Sodium 487mg; Sugar 7g;*
ROASTED CARROTS - *PER ⅔-CUP SERVING: Calories 97; Carbs 14g; Fat 5g; Protein 1g; Sodium 103mg; Sugar 8g*

Savoury Holiday Tart

prep time: 50 minutes | cook time: 75 minutes | makes: one 9" pie (6 servings)

Rich in: A, Fe, C, K

Our Savoury Holiday Tart will surely add to your holiday merriment. So, whatever you're celebrating, whether it be Thanksgiving, Christmas, or any other special occasion, you deserve a feast that can live up to the celebration. We reckon this vegan mushroom, hazelnut, and cranberry tart is tasty enough, pretty enough, and special enough to serve as your holiday main. This meal is sure to pass the hoopla test with flying colours, especially when set out along with all our Holiday Sides. Trust us, your kinfolk'll be hellabalooing for a second serving.

Cook up some dried chickpeas in advance or save the chickpea water from the can for later use as aquafaba, aka: egg white substitute (page 14).
You can make the tart in advance and freeze it before baking. To serve, just pull it straight from the freezer and cook in a preheated 400°F oven for 10 minutes, reduce the heat to 375°F, and cook for an additional 40–50 minutes. Alternatively, you can make the pastry a day or two in advance, wrap it up tightly, and refrigerate it until ready to make the filling. Just be sure to remove it from the fridge for at least 3 hours before rolling the dough to let the dough reach room temperature.

HOLIDAY MEAL - HOLIDAY MAINS

INGREDIENTS

1 cup + 2 tbsp raw hazelnuts

GARLIC CASHEW CREME CHEEZ (makes 1 cup)

- ½ head of Roasted Bulb of Garlic (page 139)
- ⅔ cup raw cashews, soaked in water for at least 4 hours
- ¼ cup pine nuts, soaked in water for at least 4 hours
- 2 tbsp cashew milk
- 1½ tbsp apple cider vinegar
- 1½ tbsp coconut oil
- 2 tsp lemon juice (from ½ lemon)
- 1½ tsp arrowroot powder
- 1½ tsp nutritional yeast
- ½ tsp salt
- ⅛ tsp ground nutmeg

HEALTHIER PASTRY (makes 1¾ cups)

- 1¾ cups whole-wheat pastry flour + small amount for rolling the dough
- 1 tsp sugar
- ¾ tsp salt
- 3 tbsp cold water + more if needed
- ¾ tsp white wine vinegar
- ½ cup semi-solid coconut oil (page 17)

DIRECTIONS

1. Roast hazelnuts. Place 1 cup + 2 tbsp hazelnuts in a frying pan over medium heat and cook for 5–10 minutes or until nuts brown. Gently stir them every few minutes. Remove from heat and divide into 1 cup + 2 tbsp for topping.

2. Prepare *Garlic Cashew Creme Cheez*:

   a. Peel 6–8 roasted garlic cloves from ½ head of Roasted Bulb of Garlic.

   b. Drain and rinse the soaked cashews and pine nuts. Put in a food processor or blender along with the peeled roasted garlic cloves, 2 tbsp cashew milk, 1½ tbsp each apple cider vinegar and coconut oil, 2 tsp lemon juice, 1½ tsp each arrowroot powder and nutritional yeast, ½ tsp salt, and ⅛ tsp ground nutmeg. Process until smooth and creamy (3–5 minutes), scraping down sides as needed with a rubber spatula.

3. Prepare *Healthier Pastry*:

   a. In a medium bowl, sift 1¾ cups whole-wheat pastry flour, 1 tsp sugar, and ¾ tsp salt. Stir a few times to ensure all ingredients are well mixed.

   b. In a small dish, mix 3 tbsp cold water with ¾ tsp white wine vinegar.

   c. Slowly add ½ cup semi-solid coconut oil to the flour mixture, 1 tbsp at a time. Using a pastry cutter (or 2 butter knives, cutting in opposite directions, or a balloon whisk), press straight down, repeating in different spots. Cut the oil into the flour mixture until it looks like crumbs. Do not overdo it, or the dough may become tough.

   d. Slowly pour the cold-water mixture over the flour mixture, 1 tbsp at a time. Mix continuously with a fork until no dry patches remain, and the dough starts to form a ball. If the dough gathers into a ball before using all the water, leave any remaining water. If the pastry is too dry after adding all the water, slowly add more cold water 1 tbsp at a time. Note: If the dough feels too sticky, add a little more flour. Try not to overhandle the dough, or it may become tough.

   e. Immediately roll out the dough using 2 sheets of parchment paper. Place one sheet of parchment paper on the counter and lightly sprinkle flour over it. Shape the dough into a nice round ball and place it on top of the first sheet of parchment paper. Sprinkle lightly with flour. Place the second sheet of parchment paper over the dough. Using a pastry roller, roll out the dough until it is ⅛-inch thick and at least 2 inches larger than the diameter and sides of your pie dish (14 inches in diameter for a 9-inch pie dish). To get an even thickness, rotate the bottom sheet of parchment clockwise after each roll. Gently peel off the top sheet of parchment paper.

INGREDIENTS, con't

OTHER INGREDIENTS

2 tbsp ground flax seeds

⅓ cup water

2 tbsp olive oil

1 cup diced onion (about ½ medium)

4 cups sliced mushroom (about 16 medium)

1½ cups chopped carrot (about 3 medium)

1 tsp Spike all-purpose seasoning or Old Bay seasoning

1 tsp dried mushroom powder

1 cup cooked chickpeas

½ cup fresh cranberries

2 tbsp minced parsley leaves + a few leaves for garnish

1 tbsp minced thyme leaves

DIRECTIONS, con't

f. Using a pastry knife, cut around the outside rim of the dough to make a nice clean edge. Using the bottom sheet of the parchment paper for leverage, lift the pastry and carefully invert it over the pie dish. Lay the pastry down gently with the parchment paper on top. Gently arrange pastry in pan to ensure it is evenly placed. Slowly peel off the parchment paper. The pastry should hang over the edges of the pie dish by at least 1 inch.

4. Preheat oven to 375°F.

5. In a small dish, mix 2 tbsp ground flax seeds with ⅓ cup water and let thicken for at least 5 minutes.

6. Place frying pan on medium-high heat and add 2 tbsp olive oil. Once hot, add 1 cup diced onion and sauté until translucent and beginning to darken (about 5 minutes). Add a little water if onions start to stick.

7. Add 4 cups sliced mushroom, 1½ cups chopped carrot, and 1 tsp each Spike seasoning and dried mushroom powder. Stir until well combined. Cook until mushrooms brown and carrots soften (10–15 minutes).

8. In a medium bowl, mix mushroom mixture, 1 cup each roasted hazelnuts and cooked chickpeas, ½ cup fresh cranberries, 2 tbsp minced parsley, 1 tbsp minced thyme, thickened flax seed mixture, and 1 cup Garlic Cashew Creme Cheez. Stir until well combined.

9. Spoon into the prepared pastry, and top with 2 tbsp roasted hazelnuts. Gently fold excess pastry over the filling.

10. Cover top edge of tart with foil and bake for 45 minutes or until filling is bubbling and pastry is light golden brown. Remove from oven and let set for 10 minutes. Garnish with a few parsley leaves and serve as a festive main dish.

NUTRITION: PER SERVING: Calories 741; Carbs 54g; Fat 52g; Protein 14g; Sodium 698mg; Sugar 7g

Creamy Pumpkin Pie

prep time: 30 minutes cook time: 50 minutes makes: one 9" pie (6 servings)

Rich in A, Fe, K, Ca

We absolutely love pumpkin pie and have created a vegan version that's a cut above the traditional variety. Fall harvest season is always exciting 'cause that's when pumpkin patches appear around the homestead. It's a lot of fun going to the patch and picking out your own pumpkin. But be forewarned, the jack-o'-lantern type doesn't hold a candle to sweet cooking pumpkins when it comes to pie. While carved pumpkins may be a tradition in some places, that's all they're good for 'cause they lack flavour and are overly watery when it comes to cooking. Ours starts with sweet cooking pumpkins and is creamy with an incredible depth of flavour that comes from freshly roasted pumpkin and decadent dates. We like to make several pies at once and then freeze a few, especially when we want a fresh pumpkin pie for Christmas. 'Cause once October 31 rolls by, pumpkins just seem to disappear. To double the creaminess, serve a slice with a scoop of Coconut Whipped Creme. Plus, it's fun to dish it out with a couple of cinnamon sticks on the side.

You can make the pie in advance and freeze it before baking. For previously frozen pies, unwrap the frozen pie, line the top edge of the pie crust with a thin layer of aluminum foil, and place it directly in a preheated 425°F oven for 20 minutes. Then, reduce the heat to 350°F for 55-60 minutes or until the filling is bubbling.
For a nut-free version, replace cashew milk with your favourite nut-free vegan milk.
If you want to avoid corn, substitute arrowroot powder for cornstarch.

INGREDIENTS

1¾ cups Healthier Pastry (page 216)

whole-wheat pastry flour for rolling the dough

¾ cup pitted Medjool dates (8–10 medium) + boiling water for soaking

2 cups fresh roasted pumpkin meat (page 21)

Milk Mixture (makes 1 cup)
   ⅔ cup oat milk
   ¼ cup cashew milk
   4 tsp coconut milk

¼ cup cornstarch

2 tbsp brown sugar

2 tsp ground cinnamon

1 tsp molasses

1 tsp vanilla extract

½ tsp ground ginger

½ tsp ground nutmeg

½ tsp ground allspice

½ tsp salt

¼ tsp ground cloves

Coconut Whipped Creme (page 33) (optional)

DIRECTIONS

1. Preheat oven to 425°F.

2. Roll out 1¾ cups Healthier Pastry dough using 2 sheets of parchment paper. Place one sheet of parchment paper on the counter and lightly sprinkle flour over it. Shape the dough into a nice round ball and place it on top of the first sheet of parchment paper. Sprinkle lightly with flour. Place the second sheet of parchment paper over the dough. Using a pastry roller, roll out the dough until it is ⅛-inch thick and at least ½ inch larger than the diameter of the bottom and sides of your pie dish (12½ inches in diameter for a 9-inch pie dish). To get an even thickness, rotate the bottom sheet of the parchment clockwise after each roll. Then, gently peel off the top piece of parchment paper.

3. Using a pastry knife, cut around the outside rim of the dough to make a nice clean edge. Using the bottom sheet of the parchment paper for leverage, lift the pastry and carefully invert it over the pie dish. Lay the pastry down gently with the parchment paper on top. Gently arrange the pastry in the pan to ensure it is evenly placed. Slowly peel off the parchment paper.

4. Place ¾ cup pitted Medjool dates in a small bowl and cover with boiling water. Let sit for 10 minutes, drain water, and place in a food processor or blender.

5. Add 2 cups fresh roasted pumpkin meat, 1 cup Milk Mixture (⅔ cup oat milk, ¼ cup cashew milk, and 4 tsp coconut milk), ¼ cup cornstarch, 2 tbsp brown sugar, 2 tsp ground cinnamon, 1 tsp each molasses and vanilla extract, ½ tsp each ground ginger, ground nutmeg, ground allspice, and salt, and ¼ tsp ground cloves. Process until well blended and smooth.

6. Pour pumpkin mixture into the prepared pastry shell. Line the top edge of the pie crust (but not the entire top) with a thin layer of aluminum foil to prevent over-browning around the edges.

7. Bake for 10 minutes, reduce heat to 350°F, and cook for an additional 35–40 minutes or until the filling is bubbling and the pastry is golden brown.

8. Let pie cool and serve with Coconut Whipped Creme.

NUTRITION: PIE ONLY (without Coconut Whipped Creme) *PER SERVING:* Calories 491; Carbs 61g; Fat 24g; Protein 7g; Sodium 785mg; Sugar 22g

Mulled Wine

prep time: 15 minutes cook time: 15 minutes makes: 6 x ¾-cup servings

Rich in

Gather around a cozy fireplace and merrily bring in the holidays with a mug of warm Mulled Wine (aka: spiced wine). It's traditionally served during the holidays 'cause it really hits the spot on a cold winter's eve. These spices truly do warm the hearth and the heart. Just heat up some red wine along with a drop of maple syrup, a splash of apple cider, and a smattering of Christmas spices — and just for fun, we like to spike the pot with a bit of rum or brandy. This delicious drink is easy to make, easy to drink, and pleasant to enjoy with friends or family.

INGREDIENTS

SPECIAL SPICE BALL

- 3 whole star anise or 1½ tsp anise seed
- ½ tsp whole cloves
- ½ tsp whole peppercorns
- 2 crushed cardamom pods
- 1 cinnamon stick, broken into pieces
- cheesecloth or tea bag filter to wrap spices

OTHER INGREDIENTS

- 1 orange
- whole cloves
- 750-ml bottle red wine (medium-bodied, like a merlot)
- 1 cup apple cider or juice
- ¼ cup maple syrup
- ¼ cup brandy or rum
- cinnamon sticks for garnish

DIRECTIONS

1. Prepare *Special Spice Ball*. Mix 3 whole star anise, ½ tsp each whole cloves and whole peppercorns, 2 crushed cardamom pods, and 1 cinnamon stick broken into pieces. Place in a piece of cheesecloth or a tea bag filter and tie into a ball.

2. Slice an orange into rings, then cut into halves (shaped like Ds). Select 8 slices for garnish. Cut these 8 slices in half again and put them in a small dish. Press a whole clove into the centre of the remaining sliced orange halves.

3. In a medium saucepan, combine 750-ml bottle red wine (the whole bottle), 1 cup apple cider, ¼ cup maple syrup, Special Spice Ball, and the sliced orange halves with cloves. Heat on medium-low until the wine almost reaches a simmer (avoid letting it bubble and keep below 172°F as that is when alcohol begins to vaporize). Reduce heat to low, cover completely, and let the wine simmer for 10 minutes. Remove the spice ball.

4. Add ¼ cup brandy, stir, and serve warm. Garnish each glass with a slice of orange and a cinnamon stick.

NUTRITION: PER ¾-CUP SERVING: *Calories 192; Carbs 20g; Fat 0g; Protein 0g; Sodium 17mg; Sugar 15g*

Nicely Spiced Cran-Apple Cider

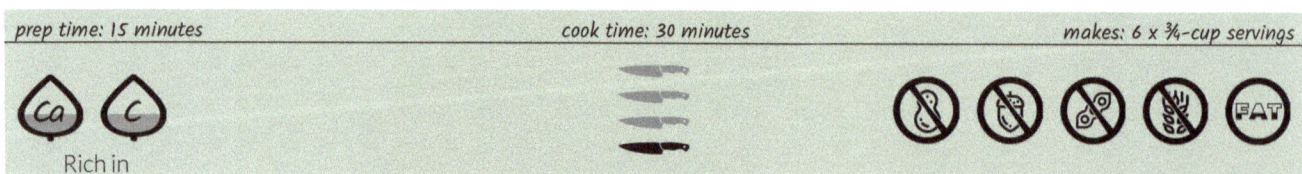

prep time: 15 minutes   cook time: 30 minutes   makes: 6 x ¾-cup servings

Rich in: Ca, C

The ole homestead will feel like Christmas when you're steeping some Nicely Spiced Cran-Apple Cider. We like to use a Crock-Pot, but a saucepan or Dutch oven works just as well. This drink is soothing for the soul and pleasing to the senses, plus it comes together in a snap. It looks pretty with fresh cranberries and studded orange slices. This cider is a real treat for folks who don't want to indulge in anything stronger but still like to enjoy a festive drink.

INGREDIENTS

1 orange
1 lemon
whole cloves
2 cups cranberry juice
2 cups apple cider
2 tbsp maple syrup
2 tbsp fresh cranberries
1 tbsp lemon juice (about ½ lemon)
Spice Ball (page 209)
cinnamon sticks for garnish

DIRECTIONS

1. Slice an orange into rings, then cut into halves (shaped like Ds). Select a few slices for garnish, cut these in half again, and place them in a small dish. For the remaining sliced orange halves, press a whole clove into the centre of each.

2. Slice a lemon into rings, then cut into halves (shaped like Ds). Select a few slices for garnish, cut these in half again, and place them in a small dish. For the remaining sliced lemon halves, press a whole clove into the centre of each.

3. In a large saucepan, Dutch Oven, or slow cooker, mix 2 cups each cranberry juice and apple cider, the prepared orange and lemon slices studded with whole cloves, 2 tbsp each maple syrup and fresh cranberries, 1 tbsp lemon juice, and the Spice Ball. Bring to a low boil, then reduce to medium-low and simmer for 15 minutes to blend the flavours. Reduce to low, cover, and simmer for 10 minutes.

4. Discard the spice ball and serve the cider hot. Garnish each drink with remaining orange and lemon slices and a cinnamon stick.

NUTRITION: PER ¾-CUP SERVING: *Calories 114; Carbs 29g; Fat 0g; Protein 0g; Sodium 26g; Sugar 25g*

DESSERTS

With Chocolate

Strawberries with Chocolate Sauce	227
Nutty Chocolate Pudding with Raspberry Purée	229

Cupcakes and Cookies

Carrot-Ginger-Orange Cupcakes	231
Very Berry Almond Cookies	233
AquaFabulous Meringues	235

Fruity Treats

Rhubarb and Strawberry Treat	237
Gooey Baked Apples	239
Kumquat Candy	241

Pastries

Sinnamon Wheels	243
Unbutter Tarts	245

Strawberries with Chocolate Sauce

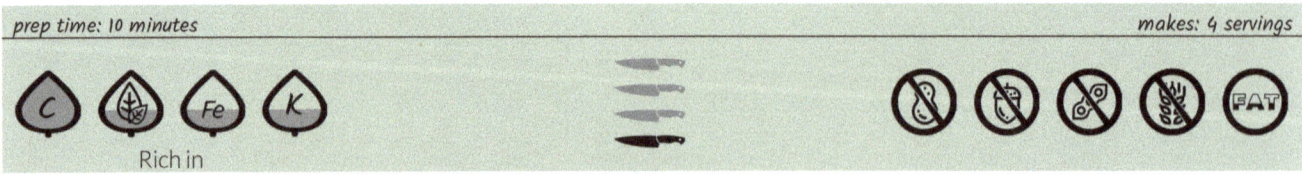

prep time: 10 minutes
makes: 4 servings

Rich in

Strawberries are hard to beat! They're luscious, juicy, and sweet, with just a smidgeon of tartness that perfectly complements the delightful depth of chocolatey-ness in this sauce. There's no better way to be cooling yer heels than munching on this treat. Just dip 'em in the chocolate sauce and scoop up big dollops of deliciousness! Our sauce is thick and creamy with an occasional crunch from the cacao nibs, plus it's low in fat. Agave syrup provides the smoothest texture and the best flavour with cocoa powder, but maple syrup also works well.

INGREDIENTS

CHOCOLATE SAUCE *(makes ½ cup)*

½ cup cocoa powder

3 tbsp raw blue agave nectar or maple syrup

1 tbsp cacao nibs + a few for garnish

1 tsp vanilla extract

1 tbsp–¼ cup oat milk

OTHER INGREDIENTS

32 fresh whole strawberries, stems attached, washed and dried

DIRECTIONS

1. Prepare **Chocolate Sauce**:

    a. Sift ½ cup cocoa powder into a small bowl. Do not skip this step, as sifting helps create a smooth and creamy texture for the chocolate sauce.

    b. Slowly add 3 tbsp agave nectar, continuously mixing with a spoon until syrup is absorbed into cocoa powder. The mixture should become a bit moist but will still be quite dry.

    c. Stir in 1 tbsp cacao nibs and 1 tsp vanilla extract.

    d. Add oat milk, 1 tbsp at a time, stirring continuously until the sauce is thick and creamy. You should be able to scoop up the sauce, but you do not want it to be too runny.

2. Scoop 2 tbsp of chocolate sauce onto 4 small individual plates along with a few cacao nibs for garnish. Serve with 8 fresh strawberries per person.

NUTRITION: PER SERVING: *Calories 131; Carbs 24g; Fat 2g; Protein 3g; Sodium 8mg; Sugar 16g*

Nutty Chocolate Pudding with Raspberry Purée

prep time: 20 minutes   cook time: 15 minutes   makes: 6 servings

Rich in

Potato Pat is nuts for this creamy, yummy pudding 'cause it fits the bill when only chocolate'll do. Wrapped up in velvety smoothness, this dessert's got it all. You'll find nutty lusciousness from cashew butter and tangy sweetness from raspberries, plus a double hit of chocolate enjoyment. After just one taste, you too will be nuts for more. Serve this treasure chilled and bask in the warmth of happy smiles from your mates.

INGREDIENTS

RASPBERRY PURÉE (makes ¾ cup)
- 2 cups raspberries, fresh or frozen
- 2 tbsp raw blue agave nectar
- 2 tsp lemon juice (from ½ lemon)

OTHER INGREDIENTS

- ⅓ cup unsweetened cocoa powder
- 2 tbsp tapioca flour
- Milk Mixture (makes 1½ cups)
  - 1 cup oat milk
  - ⅓ cup cashew milk
  - 2 tbsp + 1 tsp coconut milk
- ¼ cup raw blue agave nectar
- 1 tbsp cacao nibs
- 1 tsp vanilla extract
- ¼ tsp ground cinnamon
- ⅛ tsp ground allspice
- ¼ cup cashew butter
- 6 hazelnuts for garnish
- 6 raspberries for garnish
- Coconut Whipped Creme (page 33) (optional)

DIRECTIONS

1. Prepare *Raspberry Purée*:

    a. Place medium saucepan on medium heat and add 2 cups raspberries, 2 tbsp agave nectar, and 2 tsp lemon juice. Stir until well combined. Once berries come to a low boil, reduce to medium-low. Cook until berries are soft and mushy (about 10 minutes), stirring often. Remove from stovetop and let cool.

    b. Once the mixture cools, push it through a sieve into a small bowl using the back of a spoon. Scrape any pulp that gathers on the outside of the sieve but leave the seeds behind. Discard seeds and set purée aside.

2. Sift ⅓ cup unsweetened cocoa powder and 2 tbsp tapioca flour into a medium saucepan. Do not skip this step, as sifting helps create a smooth and creamy chocolate pudding. Next, slowly stir in 1½ cups Milk Mixture (1 cup oat milk, ⅓ cup cashew milk, and 2 tbsp + 1 tsp coconut milk) and mix with a whisk until well blended. Add ¼ cup agave nectar, 1 tbsp cacao nibs, 1 tsp vanilla extract, ¼ tsp ground cinnamon, and ⅛ tsp ground allspice. Mix with a whisk until well blended.

3. Cook on medium heat, whisking continuously until mixture becomes smooth and starts to heat up (about 3 minutes). Once the mixture comes to a low boil, cook until pudding thickens (about 2 minutes). Remove from heat and whisk in ¼ cup cashew butter until pudding is smooth and creamy.

4. Fill 6 martini glasses or parfait dishes, layering the components in this order: 1 tbsp raspberry purée in the bottom, then ⅓ cup chocolate pudding, and top with 1 tbsp raspberry purée. Add 1 whole hazelnut and 1 whole raspberry for garnish. If you are feeling energetic, add a dollop of Whipped Coconut Creme. Chill the puddings for at least 1 hour before serving.

NUTRITION: *PER SERVING: Calories 227; Carbs 34g; Fat 10g; Protein 4g; Sodium 29mg; Sugar 21g*

Carrot-Ginger-Orange Cupcakes

Cupcakes: prep time: 30 minutes + time to chill pan
Cashew Date Icing: prep time: 15 minutes + time to set

cook time: 45 minutes

makes: 18 cupcakes
makes: 18 x 5-tsp servings

Rich in

Golly, but we do love these moist little cakes. It's sure as Sunday morning that Carrot Rick'll be the first one in line when they're placed on the table. Not only 'cause they taste amazing, but they're full of vitamins, minerals, and dietary fibre. By-the-bye, if you're in the mood, you could create a beautiful deep-dish carrot cake instead of cupcakes. Whether small or large, these cakes are tender and perfectly spiced. Dish them up unadorned or top them with Cashew-Date Icing. Regardless of the form, you're guaranteed a spectacular taste explosion, resulting in pure bliss.

If you make a full-sized cake, cook in two 9-inch layer pans for an additional 10–15 minutes or in a 10-inch Bundt pan for an additional 15–20 minutes.
Zest the orange before cutting and juicing.
Refrigerating the icing lets it harden up and makes it easier to spread.

INGREDIENTS

CASHEW-DATE ICING (makes 2 cups) (optional)

- 1 cup Medjool dates, pitted (about 8 medium) + boiling water for soaking
- ¾ cup raw cashews, soaked in water for at least 4 hours
- ¼ cup pine nuts, soaked in water for at least 4 hours
- 2 tbsp cashew milk
- 2 tbsp coconut oil
- 1 tbsp lemon juice (about ½ lemon)
- 1 tbsp apple cider vinegar
- 1½ tsp nutritional yeast
- ½ tsp salt
- pinch of ground nutmeg
- 1 tsp vanilla extract

OTHER INGREDIENTS

- 1 cup + 1 tsp grapeseed oil, divided into 1 cup + 2 x ½ tsp for greasing the pan
- 2 tbsp ground flax seeds
- ⅓ cup water
- ½ cup raisins + boiling water for soaking
- 2½ cups whole-wheat pastry flour
- 1 tbsp baking powder
- 2 tsp ground ginger
- 1 tsp baking soda
- 1 tsp ground cinnamon
- ¾ tsp salt
- ½ tsp ground cloves
- ½ tsp ground allspice
- 1½ cups unsweetened applesauce
- 1 cup orange juice (about 4 oranges)
- ½ cup maple syrup
- ¼ cup sugar
- 1 tsp vanilla extract
- 2 cups peeled and grated carrot (5–6 medium)
- 1 cup chopped candied ginger
- 1 cup chopped walnuts
- 1½ tbsp orange zest, divided into 1 tbsp + ½ tsp for topping

DIRECTIONS

1. Prepare **Cashew-Date Icing**:

   a. Place 1 cup pitted Medjool dates in a small bowl and cover with boiling water. Let sit for 10 minutes, then drain water.

   b. While the dates soak, drain and rinse the cashews and pine nuts. Place in a food processor or blender with 2 tbsp each cashew milk and coconut oil, 1 tbsp each lemon juice and apple cider vinegar, 1½ tsp nutritional yeast, ½ tsp salt, and a pinch of ground nutmeg. Process until smooth (3–5 minutes), scraping down sides as needed with a rubber spatula. Add soaked and drained dates and 1 tsp vanilla extract. Blend until creamy (3–5 minutes), scraping down sides as needed with a rubber spatula.

   c. Refrigerate for at least 30 minutes before applying.

2. Preheat oven to 325°F. Spray a 6-hole and a 12-hole muffin tin with oil or, using a pastry brush, spread a thin layer of oil in each muffin hole (½ tsp oil). Add muffin liners (if using) and spray or oil bottom of liners to ensure the muffins easily separate from liners (½ tsp oil).

3. In a large bowl, mix 2 tbsp ground flax seeds with ⅓ cup water and let thicken for at least 5 minutes. Cover ½ cup raisins with boiling water and soak for about 5 minutes, then drain water and set aside.

4. In a separate large bowl, sift 2½ cups whole-wheat pastry flour, 1 tbsp baking powder, 2 tsp ground ginger, 1 tsp each baking soda and ground cinnamon, ¾ tsp salt, and ½ tsp each ground cloves and ground allspice. Stir until well combined.

5. To thickened flax seed mixture, add 1½ cups applesauce, 1 cup each grapeseed oil and orange juice, ½ cup maple syrup, ¼ cup sugar, and 1 tsp vanilla extract. Using a hand mixer, beat on high for 2–3 minutes, making sure to create some bubbles. This is an essential step as it helps cupcakes rise during cooking.

6. Make a well in the centre of dry ingredients and pour in liquid ingredients, stirring gently until dry ingredients are moistened. Do not overmix, or cupcakes may become tough.

7. Fold in 2 cups grated carrot, 1 cup each chopped candied ginger and chopped walnuts, ½ cup soaked and drained raisins, and 1 tbsp orange zest.

8. Spoon batter into prepared muffin tins filling to just below the rim in each hole (about ½ cup per cupcake). Refrigerate for 10–15 minutes before cooking. This step lets the gluten relax (important when using whole-wheat flour) and chills the oil, giving the muffins more time to rise. Bake for 35–45 minutes or until the cupcake tops spring back when touched, a toothpick comes out clean when inserted in the centre, and cooked batter has pulled away from the top edge of the muffin tin.

9. Let cool for 10 minutes in the pan, then remove to wire rack to continue cooling. Cool thoroughly before topping with Cashew-Date Icing. Garnish each cupcake with a sprinkle of orange zest. Serve immediately or refrigerate in an air-tight container until needed.

NUTRITION: CUPCAKES ONLY (without icing) - *PER CUPCAKE:* Calories 258; Carbs 38g; Fat 11g; Protein 4g; Sodium 277mg; Sugar 15g; **CASHEW-DATE ICING** - *PER 5-TSP SERVING:* Calories 81; Carbs 9g; Fat 5g; Protein 1g; Sodium 66mg; Sugar 0g

Very Berry Almond Cookies

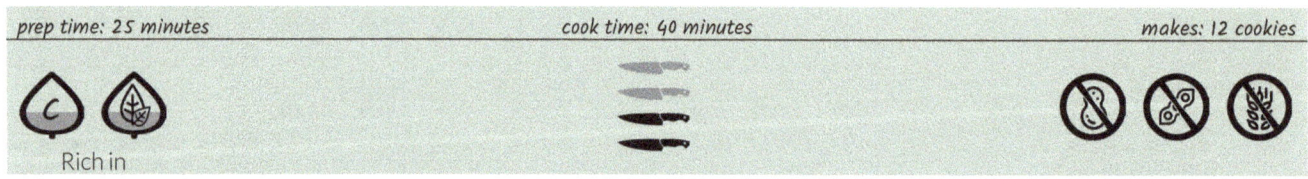

prep time: 25 minutes   cook time: 40 minutes   makes: 12 cookies

Rich in

Adding berries, lemon, and lavender takes yer garden-variety almond cookie to a whole new level. It is so worth the time and effort to seek out culinary lavender (page 19) and dried golden berries (page 19). But, in true Veggie OUTLAWS style, you can skip the lavender if you don't have it and sub in dried cranberries in place of gooseberries. We use almond flour for this recipe (where the almond skins are removed before milling) 'cause this makes for a prettier cookie. Almond meal works equally well, but the flecks of almond skin give the cookies a more rustic look. You will enjoy these cookies without the lemon glaze, but if you take the time to add it, you'll be well rewarded.

Zest the lemon before cutting and juicing.

INGREDIENTS

2 tbsp ground flax seeds
⅓ cup water
2 cups almond flour (page 13)
2 tbsp lemon zest (about 2 lemons)
1 tsp baking soda
½ tsp dried culinary lavender
¼ tsp salt
¼ cup maple syrup
1 tsp lemon juice (from ½ lemon)
⅛ tsp lemon extract
¼ cup dried golden berries
¼ cup dried currants
¼ cup fresh or frozen blueberries
1 tbsp sliced almonds
½ cup Lemon Glaze (page 31)

DIRECTIONS

1. Preheat oven to 325°F. Line a baking sheet with parchment paper.
2. In a medium bowl, mix 2 tbsp ground flax seeds with ⅓ cup water and let thicken for at least 5 minutes.
3. In a large bowl, add 2 cups almond flour, 2 tbsp lemon zest, 1 tsp baking soda, ½ tsp dried culinary lavender, and ¼ tsp salt. Stir until well combined.
4. To thickened flax seed mixture, add ¼ cup maple syrup, 1 tsp lemon juice, and ⅛ tsp lemon extract. Beat with an electric hand mixer for 2–3 minutes, making sure to create some bubbles. This is a crucial step as it helps cookies to rise during cooking.
5. Make a well in the centre of dry ingredients and pour in wet ingredients, stirring until well combined. Do not overmix.
6. Gently fold in ¼ cup each dried golden berries, dried currants, and fresh or frozen (but not thawed) blueberries.
7. Using a 2 tbsp measuring spoon, drop batter onto the parchment-lined baking sheet. The cookies expand a little as they bake, so leave about 1 inch between each. Place a few sliced almonds on the top of each cookie. Bake for 30–40 minutes or until golden brown and a toothpick comes out clean when inserted.
8. Remove from oven and cool slightly (about 10 minutes). Spread lemon glaze over the tops of the cookies before removing them to a wire rack to cool completely.

NUTRITION: PER COOKIE: *Calories 217; Carbs 25g; Fat 10g; Protein 5g; Sodium 192mg; Sugar 20g*

AquaFabulous Meringues

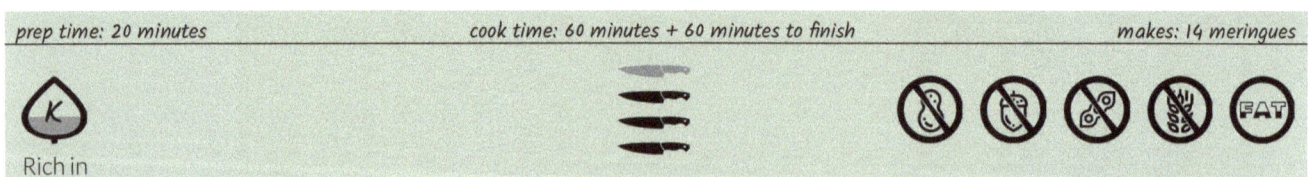

| prep time: 20 minutes | cook time: 60 minutes + 60 minutes to finish | makes: 14 meringues |

Rich in

If you like meringues, you're gonna love these 'cause they're simply "aquafaba-lous"! These little cookies are crispy on the outside, slightly chewy on the inside, and oh so light and delicious. Aquafaba is a plant-based substitute for egg whites and is easily found. All you need do is open a can of salt-free chickpeas — then drain and save the liquid. Voila, just like magic, the aquafaba elixir appears. The liquid has very little taste, but we add a little orange extract and colouring to remove any trace of chickpea flavour. We have also made these meringues with rose water, which gives them a lovely flowery flavour. A nice option is to add a sprinkle of chocolate powder and a dash of cardamom on each meringue.

INGREDIENTS

¼ cup cane sugar

¼ cup aquafaba (page 14)

¼ tsp cream of tartar

½ tsp vanilla extract

¼ tsp orange extract or 1 tbsp rose water

small amount of natural orange or pink food colouring (optional)

chocolate powder for sprinkling (optional)

dash of cardamom for sprinkling (optional)

DIRECTIONS

1. Preheat oven to 200°F. Line a baking sheet with parchment paper.
2. Grind ¼ cup cane sugar in a spice or coffee grinder until fine (about 5 seconds). Set aside.
3. Into a deep bowl, pour ¼ cup aquafaba and add ¼ tsp cream of tartar.
4. Using a balloon whisk on an electric hand mixer or stand mixer, beat liquid at high speed for about 10 minutes or until firm peaks form. Slowly add ground cane sugar, beating continuously. Slowly add ½ tsp vanilla extract, ¼ tsp orange extract, and food colouring, if using, and continue to beat until well combined, thick and glossy, and stiff peaks form.
5. Spoon the mixture into a piping bag fitted with your favourite decorating tip. Pipe 14 meringues, each 1 inch in diameter, onto the prepared baking sheet.
6. Bake for 1 hour or until meringues start to harden. Then turn off the heat and let them finish cooking in the cooling oven for an additional hour. This extra time allows the meringues to continue to harden without becoming brittle.
7. Remove from the oven, place meringues on a wire rack, and sprinkle a little chocolate powder and ground cardamom over each one. Cool completely before serving. You can store leftover meringues in an airtight container for a few days or freeze them for a few weeks.

NUTRITION: *PER MERINGUE:* Calories 14; Carbs 3g; Fat 0g; Protein 0g; Sodium 0mg; Sugar 3g

Rhubarb and Strawberry Treat

prep time: 10 minutes   cook time: 20 minutes   makes: 8 x ½-cup servings

Rich in

Rhubarb and strawberry make a great team when you've a mind for something sweet with a touch of tartness, especially when a little orange and ginger are added. Just for fun, a sprinkle of fresh basil makes things interesting and adds a nice touch. This fast and simple recipe can be enjoyed in several ways —over vegan ice cream, slathered on toast, or all on its own scooped up by the spoonful. A toothsome treat! You'll be hankering for more after just one taste of Rhubarb and Strawberry Treat.

Zest the orange before cutting and juicing.

INGREDIENTS

4 cups chopped rhubarb (about 6 medium stalks)

2 cups sliced fresh or frozen strawberries (about 24 medium) + a few slices for garnish

½ cup orange juice (about 2 oranges)

¼ cup maple syrup

2 tbsp orange zest (about 1 orange) + a few for garnish

2 tsp grated ginger root

1 tsp vanilla extract

1 tsp snipped basil leaves for garnish

DIRECTIONS

1. In a medium saucepan, place 4 cups chopped rhubarb, 2 cups sliced strawberries, ½ cup orange juice, ¼ cup maple syrup, 2 tbsp orange zest, 2 tsp grated ginger root, and 1 tsp vanilla extract. Cook on medium heat for about 20 minutes or until fruit softens, rhubarb is stewed, and all the flavours have combined. Stir often.

2. Serve warm or cold, garnished with a few slices of strawberry, fresh snipped basil, and a little orange zest.

NUTRITION: PER ½-CUP SERVING: Calories 61; Carbs 14g; Fat 0g; Protein 1g; Sodium 4mg; Sugar 10g

Gooey Baked Apples

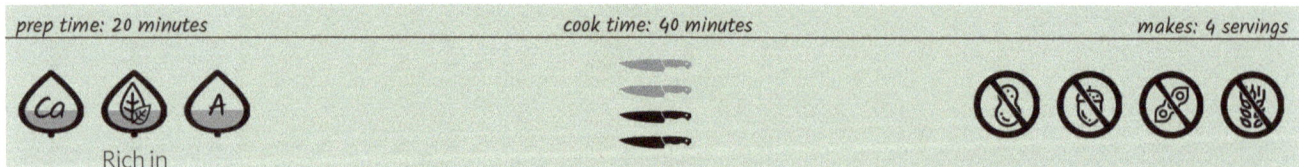

prep time: 20 minutes cook time: 40 minutes makes: 4 servings

Rich in

Baked apples are, as you guessed it, baked in the oven until the fruit becomes soft — and when stuffed with just the right ingredients, they're sweet and gooey. It's a great way to use up apples that have over-ripened but are still edible. The recipe works with just about any variety. However, our favourite apples are galas ('cause we love that apple the best). This is an easy, peasy recipe. All you need do is remove the top three-quarters of the core and stuff the apple with nummy ingredients. Then bake and enjoy the plumb good pleasure that warms your body from head to toes.

INGREDIENTS

4 medium apples

¼ cup brown sugar

2 tsp ground cinnamon

4 tsp spiced rum, divided into 4 x 1 tsp

4 tsp vegan butter, divided into 4 x 1 tsp

DIRECTIONS

1. Preheat oven to 350°F.
2. Wash 4 medium apples. Keep each apple whole, and using a paring knife, remove the top ¾ of the core. Be sure to leave the bottom ¼ of the core intact so the apple can hold the yummy filling.
3. In a small bowl, mix ¼ cup brown sugar and 2 tsp ground cinnamon. Stir until well combined.
4. Evenly divide the mixture among the apples (about 2 tbsp per apple), packing it into the hole left by the core. Next, pour 1 tsp spiced rum into each apple and dab 1 tsp vegan butter on top.
5. Place apples on a baking dish and bake for 30–40 minutes or until apples are tender and the filling is bubbling.
6. Remove from oven and cool for 10–15 minutes. Serve warm.

NUTRITION: *PER SERVING: Calories 191; Carbs 36g; Fat 4g; Protein 0g; Sodium 42mg; Sugar 29g*

DESSERTS - FRUITY TREATS

Kumquat Candy

prep time: 15 minutes   cook time: 25 minutes   makes: 8 x ½-cup servings

Rich in

Kumquat Candy is an exotic treat that's sure to be a hot item in the ole homestead. They look and taste like tiny little oranges. Although they're not much bigger than a grape, they fill your mouth with a burst of sweetly-tart citrus flavour. Since they're so small, they're next to impossible to peel. That's why it's best to cut them in half, then toss them on the stovetop with a bit of water, sugar, and spice. After 15 minutes, they transform into tasty Kumquat Candies. We love to dish them up as is, but they also go great in a bowl spooned over vegan ice cream or topped with Coconut Whipped Creme (page 33). No matter how you enjoy them, they're wickedly delicious.

INGREDIENTS

4 cups kumquats (1–1½ lbs)
1 cup hot water
1 cup sugar
¼ tsp ground anise
¼ tsp ground cloves
¼ tsp orange extract

DIRECTIONS

1. Cut 4 cups kumquats into halves. Discard any seeds that pop loose, but do not worry about any other seeds as they will soften as the fruit cooks. Feel free to leave a few small kumquats whole.

2. Place a small saucepan on medium-high heat and add 1 cup each hot water and sugar. Cook until mixture comes to a boil, then reduce heat and simmer for 4 minutes. Be sure sugar dissolves completely.

3. To the sugar mixture, add 4 cups halved kumquats, ¼ tsp each ground anise, ground cloves, and orange extract. Simmer for 15 minutes.

4. Drain kumquats through a sieve set over a bowl. Return syrup to the pan and simmer for 5 minutes to reduce the syrup by half. Combine kumquats and remaining syrup.

5. Serve immediately or refrigerate in an airtight jar for up to 2 weeks.

NUTRITION: PER ½-CUP SERVING: *Calories 140; Carbs 35g; Fat 0g; Protein 1g; Sodium 0mg; Sugar 24g*

Sinnamon Wheels

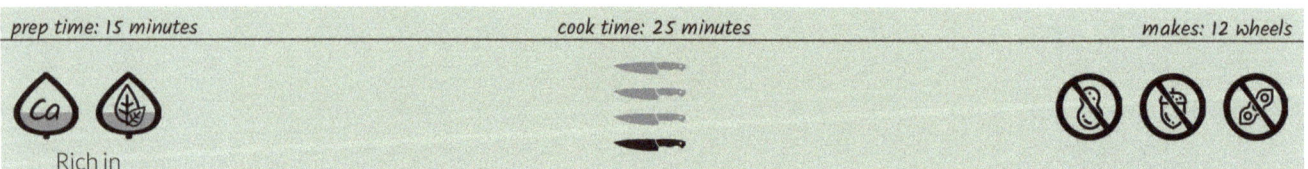

prep time: 15 minutes   cook time: 25 minutes   makes: 12 wheels

Rich in

We call these little circles of cinnamon delight Sinnamon Wheels 'cause they taste so good it's gotta be a sin. They're filled with vegan butter, brown sugar, and, of course, cinnamon, making them so yummy. We love to make Sinnamon Wheels with leftover pastry. But 'cause they're so good, sometimes we'll make pastry just so we can enjoy these decadent pastry treats.

INGREDIENTS

1¾ cups Healthier Pastry (page 216)
flour for rolling the dough
2 tbsp vegan butter
½ cup brown sugar
1 tsp ground cinnamon

DIRECTIONS

1. Preheat oven to 375°F.
2. Place a piece of parchment paper on the counter and sprinkle lightly with flour. Place a ball of dough made from 1¾ cups Healthier Pastry on the parchment and, using your hands, form it into a rough rectangle shape. Sprinkle lightly with flour and place another sheet of parchment paper over the dough. Using a pastry roller, roll out the dough until it is ⅛-inch thick and 9- x 12-inch in size. (To get an even thickness, rotate the dough 90° after each roll and try to maintain a rectangle shape.) Gently peel off the top sheet of parchment paper.
3. Spread 2 tbsp vegan butter evenly over the dough. Evenly sprinkle ½ cup brown sugar and 1 tsp ground cinnamon on top.
4. Starting at one of the long edges, tightly roll the pastry into a log. Cut the log into 12 x 1-inch pieces. Place the wheels flat on a baking sheet, leaving about ½ inch between each one. Bake for 20–25 minutes or until the wheels become nicely brown.
5. Remove from oven and let cool for 10 minutes before serving.

NUTRITION: *PER 1-INCH WHEEL: Calories 199; Carbs 23g; Fat 11g; Protein 2g; Sodium 165mg; Sugar 9g*

Unbutter Tarts

prep time: 35 minutes   cook time: 25 minutes   makes: 12 tarts

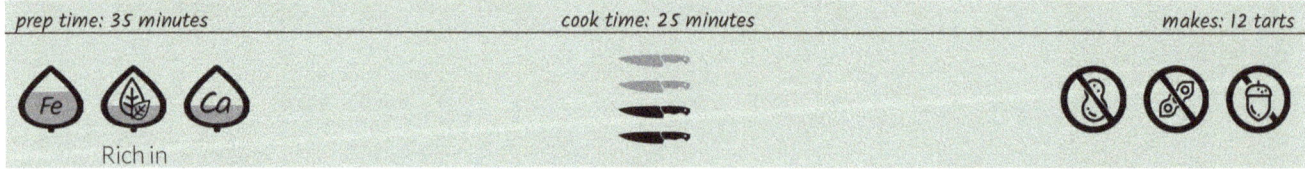

These little sweet treats are a vegan alternative to the great Canadian butter tart. Butter tarts, a Canadian invention, are considered one of Canada's quintessential treats. The classic tart, which typically combines butter, sugar, and raisins in a pastry shell, doesn't hold a candle to our version. We turned the old-fashioned Canadian original on its head and removed the butter. Instead, we use coconut oil and add a few coconut flakes for good measure. Whenever these are served, they disappear fast, getting rave reviews. If fact, they're sooo good that you'll be slapping away folks' hands as they reach for a tart coming straight out of the oven.

For a twist on the Unbutter Tart, leave out the raisins and use an equal amount of unsoaked pecans instead. Presto, the Unbutter Tart becomes a Pecan Tart.

This pastry makes enough dough for two single-crust 9-inch pies, one double-crust 9-inch pie, 12 regular tarts, or 24 small tarts. You can make the dough in advance, wrap it tightly in plastic wrap, and refrigerate it for up to a week. Then, remove from the fridge at least 3 hours before rolling to let the dough come to room temperature.

For nut-free, replace cashew milk with vegan nut-free milk of your choice.

INGREDIENTS

HEALTHIER PASTRY *(makes 2½ cups)*

- 2½ cups whole-wheat pastry flour + small amount for rolling the dough
- 2 tsp sugar
- 1 tsp salt
- 5 tbsp cold water + more if needed
- 1 tsp white wine vinegar
- ⅔ cup semi-solid coconut oil (page 17)

DIRECTIONS

1. Prepare *Healthier Pastry*:

    a. In a medium bowl, sift 2½ cups whole-wheat pastry flour, 2 tsp sugar, and 1 tsp salt. Stir a few times to ensure all ingredients are well mixed.

    b. In a small dish, mix 5 tbsp cold water with 1 tsp white wine vinegar and set aside.

    c. Scoop ⅔ cup semi-solid coconut oil, 1 tbsp at a time, into flour mixture. Using a pastry cutter (or 2 butter knives, cutting in opposite directions, or a balloon whisk), press straight down, repeating in different spots. Cut the oil into the flour mixture until it looks like crumbs. Do not overdo it, or the dough may become tough.

    d. Slowly pour cold-water mixture over flour, 1 tbsp at a time, mixing continuously with a fork until no dry patches remain and dough starts to form a ball. Depending on your flour, you may not need all the water. If pastry is still too dry after adding all the water, slowly add more cold water 1 tbsp at a time. If dough feels too sticky, add a little more flour. Do not overhandle dough, or it may become tough.

    e. Once dough forms into a ball, separate it into 2 equal-sized balls.

    f. Immediately roll out the dough using 2 sheets of parchment paper. Place one sheet on the counter and sprinkle lightly with flour. Place one of the dough balls on top and sprinkle lightly with flour. Place the second sheet of parchment paper over the dough. Using a pastry roller, roll out the dough until it is ⅛-inch thick. (To get an even thickness, rotate the dough after each roll.) Gently peel off the top sheet of parchment paper, keeping it close for use on the second dough ball.

    g. Have ready a 12-hole muffin tin or 12 x 2-inch tart pans. Use a 24-hole mini-muffin tin or 24 x 1-inch tart pans for small tarts.

    h. Cut out pastry circles using a cookie cutter, a drinking glass, or any circular object with a 4½-inch diameter (a martini glass works well). For small tarts, use a 3¼-inch cutter instead. Gather any excess pastry and set it aside.

    i. Using scissors, cut the bottom sheet of parchment paper around each pastry circle, leaving a little extra space and separating one from another. Place pastry circles, parchment paper and all, in tart pans, paper side down.

    j. Cut and lightly flour a new sheet of parchment. Set the second ball of dough on top, lightly flour, and cover with the remaining sheet of parchment. Roll and cut out pastry circles from the second ball of dough. (If you don't have a total of 12 tart shells, roll out some of the excess pastry until you have enough.) Using scissors, cut the bottom sheet of parchment paper around each pastry circle, leaving a little extra space and separating one from another. Place pastry circles, parchment paper and all, in tart pans, paper side down.

INGREDIENTS, con't

FILLING

1 cup golden raisins + boiling water for soaking

1 tbsp ground flax seeds

3 tbsp water

3 tbsp coconut oil

1 cup brown sugar

2 tbsp + 1 tsp unsweetened applesauce

2 tbsp cashew milk

2 tbsp shredded coconut flakes

1 tsp vanilla extract

DIRECTIONS, con't

2. Preheat oven to 375°F for large tarts and 350°F for small tarts.
3. In a medium bowl, soak 1 cup golden raisins in boiling water for 10 minutes. Drain and rinse.
4. In a large bowl, mix 1 tbsp ground flax seeds with 3 tbsp water and let thicken for at least 5 minutes.
5. In a small saucepan, melt 3 tbsp coconut oil on low heat.
6. To thickened flax seed mixture, add drained and rinsed raisins, 1 cup brown sugar, 3 tbsp melted coconut oil, 2 tbsp + 1 tsp applesauce, 2 tbsp each cashew milk and shredded coconut flakes, and 1 tsp vanilla extract. Stir until well combined.
7. Fill each tart evenly with raisin mixture, using about 2½ tbsp filling per large tart (and 4 tsp per small tart).
8. Bake large tarts for 20–25 minutes and small tarts for 15–20 minutes. Remove from oven when pastry browns and filling bubbles. Set on a wire rack to cool for 10 minutes. Then remove tarts from the pan and place them on a wire rack to cool completely. If there are any tarts left once your family and friends have a go at them, store them in an airtight container.

NUTRITION: PER 4½-INCH TART: *Calories 383; Carbs 63g; Fat 14g; Protein 5g; Sodium 205mg; Sugar 30g*

A Quick Message from the Veggie OUTLAWS

Howdy! We're so glad you hopped on board.

Did you enjoy Veggie Outlaws – Most Wanted Vegan Recipes? If you and everyone on your homestead loved devouring good eats made with delicious plant-based foods, please post a short review on Amazon. It'll take less than a minute. Sharing your honest review is a swell way to spread the word that vegan food tastes good. Even a two-sentence review is dang good. We read the reviews every week and are right grateful for your support.

Just click on the QR code below and go straight to the review form.

Amazon.com

Amazon.ca

Goodreads

Y'all are the best! Thanks for buying our book and posting your review. We're here to spread the truth about plant-based eating and do appreciate your help.

Index

A
a little longer
- about, 10
- AquaFabulous Meringues, 235
- Cabbage Roll Casserole, 191
- Desperado Pizza with Dipping Sauce, 161
- Friendly Mac 'n' Cheez, 145
- Grandma's Macaroni, Creamy Style, 147
- Lemon and Hemp Loaf, 31
- Mexican-Style Rice and Beans with Fresh Tomato Salsa, 51
- Pumpkin Lentil Risotto, 155,
- Red Currant and Mushroom Gravy, 211
- Saloon Gumbo with Cajun Rice and Tofu, 188
- Savoury Holiday Tart, 216
- Seriously the Best Chili con Veggies, 175
- Shepherdless Pie, 172
- Succulent Bread Dressing, 207
- Vegan Caesar Salad with Tender and Crispy Croutons, 89
- Versatile Pot Pie, 169

agave nectar, about, 13
aioli, chipotle, 135
allergens, about, 10
almond(s)
- cookies, 233
- Farmesan, 89
- flour and meal, about, 13
- and salad, 81, 85, 89
- Sun-Dried Tomato Pesto, 197

amchur powder (dried mango powder), about, 13
American saffron, about, 13
ancho chili pepper, ground, about, 13
Appies, 53
apple cider vinegar
- about, 13
- dressing, 77, 81, 87, 93

apple(s)
- and bread dressing, 207
- compote, 49
- and fennel salad, 87
- Gooey Baked Apples, 239
- and pumpkin soup, 103
- salad with sliced cabbage, 93

aquafaba
- about, 14
- AquaFabulous Meringues, 235

arrowroot powder, about, 14
artichoke(s)
- and frittata, 44
- filling, 65
- hearts with spaghetti squash, 153
- and pasta, 153
- and pizza, 163
- stuffed mushroom caps, 65

avocado(s)
- guacamole, 183
- and sun-dried tomato toast, 159

B
Badass Black Bean Soup, 109
baking powder, about, 14
baking soda, about, 14
balsamic reduction, about, 14
Basic Un-Omelet, 41
basil
- Basil Cashew Creme Fraîche, 69
- pesto, 197

beans. *See also* black beans, chickpeas, and edamame
- dried versus canned, about, 15
- canned beans, dried beans, and lentils, about, 15
- dried beans, about, 15
- canned chili-style beans, about, 17
- chili con veggies, 175
- fasolada-style bean soup, 111
- and grilled veggies, 185
- gumbo, 188
- minestrone soup, 115
- and rice, 51, 183, 185
- and tacos, 183

beet(s)
- and big bowl, 178
- Beet Greens, 121
- Beets, Rosemary, 119

Best Bechamel Sauce, 41
Best Brussels Sprouts, 203
Bestcestershire Sauce (vegan Worcestershire sauce), about, 15
Big Bowl, Yummy Style, 178
Big Daddy Dip (Baba Ghanoush), 59
biscuits, 141
black beans
- Cuban-style, 79
- dip, 57
- fajitas, 185
- and roasted veggies, 185
- soup, 109
- and salad, 79, 95

black Indian salt (Kala Namak), about, 15
Boxcar Green Chile Sauce, 175
Bragg seasoning, about, 15
Breadcrumb Topping, 145
breakfast standards, 26
breakout tricks explained, 12
broccoli
- Broccoli Bandit Soup with Cashew Creme Fraîche, 101
- Broccoli Fritters, 47
- and soup, 109
- and pot pie, 169
- and stir-fry, 195

Broccoli Bandit, about, 6
Brunch, 25
Brussels Sprouts, Best, 203
butters, vegan, about, 16
butternut squash. *See* squash

C
cabbage
- Cabbage Roll Casserole, 191
- salad, 93, 95

cacao, about, 17
Cajun
- Rice, 188
- roasted veggies, 188
- tofu, 188

calcium, content, about, 11
calcium, content recipe has
- Badass Black Bean Soup, 109
- Best Brussels Sprouts, 203
- Big Bowl, Yummy Style, 178
- Creamy Artichoke Hearts with Spaghetti Squash, 153
- Creamy Pumpkin Pie, 219
- Fancy Cranberry Sauce, 209
- Friendly Mac 'n' Cheez, 145
- Gooey Baked Apples, 239
- Grilled Zucchini and Leeks with Walnuts, 125
- Guiltless French Toast, 37
- Hardy Mushroom Soup with Tender and Crispy Croutons, 99
- Infamous Ramen, 113
- Lemon and Garlic Oyster Mushrooms with Black-Eyed Peas, 129
- Mexican-Style Rice and Beans with Fresh Tomato Salsa, 51
- Millet and Spinach Patties with Sun-Dried Tomato Pesto, 197
- Mulled Wine, 221
- Nicely Spiced Cran-Apple Cider, 223
- Nuggets from Heaven: Squash, Lentil, and Chickpea Soup, 107
- Pasta Primavera with Rhubarb Tomato Sauce, 149
- Portobello Mushroom Fajitas with Chili-Lime Sauce, 185
- Red Currant and Mushroom Gravy, 211
- Rhubarb and Strawberry Treat, 237
- Roasted Pumpkin Soup, 103
- Roasted Tofu, 131
- Sautéed Greens, 121
- Savoury Latke-Style Sweet Potato Cakes with Saucy Apple Compote, 49
- Seriously the Best Chili con Veggies, 175
- Shepherdless Pie, 172
- Sinnamon Wheels, 243
- Southwestern Salad, 95
- Unbutter Tarts, 245

calcium, content recipe high
- Broccoli Bandit Soup with Cashew Creme Fraîche, 101
- Broccoli Fritters, 47
- Cabbage Roll Casserole, 191
- Chipotle Cornbread, 137
- Crunchy Lettuce Wraps, 164
- Crunchy Nut Roast with Roasted Carrots, 213
- Fast Teriyaki Stir-Fry, 195
- Grandma's Macaroni, Creamy Style, 147
- Let's Flex Tacos, 183
- Mandarin Bliss Salad with Pecans and Slivered Almonds, 81
- Mighty Minestrone, 115
- On-the-Go Layered Salad with Orange-Tarragon Dressing, 77
- Peanutty Tofu Stir-Fry, 193
- Saloon Gumbo with Cajun Rice and Tofu, 188
- Succulent Bread Dressing, 207

calcium, content recipe very high
- Chickpea Frittata with Tarragon Sauce, 44
- Desperado Pizza with Dipping Sauce, 161
- Fancy Un-Omelet with Best Bechamel Sauce, 41
- Green Bean and Squash Curry with Cucumber Raita, 123
- Krispy Kale Chips, 71
- Lemon and Hemp Loaf, 31
- Quinoa Power Salad with Cilantro-Lime Dressing, 79
- Scrumptious Spinach Salad with Strawberries, Slivered Almonds, and Mint-Balsamic Dressing, 85
- Vegan Caesar Salad with Tender and Crispy Croutons, 89
- Versatile Pot Pie, 169

Carrot Rick, about, 5
carrot(s)
- Carrot-Ginger-Orange Cupcakes, 231
- Roasted Carrots, 213

Cashew Sue, about, 4
cashew(s)
- cashew base, 213
- cashew cremes
  - about, 16
  - Basil Cashew Creme Fraîche, 69
  - Cashew Cheez, 145
  - Cashew Creme, 155
  - Cashew Creme Fraîche, 101
  - Cashew-Date Icing, 231
  - Chipotle Aioli, 135
  - Creamy Sauce, 205
  - Cucumber Raita, 123
  - Emerald Dip, 61
  - Garlic Cashew Creme Cheez, 216

Cheezy Artichoke-Stuffed Mushroom Caps, 65
cherry tomatoes
　big bowl, 178
　and pasta, 145
chickpea flour, about, 16
chickpeas
　about, 16
　crunchy Asian-style, 164
　frittata, 44
　Herb Hummus, 55
　and lettuce wraps, 164
　and pumpkin soup, 103
　and spaghetti squash, 153
　and squash and lentil soup, 107
chili and chile peppers. *See also* jalapeño peppers and Hatch chiles
　about, 17
　Boxcar Green Chile Sauce, 175
　chili con veggies, 175
　Chili-Lime Sauce, 185
　fritters, 47
chipotle peppers in adobo sauce
　about, 17
　Chipotle Aioli, 135
　cornbread, 137
Cilantro-Lime Dressing, 79
cocoa
　about, 17
　chocolate pudding, 229
　chocolate sauce, 227
　Choco-Razzmatazz Muffins, 27
coconut oil, about, 17
Coconut Whipped Creme, 33
Comfort Soups, 98
conventional versus organic, about, 21
cookies
　AquaFabulous Meringues, 235
　Very Berry Almond Cookies, 233
cooking time, about, 9
corn
　and big bowl, 178
　bread, 137
　and salad, 79, 95
cornstarch, about, 17
cranberry
　and apple cider, 223
　and apple sauce, 49
　dressing, 83
　dried
　　and bread dressing, 207
　　and cookies, 233
　　and granola, 39
　　and salad, 81, 83, 93
　sauce, 209
　Savoury Holiday Tart, 216
Creamy Artichoke Hearts with Spaghetti Squash, 153
Creamy, Dreamy Rice Pudding with Steeped Strawberries and Coconut Whipped Creme, 33
Creamy Pumpkin Pie, 219
Creamy Soups, 98
Crunchy Appies, 54
Crunchy Lettuce Wraps, 164
Crunchy Nut Roast with Roasted Carrots, 213
Cuban-Style Black Beans, 79
Cucumber Raita, 123
cupcakes
　Cupcakes and Cookies, 226
　Carrot-Ginger-Orange Cupcakes, 231

D

Desperado Pizza with Dipping Sauce, 161
Desserts, 225
dietary fibre, about, 12
dietary fibre, recipe has
　Broccoli Bandit Soup with Cashew Creme Fraîche, 101
　Broccoli Fritters, 47
　Carrot-Ginger-Orange Cupcakes, 231
　Cheezy Artichoke-Stuffed Mushroom Caps, 65
　Chipotle Cornbread, 137
　Creamy, Dreamy Rice Pudding with Steeped Strawberries and Coconut Whipped Creme, 33
　Crunchy Nut Roast with Roasted Carrots, 213
　Desperado Pizza with Dipping Sauce, 161
　Emerald Dip, 61
　Fancy Cranberry Sauce, 209
　Fasolada Greek-Style Bean Soup, 111
　Fresh Apple and Fennel Salad with Candied Pecans, 87
　Gold Rush Potato Nuggets, 133
　Golden Granola, 39
　Gooey Baked Apples, 239
　Grilled Zucchini and Leeks with Walnuts, 125
　Guiltless French Toast, 37
　Hardy Mushroom Soup with Tender and Crispy Croutons, 99
　Herb Hummus, 55
　Herbed Biscuits, 141
　Infamous Ramen, 113
　Krispy Kale Chips, 71
　Kumquat Candy, 241
　Lemon and Garlic Oyster Mushrooms with Black-Eyed Peas, 129
　Lemon and Hemp Loaf, 31
　Mandarin Bliss Salad with Pecans and Slivered Almonds, 81
　Marinated Edamame, 127
　Mashed Sweet and Russet Potatoes, 205
　Mediterranean Pasta, 151
　Melt-in-Your-Mouth Pancakes, 35
　Nutty Chocolate Pudding with Raspberry Purée, 229
　Orange, Zucchini, Date, Walnut Spice Muffins, 29
　Portobello Carpaccio, 69
　Rosemary Beets, 119
　Salad with Sliced Cabbage, Apple, Vinegar, and Caraway, 93
　Sautéed Greens, 121
　Sinnamon Wheels, 243
　Southwestern Salad, 95
　Spicy Black Bean Dip, 57
　Spicy Chili Unfries with Chipotle Aioli, 135
　Strawberries with Chocolate Sauce, 227
　Unbutter Tarts, 245
　Very Berry Almond Cookies, 233
　Zesty Chickpeas, 73
dietary fibre, recipe high
　Avocado and Sun-Dried Tomato Toast, 159
　Badass Black Bean Soup, 109
　Big Bowl, Yummy Style, 178
　Big Daddy Dip (Baba Ghanoush), 59
　Cabbage Roll Casserole, 191
　Chickpea Frittata with Tarragon Sauce, 44
　Choco-Razzmatazz Muffins, 27
　Creamy Artichoke Hearts with Spaghetti Squash, 153
　Creamy Pumpkin Pie, 219
　Fancy Un-Omelet with Best Bechamel Sauce, 41
　Fast Teriyaki Stir-Fry, 195
　Friendly Mac 'n' Cheez, 145
　Grandma's Macaroni, Creamy Style, 147
　Green Bean and Squash Curry with Cucumber Raita, 123
　Mighty Minestrone, 115
　Millet and Spinach Patties with Sun-Dried Tomato Pesto, 197
　Peanutty Tofu Stir-Fry, 193
　Portobello Mushroom Fajitas with Chili-Lime Sauce, 185
　Roasted Pumpkin Soup, 103
　Savoury Holiday Tart, 216
　Savoury Latke-Style Sweet Potato Cakes with Saucy Apple Compote, 49
　Scrumptious Spinach Salad with Strawberries, Slivered Almonds, and Mint-Balsamic Dressing, 85
　Succulent Bread Dressing, 207
　Sweet and Complete Corn and Pea Salad, 91
　Tempting Toor Dal Tadka with Tangy Tomato Chutney, 199
　Versatile Pot Pie, 169
dietary fibre, recipe very high
　Crunchy Lettuce Wraps, 164
　Lentil and Vegetable Medley Soup, 105
　Let's Flex Tacos, 183
　Mexican-Style Rice and Beans with Fresh Tomato Salsa, 51
　Nuggets from Heaven: Squash, Lentil, and Chickpea Soup, 107
　On-the-Go Layered Salad with Orange-Tarragon Dressing, 77
　Pasta Primavera with Rhubarb Tomato Sauce, 149
　Pumpkin Lentil Risotto, 155
　Quinoa Power Salad with Cilantro-Lime Dressing, 79
　Saloon Gumbo with Cajun Rice and Tofu, 188
　Seriously the Best Chili con Veggies, 175
　Shepherdless Pie, 172
　Vegan Caesar Salad with Tender and Crispy Croutons, 89
dietary information, about, 10
difficulty level, about, 9
Dips and Spreads, 54
dressings
　Cilantro-Lime Dressing, 79
　Cranberry Vinegar Dressing, 83
　Ginger-Mint Dressing, 91
　Lemon-Tarragon Dressing, 87
　Mint-Balsamic Dressing, 85
　Orange-Tarragon Dressing, 77
　Sweet Apple Cider Vinegar Dressing, 81
　Tahini Dressing, 178
　Vegan Caesar Dressing, 89
dried mushroom powder, about, 18

E

Easy Guacamole, 183
Easy Pizza Crust, 161
Easy Salads, 93
edamame beans
　and big bowl, 178
　Marinated Edamame, 127
　and salad, 77
　and stir-fry, 195
eggplant
　about, 18
　Big Daddy Dip (Baba Ghanoush), 59
　Roasted Eggplant and Mushrooms, 213
　and salad, 77
Emerald Dip, 61
Extras, 118

F

Fajita Rice, 185
Fake'n Bacon, 147
Fancy Cranberry Sauce, 209
Fancy Un-Omelet with Best Bechamel Sauce, 41
Farmesan, 89
Fasolada Greek-Style Bean Soup, 111
Fast Teriyaki Stir-Fry, 195
fennel
　and apple salad, 87
　and pasta, 149
five-spice powder, about, 18
flour, whole-wheat, all-purpose, pastry flour, about, 18
French toast, 37
Fresh Apple and Fennel Salad with Candied Pecans, 87

Fresh Tomato Salsa, 51
Friendly Mac 'n' Cheez, 145
Fruity Treats, 226
Full-Meal Salads, 76

G

Garlic Cashew Creme Cheez, 216
Garlic-Ginger Dipping Sauce, 164
Garlic Parsley Bread, 139
Ginger-Mint Dressing, 91
Glaze for Carrots, 213
gluten-free
  about, 11
  AquaFabulous Meringues, 235
  Badass Black Bean Soup, 109
  Best Brussels Sprouts, 203
  Big Bowl, Yummy Style, 178
  Big Daddy Dip (Baba Ghanoush), 59
  Broccoli Bandit Soup with Cashew Creme Fraîche, 101
  Broccoli Fritters, 47
  Cabbage Roll Casserole, 191
  Cheezy Artichoke-Stuffed Mushroom Caps, 65
  Creamy, Dreamy Rice Pudding with Steeped Strawberries and Coconut Whipped Creme, 33
  Crunchy Lettuce Wraps, 164
  Crunchy Nut Roast with Roasted Carrots, 213
  Emerald Dip, 61
  Fancy Cranberry Sauce, 209
  Fasolada Greek-Style Bean Soup, 111
  Fast Teriyaki Stir-Fry, 195
  Fresh Apple and Fennel Salad with Candied Pecans, 87
  Gold Rush Potato Nuggets, 133
  Gooey Baked Apples, 239
  Green Bean and Squash Curry with Cucumber Raita, 123
  Grilled Zucchini and Leeks with Walnuts, 125
  Herb Hummus, 55
  Infamous Ramen, 113
  Krispy Kale Chips, 71
  Kumquat Candy, 241
  Lemon and Garlic Oyster Mushrooms with Black-Eyed Peas, 129
  Lentil and Vegetable Medley Soup, 105
  Let's Flex Tacos, 183
  Mandarin Bliss Salad with Pecans and Slivered Almonds, 81
  Marinated Edamame, 127
  Marinated Mushroom Bites, 67
  Mashed Sweet and Russet Potatoes, 205
  Mexican-Style Rice and Beans with Fresh Tomato Salsa, 51
  Millet and Spinach Patties with Sun-Dried Tomato Pesto, 197
  Mulled Wine, 221
  Nicely Spiced Cran-Apple Cider, 223
  Nuggets from Heaven: Squash, Lentil, and Chickpea Soup, 107
  Nutty Chocolate Pudding with Raspberry Purée, 229
  On-the-Go Layered Salad with Orange-Tarragon Dressing, 77
  Portobello Carpaccio, 69
  Pumpkin Lentil Risotto, 155
  Quinoa Power Salad with Cilantro-Lime Dressing, 79
  Rainbow Rice Wraps, 167
  Rhubarb and Strawberry Treat, 237
  Roasted Pumpkin Soup, 103
  Roasted Tofu, 131
  Rosemary Beets, 119
  Salad with Sliced Cabbage, Apple, Vinegar, and Caraway, 93
  Saloon Gumbo with Cajun Rice and Tofu, 188
  Sautéed Greens, 121
  Savoury Latke-Style Sweet Potato Cakes with
  Saucy Apple Compote, 49
  Scrumptious Spinach Salad with Strawberries, Slivered Almonds, and Mint-Balsamic Dressing, 85
  Seriously the Best Chili con Veggies, 175
  Snap'n Tapenade, 63
  Southwestern Salad, 95
  Spicy Black Bean Dip, 57
  Spicy Chili Unfries with Chipotle Aioli, 135
  Strawberries with Chocolate Sauce, 227
  Sweet and Complete Corn and Pea Salad, 91
  Tasty Pear and Candied Walnut Salad with Cranberry Vinegar Dressing, 83
  Tempting Toor Dal Tadka with Tangy Tomato Chutney, 199
  Very Berry Almond Cookies, 233
  Zesty Chickpeas, 73
gluten-free optional
  about, 11
  Avocado and Sun-Dried Tomato Toast, 159
  Creamy Artichoke Hearts with Spaghetti Squash, 153
  Hardy Mushroom Soup with Tender and Crispy Croutons, 99
  Mediterranean Pasta, 151
  Mighty Minestrone, 115
  Golden Granola, 39
  Peanutty Tofu Stir-Fry, 193
  Portobello Mushroom Fajitas with Chili-Lime Sauce, 185
  Red Currant and Mushroom Gravy, 211
  Shepherdless Pie, 172
  Vegan Caesar Salad with Tender and Crispy Croutons, 89
Gold Rush Potato Nuggets, 133
golden berries, dried
  about, 19
  cookies, 233
Golden Granola, 39
Gooey Baked Apples, 239
Grandma's Macaroni, Creamy Style, 147
gravy
  Quick and Creamy Mushroom Gravy, 172
  Red Currant and Mushroom Gravy, 211
Great Additions, 202
green beans
  about, 19
  big bowl, 178
  curry, 123
  soup, 115
greens, sautéed, 121
Grilled Zucchini and Leeks with Walnuts, 125
Guiltless French Toast, 37

H

Hardy Mushroom Soup with Tender and Crispy Croutons, 99
Hatch chile: Boxcar Green Chile Sauce, 175
Healthier Pastry, 216, 245
hemp hearts, about, 19
Herb Hummus, 55
Herbed Biscuits, 141
herbs, about, 19
Holiday Mains, 202
Holiday Meal, 201
hoisin sauce, 164
Hows and Whys to Veggie OUTLAWS Recipes, 1
Humble Rice, 191
Hummus, 55

I

Icons Explained, 8
Imagine Creamy Tomato Soup, about, 18
in a snap
  about, 9
  Avocado and Sun-Dried Tomato Toast, 159

Best Brussels Sprouts, 203
Big Daddy Dip (Baba Ghanoush), 59
Broccoli Fritters, 47
Chipotle Cornbread, 137
Choco-Razzmatazz Muffins, 27
Emerald Dip, 61
Fancy Cranberry Sauce, 209
Fast Teriyaki Stir-Fry, 195
Gold Rush Potato Nuggets, 133
Guiltless French Toast, 37
Herb Hummus, 55
Krispy Kale Chips, 71
Kumquat Candy, 241
Mandarin Bliss Salad with Pecans and Slivered Almonds, 81
Marinated Edamame, 127
Marinated Mushroom Bites, 67
Melt-in-Your-Mouth Pancakes, 35
Mighty Minestrone, 115
Mulled Wine, 221
Nicely Spiced Cran-Apple Cider, 223
Nuggets from Heaven: Squash, Lentil, and Chickpea Soup, 107
Nutty Chocolate Pudding with Raspberry Purée, 229
Rainbow Rice Wraps, 167
Rhubarb and Strawberry Treat, 237
Roasted Pumpkin Soup, 103
Roasted Tofu, 131
Salad with Sliced Cabbage, Apple, Vinegar, and Caraway, 93
Sautéed Greens, 121
Scrumptious Spinach Salad with Strawberries, Slivered Almonds, and Mint-Balsamic Dressing, 85
Sinnamon Wheels, 243
Snap'n Tapenade, 63
Southwestern Salad, 95
Spicy Black Bean Dip, 57
Strawberries with Chocolate Sauce, 227
Tasty Pear and Candied Walnut Salad with Cranberry Vinegar Dressing, 83
Zesty Chickpeas, 73
in short order
  about, 10
  Badass Black Bean Soup, 109
  Big Bowl, Yummy Style, 178
  Broccoli Bandit Soup with Cashew Creme Fraîche, 101
  Carrot-Ginger-Orange Cupcakes, 231
  Cheezy Artichoke-Stuffed Mushroom Caps, 65
  Chickpea Frittata with Tarragon Sauce, 44
  Creamy Artichoke Hearts with Spaghetti Squash, 153
  Creamy Pumpkin Pie, 219
  Creamy, Dreamy Rice Pudding with Steeped Strawberries and Coconut Whipped Creme, 33
  Crunchy Lettuce Wraps, 164
  Fancy Un-Omelet with Best Bechamel Sauce, 41
  Fresh Apple and Fennel Salad with Candied Pecans, 87
  Garlic Parsley Bread, 139
  Gooey Baked Apples, 239
  Green Bean and Squash Curry with Cucumber Raita, 123
  Hardy Mushroom Soup with Tender and Crispy Croutons, 99
  Herbed Biscuits, 141
  Infamous Ramen, 113
  Lemon and Garlic Oyster Mushrooms with Black-Eyed Peas, 129
  Lentil and Vegetable Medley Soup, 105
  Let's Flex Tacos, 183
  Mediterranean Pasta, 151
  Millet and Spinach Patties with Sun-Dried Tomato Pesto, 197
  On-the-Go Layered Salad with Orange-Tarragon Dressing, 77

251

Orange, Zucchini, Date, Walnut Spice Muffins, 29
Pasta Primavera with Rhubarb Tomato Sauce, 149
Peanutty Tofu Stir-Fry, 193
Portobello Carpaccio, 69
Quinoa Power Salad with Cilantro-Lime Dressing, 79
Rosemary Beets, 119
Savoury Latke-Style Sweet Potato Cakes with Saucy Apple Compote, 49
Spicy Chili Unfries with Chipotle Aioli, 135
Sweet and Complete Corn and Pea Salad, 91
Tempting Toor Dal Tadka with Tangy Tomato Chutney, 199
Unbutter Tarts, 245
Very Berry Almond Cookies, 233
Infamous Ramen, 113
ingredients explained, about, 13
Instant Pot
  Cuban-Style Black Beans, 79
  dried beans, 15
iron, about, 11
iron, recipe has
  Badass Black Bean Soup, 109
  Big Bowl, Yummy Style, 178
  Cabbage Roll Casserole, 191
  Cheezy Artichoke-Stuffed Mushroom Caps, 65
  Choco-Razzmatazz Muffins, 27
  Creamy Artichoke Hearts with Spaghetti Squash, 153
  Creamy Pumpkin Pie, 219
  Crunchy Lettuce Wraps, 164
  Crunchy Nut Roast with Roasted Carrots, 213
  Fancy Un-Omelet with Best Bechamel Sauce, 41
  Fasolada Greek-Style Bean Soup, 111
  Fast Teriyaki Stir-Fry, 195
  Fresh Apple and Fennel Salad with Candied Pecans, 87
  Golden Granola, 39
  Grilled Zucchini and Leeks with Walnuts, 125
  Hardy Mushroom Soup with Tender and Crispy Croutons, 99
  Infamous Ramen, 113
  Kumquat Candy, 241
  Lemon and Garlic Oyster Mushrooms with Black-Eyed Peas, 129
  Lentil and Vegetable Medley Soup, 105
  Mashed Sweet and Russet Potatoes, 205
  Mexican-Style Rice and Beans with Fresh Tomato Salsa, 51
  Mighty Minestrone, 115
  On-the-Go Layered Salad with Orange-Tarragon Dressing, 77
  Peanutty Tofu Stir-Fry, 193
  Pumpkin Lentil Risotto, 155
  Savoury Latke-Style Sweet Potato Cakes with Saucy Apple Compote, 49
  Snap'n Tapenade, 63
  Spicy Chili Unfries with Chipotle Aioli, 135
  Strawberries with Chocolate Sauce, 227
  Sweet and Complete Corn and Pea Salad, 91
  Tempting Toor Dal Tadka with Tangy Tomato Chutney, 199
iron, recipe high
  Carrot-Ginger-Orange Cupcakes, 231
  Friendly Mac 'n' Cheez, 145
  Grandma's Macaroni, Creamy Style, 147
  Mediterranean Pasta, 151
  Millet and Spinach Patties with Sun-Dried Tomato Pesto, 197
  Nuggets from Heaven: Squash, Lentil, and Chickpea Soup, 107
  Pasta Primavera with Rhubarb Tomato Sauce, 149
  Portobello Mushroom Fajitas with Chili-Lime Sauce, 185
  Quinoa Power Salad with Cilantro-Lime Dressing, 79
  Saloon Gumbo with Cajun Rice and Tofu, 188
  Savoury Holiday Tart, 216
  Seriously the Best Chili con Veggies, 175

Shepherdless Pie, 172
Succulent Bread Dressing, 207
Unbutter Tarts, 245
Versatile Pot Pie, 169
iron, recipe very high
  Green Bean and Squash Curry with Cucumber Raita, 123
  Vegan Caesar Salad with Tender and Crispy Croutons, 89

J
jalapeño peppers
  about, 17
  Chili-Lime Sauce, 185
  and curry, 123
  Emerald Dip, 61
  and salad, 91
  and soup, 109
  salsa, 51
  tomato chutney, 199
  toor dal, 199

K
kale
  Big Bowl, 178
  chips, 71
  lentil soup, 105
  rice wraps, 167
  Sautéed Greens, 121
  Un-Omelet Filling, 41
kamut flakes: granola, 39
Krispy Kale Chips, 71
Kumquat Candy, 241

L
lavender
  about, 19
  almond cookies, 233
leek(s)
  grilled, 125
  lentil soup, 105
lemon
  dressing, 87
  glaze, 31
  lemon & herb seasoning, about, 19
  lemon loaf, 31
  and oyster mushrooms, 129
lentils: soup, 105, 107
Let's Flex Tacos, 183
Lettuce Wraps, Crunchy, 164
lime leaf, about, 19
low-fat
  about, 11
  AquaFabulous Meringues, 235
  Badass Black Bean Soup, 109
  Best Brussels Sprouts, 203
  Chipotle Cornbread, 137
  Fancy Cranberry Sauce, 209
  Gold Rush Potato Nuggets, 133
  Guiltless French Toast, 37
  Kumquat Candy, 241
  Lentil and Vegetable Medley Soup, 105
  Mighty Minestrone, 115
  Mulled Wine, 221
  Nicely Spiced Cran-Apple Cider, 223
  Nuggets from Heaven: Squash, Lentil, and Chickpea Soup, 107
  Seriously the Best Chili con Veggies, 175
  Spicy Black Bean Dip, 57
  Strawberries with Chocolate Sauce, 227
low-fat optional
  about, 11
  Broccoli Bandit Soup with Cashew Creme Fraîche, 101
  Hardy Mushroom Soup with Tender and Crispy Croutons, 99

M
Macaroni
  Grandma's Macaroni, 147
  mac 'n' cheez, 145
Mains, 181
Mandarin Bliss Salad with Pecans and Slivered Almonds, 81
mango(s)
  dried, about, 13
  salad, 81
Marinated Edamame, 127
Marinated Mushroom Bites, 67
Mashed Potatoes, 172
Mashed Sweet and Russet Potatoes, 205
Meals, 157
Mediterranean Pasta, 151
Melt-in-Your-Mouth Pancakes, 35
Mexican-Style Rice and Beans with Fresh Tomato Salsa, 51
Mighty Minestrone, 115
milk
  about, 19
  milk mixture, 27
Millet and Spinach Patties with Sun-dried Tomato Pesto, 197
mint
  and bean soup, 111
  and broccoli soup, 101
  and grilled vegetables, 125
  and pea dip, 61
  dressing, 85, 91
mixed bean sprouts
  about, 22
  Big Bowl, 178
  and salad, 77
molasses, about, 19
more time
  about, 10
  Crunchy Nut Roast with Roasted Carrots, 213
muffins, 221
  Choco-Razzmatazz Muffins, 27
  Orange, Zucchini, Date, Walnut Spice Muffins, 29
Mulled Wine, 221
mushroom(s)
  about, 20
  big bowl, 178
  broth, 211
  carpaccio, 69
  dried, about, 18
  fajita, 185
  and frittata, 44
  gravy, 172, 211
  and holiday tart, 216
  and lemon, 129
  marinated, 67
  and nut roast, 213
  and pasta, 147, 151
  and pizza, 161
  and pot pie, 169
  and rice and beans, 51
  and risotto, 155
  roasted, 178, 185
  soup, 99, 113
  and stir-fry, 193, 195
  stuffed, 65
Must Haves, 182
Must-Try Salads, 76

N
Nicely Spiced Pie Crust, 169
Nicely Spiced Cran-Apple Cider, 223
Nuggets from Heaven: Squash, Lentil, and Chickpea Soup, 107

nut-free
  about, 10
  AquaFabulous Meringues, 235
  Avocado and Sun-Dried Tomato Toast, 159
  Best Brussels Sprouts, 203
  Big Daddy Dip (Baba Ghanoush), 59
  Broccoli Fritters, 47
  Cabbage Roll Casserole, 191
  Crunchy Lettuce Wraps, 164
  Desperado Pizza with Dipping Sauce, 161
  Fancy Cranberry Sauce, 209
  Fasolada Greek-Style Bean Soup, 111
  Garlic Parsley Bread, 139
  Gold Rush Potato Nuggets, 133
  Gooey Baked Apples, 239
  Herb Hummus, 55
  Krispy Kale Chips, 71
  Kumquat Candy, 241
  Lemon and Garlic Oyster Mushrooms with Black-Eyed Peas, 129
  Lentil and Vegetable Medley Soup, 105
  Let's Flex Tacos, 183
  Marinated Edamame, 127
  Marinated Mushroom Bites, 67
  Mexican-Style Rice and Beans with Fresh Tomato Salsa, 51
  Mighty Minestrone, 115
  Mulled Wine, 221
  Nicely Spiced Cran-Apple Cider, 223
  Nuggets from Heaven: Squash, Lentil, and Chickpea Soup, 107
  On-the-Go Layered Salad with Orange-Tarragon Dressing, 77
  Portobello Mushroom Fajitas with Chili-Lime Sauce, 185
  Quinoa Power Salad with Cilantro-Lime Dressing, 79
  Rainbow Rice Wraps, 167
  Red Currant and Mushroom Gravy, 211
  Rhubarb and Strawberry Treat, 237
  Roasted Pumpkin Soup, 103
  Roasted Tofu, 131
  Rosemary Beets, 119
  Salad with Sliced Cabbage, Apple, Vinegar, and Caraway, 93
  Saloon Gumbo with Cajun Rice and Tofu, 188
  Sautéed Greens, 121
  Savoury Latke-Style Sweet Potato Cakes with Saucy Apple Compote, 49
  Seriously the Best Chili con Veggies, 175
  Snap'n Tapenade, 63
  Southwestern Salad, 95
  Spicy Black Bean Dip, 57
  Strawberries with Chocolate Sauce, 227
  Sweet and Complete Corn and Pea Salad, 91
  Tempting Toor Dal Tadka with Tangy Tomato Chutney, 199
  Versatile Pot Pie, 169
  Zesty Chickpeas, 73
nut-free optional
  about, 10
  Badass Black Bean Soup, 109
  Big Bowl, Yummy Style, 178
  Chickpea Frittata with Tarragon Sauce, 44
  Chipotle Cornbread, 137
  Choco-Razzmatazz Muffins, 27
  Creamy Pumpkin Pie, 219
  Creamy, Dreamy Rice Pudding with Steeped Strawberries and Coconut Whipped Creme, 33
  Fancy Un-Omelet with Best Bechamel Sauce, 41
  Fast Teriyaki Stir-Fry, 195
  Hardy Mushroom Soup with Tender and Crispy Croutons, 99
  Herbed Biscuits, 141
  Lemon and Hemp Loaf, 31
  Melt-in-Your-Mouth Pancakes, 35
  Orange, Zucchini, Date, Walnut Spice Muffins, 29
  Shepherdless Pie, 172
  Unbutter Tarts, 245
nutmeg, about, 20
nutritional details, 12
nuts
  about, 20
  and Big Bowl, 178
  and Bread Dressing, 207
  candied, 83, 87
  and chocolate pudding, 229
  and cupcakes, 231
  and granola, 39
  and grilled vegetables, 77, 125
  and Holiday Tart, 216
  and muffins, 27, 29
  nut roast, 213
  and pasta, 145, 147, 149, 153, 155
  roasted nuts, 125, 149, 213
  and salads, 81, 83, 85, 87

O

oats (rolled)
  about, 20
  and granola, 39
oil spray, about, 20
oils, about, 20
okra: gumbo, 188
Old Bay seasoning, about, 22
olives
  about, 21
  tapenade, 63
On the Lighter Side, 158
On the Sweeter Side, 26
One-Dish Meals, 158
onions
  Onion Sauce, Caramelized, 161
  sautéed, about, 21
On-the-Go Layered Salad with Orange-Tarragon Dressing, 77
Orange, Zucchini, Date, Walnut Spice Muffins, 29
oranges
  cupcakes, 231
  dressing, 77, 85
  and muffins, 29
  and salad, 81
organic versus conventional, about, 21
Other High-Protein Soups, 98

P

Pasta and Risotto, 143
pastries
  Creamy Pumpkin Pie, 219
  Healthy Pastry, 216
  Nicely Spiced Pie Crust, 169
  Sinnamon Wheels, 243
  Unbutter Tarts, 245
peanut-free, about, 10
peanut(s)
  Peanutty Tofu Stir-Fry, 193
  Snappy Peanut Sauce, 193
pear(s)
  and cranberry sauce, 209
  salad, 83
peas
  Emerald Dip, 61
  and pasta, 149
  Salad, 91
  Shepherdless Pie, 172
  and stir-fry, 193
pecans
  Candied Pecans, 87
  muffin, 27
  and salad, 81, 87
  Unbutter Tarts, 245
pesto: Sun-Dried Tomato Pesto, 197

Pizza, Desperado, 161
Pizza Dipping Sauce, 161
Portobello Carpaccio, 69
Portobello Mushroom Fajitas with Chili-Lime Sauce, 185
potassium, about, 11
potassium, recipe has
  AquaFabulous Meringues, 235
  Avocado and Sun-Dried Tomato Toast, 159
  Big Daddy Dip (Baba Ghanoush), 59
  Broccoli Bandit Soup with Cashew Creme Fraîche, 101
  Cabbage Roll Casserole, 191
  Chickpea Frittata with Tarragon Sauce, 44
  Choco-Razzmatazz Muffins, 27
  Creamy Artichoke Hearts with Spaghetti Squash, 153
  Creamy Pumpkin Pie, 219
  Crunchy Lettuce Wraps, 164
  Fasolada Greek-Style Bean Soup, 111
  Fast Teriyaki Stir-Fry, 195
  Fresh Apple and Fennel Salad with Candied Pecans, 87
  Friendly Mac 'n' Cheez, 145
  Gold Rush Potato Nuggets, 133
  Grilled Zucchini and Leeks with Walnuts, 125
  Hardy Mushroom Soup with Tender and Crispy Croutons, 99
  Infamous Ramen, 113
  Krispy Kale Chips, 71
  Lemon and Garlic Oyster Mushrooms with Black-Eyed Peas, 129
  Lentil and Vegetable Medley Soup, 105
  Let's Flex Tacos, 183
  Marinated Mushroom Bites, 67
  Mediterranean Pasta, 151
  Mighty Minestrone, 115
  Pasta Primavera with Rhubarb Tomato Sauce, 149
  Peanutty Tofu Stir-Fry, 193
  Portobello Carpaccio, 69
  Portobello Mushroom Fajitas with Chili-Lime Sauce, 185
  Pumpkin Lentil Risotto, 155
  Red Currant and Mushroom Gravy, 211
  Roasted Pumpkin Soup, 103
  Rosemary Beets, 119
  Saloon Gumbo with Cajun Rice and Tofu, 188
  Sautéed Greens, 121
  Savoury Holiday Tart, 216
  Savoury Latke-Style Sweet Potato Cakes with Saucy Apple Compote, 49
  Spicy Chili Unfries with Chipotle Aioli, 135
  Strawberries with Chocolate Sauce, 227
  Succulent Bread Dressing, 207
  Sweet and Complete Corn and Pea Salad, 91
  Tasty Pear and Candied Walnut Salad with Cranberry Vinegar Dressing, 83
  Tempting Toor Dal Tadka with Tangy Tomato Chutney, 199
potassium, recipe high
  Badass Black Bean Soup, 109
  Big Bowl, Yummy Style, 178
  Fancy Un-Omelet with Best Bechamel Sauce, 41
  Grandma's Macaroni, Creamy Style, 147
  Green Bean and Squash Curry with Cucumber Raita, 123
  Mashed Sweet and Russet Potatoes, 205
  Mexican-Style Rice and Beans with Fresh Tomato Salsa, 51
  Nuggets from Heaven: Squash, Lentil, and Chickpea Soup, 107
  On-the-Go Layered Salad with Orange-Tarragon Dressing, 77
  Quinoa Power Salad with Cilantro-Lime Dressing, 79
  Seriously the Best Chili con Veggies, 175
  Shepherdless Pie, 172
potassium, very high

Vegan Caesar Salad with Tender and Crispy Croutons, 89
potato(es)
  Gold Rush Potato Nuggets, 133
  Mashed Potatoes, 172
  Mashed Sweet and Russet Potatoes, 205
  Shepherdless Pie, 172
  Spicy Chili Unfries with Chipotle Aioli, 135
prep time, about, 8
Protein Powered Side Dishes, 118
pumpkin
  about, 21
  Pumpkin Lentil Risotto, 155
  Pumpkin Pie, Creamy, 219
  Roasted Pumpkin Soup, 103

Q
Quick and Creamy Mushroom Gravy, 172
quinoa
  about, 21
  Big Bowl, 178
  Quinoa Power Salad with Cilantro-Lime Dressing, 79

R
Rainbow Rice Wraps, 167
Raspberry Purée, 229
Recipe Tricks and Tips, 8
Red Currant and Mushroom Gravy, 211
rhubarb
  Rhubarb and Strawberry Treat, 237
  Rhubarb Tomato Sauce, 149
rice
  about, 21
  Big Bowl, 178
  Cajun, 188
  fajita, 185
  Mexican-Style, 51
  pudding, 33
  With Rice, 181
  risotto, 155
Risotto, 143
Roasted Bulb of Garlic, 139
Roasted Carrots, 213
Roasted Eggplant and Mushrooms, 213
Roasted Nuts, 125, 149, 213
Roasted Pumpkin Soup, 103
Roasted Tofu, 131
Roasted Tofu and Veggies, 178
Roasted Veggies, 77
Roasted Veggies with Black Beans, 185
Rosemary Beets, 119
Rhubarb-Tomato Sauce, 149

S
Salads and Dressings, 75
Saloon Gumbo with Cajun Rice and Tofu, 188
salt, about, 22
sauces
  bechamel, 41
  cranberry, 209
  chili(e), 175, 185
  Chipotle Aioli, 135
  chocolate, 227
  creamy, 205
  garlic-ginger, 164
  hoisin, 164
  onion, 161
  peanut, 193
  Pizza Dipping Sauce, 161
  Rhubarb-Tomato Sauce, 149
  tarragon, 44
  teriyaki, 195
Savoury Holiday Tart, 216
Savoury Latke-Style Sweet Potato Cakes with Saucy Apple Compote, 49

Savoury Starts, 26
Scrumptious Spinach Salad with Strawberries, Slivered Almonds, and Mint-Balsamic Dressing, 85
Seasonal Pasta, 144
seeds
  black mustard seeds, about, 15
  black sesame seeds, about, 15
  chia seeds, ground, about, 16
  flax seeds, about, 18
Seriously the Best Chili con Veggies, 175
serving size, about, 9
Shepherdless Pie, 172
shichimi togarashi, about, 22
Sides, 117
Signposts (aka: icons) Explained, 8
Simple Breadcrumb Topping, 145
Sinnamon Wheels, 243
Snap'n Tapenade, 63
Snappy Peanut Sauce, 193
Soups, 97
Southwestern Salad, 95
soy-free
  about, 11
  AquaFabulous Meringues, 235
  Avocado and Sun-Dried Tomato Toast, 159
  Best Brussels Sprouts, 203
  Broccoli Bandit Soup with Cashew Creme Fraîche, 101
  Broccoli Fritters, 47
  Carrot-Ginger-Orange Cupcakes, 231
  Cheezy Artichoke-Stuffed Mushroom Caps, 65
  Chickpea Frittata with Tarragon Sauce, 44
  Chipotle Cornbread, 137
  Choco-Razzmatazz Muffins, 27
  Creamy Artichoke Hearts with Spaghetti Squash, 153
  Creamy Pumpkin Pie, 219
  Creamy, Dreamy Rice Pudding with Steeped Strawberries and Coconut Whipped Creme, 33
  Desperado Pizza with Dipping Sauce, 161
  Emerald Dip, 61
  Fancy Cranberry Sauce, 209
  Fresh Apple and Fennel Salad with Candied Pecans, 87
  Friendly Mac 'n' Cheez, 145
  Gold Rush Potato Nuggets, 133
  Golden Granola, 39
  Gooey Baked Apples, 239
  Green Bean and Squash Curry with Cucumber Raita, 123
  Herbed Biscuits, 141
  Krispy Kale Chips, 71
  Kumquat Candy, 241
  Lemon and Garlic Oyster Mushrooms with Black-Eyed Peas, 129
  Lemon and Hemp Loaf, 31
  Mandarin Bliss Salad with Pecans and Slivered Almonds, 81
  Marinated Mushroom Bites, 67
  Mediterranean Pasta, 151
  Melt-in-Your-Mouth Pancakes, 35
  Mighty Minestrone, 115
  Millet and Spinach Patties with Sun-Dried Tomato Pesto, 197
  Mulled Wine, 221
  Nicely Spiced Cran-Apple Cider, 223
  Nuggets from Heaven: Squash, Lentil, and Chickpea Soup, 107
  Nutty Chocolate Pudding with Raspberry Purée, 229
  Orange, Zucchini, Date, Walnut Spice Muffins, 29
  Pasta Primavera with Rhubarb Tomato Sauce, 149
  Portobello Carpaccio, 69
  Portobello Mushroom Fajitas with Chili-Lime Sauce, 185
  Quinoa Power Salad with Cilantro-Lime Dressing, 79

  Rhubarb and Strawberry Treat, 237
  Roasted Pumpkin Soup, 103
  Rosemary Beets, 119
  Salad with Sliced Cabbage, Apple, Vinegar, and Caraway, 93
  Savoury Holiday Tart, 216
  Savoury Latke-Style Sweet Potato Cakes with Saucy Apple Compote, 49
  Scrumptious Spinach Salad with Strawberries, Slivered Almonds, and Mint-Balsamic Dressing, 85
  Sinnamon Wheels, 243
  Snap'n Tapenade, 63
  Southwestern Salad, 95
  Spicy Black Bean Dip, 57
  Spicy Chili Unfries with Chipotle Aioli, 135
  Strawberries with Chocolate Sauce, 227
  Succulent Bread Dressing, 207
  Sweet and Complete Corn and Pea Salad, 91
  Tasty Pear and Candied Walnut Salad with Cranberry Vinegar Dressing, 83
  Tempting Toor Dal Tadka with Tangy Tomato Chutney, 199
  Unbutter Tarts, 245
  Very Berry Almond Cookies, 233
soy-free optional
  about, 11
  Badass Black Bean Soup, 109
  Big Daddy Dip (Baba Ghanoush), 59
  Crunchy Lettuce Wraps, 164
  Fancy Un-Omelet with Best Bechamel Sauce, 41
  Fasolada Greek-Style Bean Soup, 111
  Garlic Parsley Bread, 139
  Grandma's Macaroni, Creamy Style, 147
  Grilled Zucchini and Leeks with Walnuts, 125
  Hardy Mushroom Soup with Tender and Crispy Croutons, 99
  Herb Hummus, 55
  Lentil and Vegetable Medley Soup, 105
  Let's Flex Tacos, 183
  Mexican-Style Rice and Beans with Fresh Tomato Salsa, 51
  Pumpkin Lentil Risotto, 155
  Sautéed Greens, 121
  Seriously the Best Chili con Veggies, 175
  Shepherdless Pie, 172
  Vegan Caesar Salad with Tender and Crispy Croutons, 89
  Versatile Pot Pie, 169
  Zesty Chickpeas, 73
Special Roasted Walnuts, 125
Special Spice Ball, 221
Special Spuds, 118
Spice Ball, 209
Spicy Black Bean Dip, 57
Spicy Chili Unfries with Chipotle Aioli, 135
Spike seasoning, about, 22
spinach
  Millet and Spinach Patties, 197
  Rainbow Rice Wraps, 167
  salad, 85
  and soup, 105
sprouted lentils, 22
squash
  butternut squash and Cashew Cheez, 145
  Green Bean and Squash Curry, 123
  Pumpkin Soup, 103
  risotto, 155
  and salad, 77
  squash, lentil, and chickpea soup, 107
  spaghetti squash, 153
Steeped Strawberries, 33
Stir-Fries, 182
strawberries
  and chocolate sauce, 227
  and rhubarb, 237
  and salad, 85

Steeped Strawberries, 33
Succulent Bread Dressing, 207
sugar
　about, 16, 22
　brown, about, 16
　cane, about, 16
　powdered, about, 22
sun-dried tomatoes
　and avocado toast, 159
　and blackbean soup, 109
　Chickpea Frittata, 44
　pasta, 151
　and pizza, 161
　pot pie, 169
　Sun-Dried Tomato Pesto, 197
Sweet and Complete Corn and Pea Salad, 91
Sweet Apple Cider Vinegar Dressing, 81
tabasco sauce, about, 22

T

Taco Filling, 183
Tahini Dressing, 178
tamari, about, 15
Tangy Tomato Chutney, 199
tapioca flour, about, 22
tarragon
　broccoli soup, 101
　Tarragon Sauce, 44
　and lemon dressing, 87
　and orange dressing, 77
　pot pie, 169
Tasty Addition
　Full Listing
　　Basil Cashew Creme Fraîche, 69
　　Best Bechamel Sauce, 41
　　Breadcrumb Topping, 147
　　Cajun Rice, 188
　　Cajun Roasted Veggies, 188
　　Cajun Tofu, 188
　　Candied Pecans, 87
　　Candied Walnuts, 83
　　Caramelized Onion Sauce, 161
　　Cashew Cheez, 145
　　Cashew Creme, 155
　　Cashew Creme Fraîche, 101
　　Cashew-Date Icing, 231
　　Cheezy Artichoke Filling, 65
　　Chili-Lime Sauce, 185
　　Chipotle Aioli, 135
　　Chocolate Sauce, 227
　　Cilantro-Lime Dressing, 79
　　Coconut Whipped Creme, 33
　　Cranberry Vinegar Dressing, 83
　　Creamy Cashew Base, 213
　　Creamy Sauce, 205
　　Crumbled Tofu, 191
　　Crumbled Walnut Topping, 29
　　Crunchy Asian-Style Chickpeas, 164
　　Crunchy Nut Roast Rub, 213
　　Cuban-Style Black Beans, 79
　　Cucumber Raita, 123
　　Easy Guacamole, 89
　　Easy Pizza Crust, 161
　　Fajita Rice, 185
　　Fake'n Bacon, 147
　　Farmesan, 89
　　Fresh Tomato Salsa, 51
　　Garlic Cashew Creme Cheez, 216
　　Garlic-Ginger Dipping Sauce, 164
　　Ginger-Mint Dressing, 91
　　Glaze for Carrots, 213
　　Grain Flakes, 39
　　Healthy Pastry, 216, 245
　　Humble Rice, 191
　　Lemon Glaze, 31
　　Lemon-Tarragon Dressing, 87
　　Mashed Potatoes, 172
　　Mexican-Style Rice, 51
　　Milk Mixture, 27, 29, 31, 35, 41, 44, 100, 137, 141, 145, 153, 173, 219, 229
　　Mint-Balsamic Dressing, 85
　　Mushroom Broth, 211
　　Nicely Spiced Pie Crust, 169
　　Orange-Tarragon Dressing, 77
　　Pizza Dipping Sauce, 161
　　Quick and Creamy Mushroom Gravy, 172
　　Raspberry Purée, 229
　　Rhubarb Tomato Sauce, 149
　　Roasted Bulb of Garlic, 139
　　Roasted Carrots, 213
　　Roasted Eggplant and Mushrooms, 213
　　Roasted Nuts, 213
　　Roasted Tofu and Veggies, 178
　　Roasted Veggies, 77
　　Roasted Veggies with Black Beans, 185
　　Saucy Apple Compote, 49
　　Simple Breadcrumb Topping, 145
　　Snappy Peanut Sauce, 193
　　Special Roasted Walnuts, 125
　　Special Spice Ball, 221
　　Spice Ball, 209
　　Steeped Strawberries, 33
　　Stir-Fry Veggies, 193
　　Stir-fry Veggies with Edamame Beans, 195
　　Sun-Dried Tomato Pesto, 197
　　Sweet Apple Cider Vinegar Dressing, 81
　　Taco Filling, 183
　　Tahini Dressing, 178
　　Tangy Tomato Chutney, 199
　　Tarragon Sauce, 44
　　Tasty Tofu, 193
　　Tender Crispy Croutons, 89
　　Teriyaki Sauce, 195
　　Un-Omelet Filling, 41
　　Vegan Caesar Dressing, 89
　Quick Listing, 24
Tasty Pear and Candied Walnut Salad with Cranberry Vinegar Dressing, 83
Tempting Toor Dal Tadka with Tangy Tomato Chutney, 199
Tender and Crispy Croutons, 89
Teriyaki Sauce, 195
The Myths We Are Shooting Down, 7
tofu
　Cajun Tofu, 188
　Crumbled Tofu, 191
　French Toast, 37
　pot pie, 169
　ramen, 113
　roasted, 131
　and roasted veggies, 178
　Shepherdless pie, 172
　Tasty Tofu, 193
tomato(es), canned
　chili con veggies, 175
　gumbo, 188
　Mexican-style rice, 51
　and pasta, 149, 151
tomato(es). See also cherry tomatoes, sun-dried tomatoes, and tomatoes, canned
　avocado toast, 159
　chutney, 199
　fajita, 185
　and pasta, 145, 149, 151
　and salad, 79, 95
　salsa, 51
　and soup, 105, 109, 111, 115
　tacos, 183
　toor dal, 199
　un-omelet, 41
　vegan tomato soup, about, 18

U

Umami, about, 23
Unbutter Tarts, 245
Un-Omelet Filling, 41
Un-Omelet, basic, 41

V

Vegan Caesar Dressing, 89
Vegan Caesar Salad with Tender and Crispy Croutons, 89
Vegetable Broth, 23
Veggie OUTLAWS, about, 3
Veggie OUTLAWStlaws Hoisin Sauce, 164
Versatile Pot Pie, 169
Very Berry Almond Cookies, 233
vitamin A, about, 11
vitamin A, recipe has
　Avocado and Sun-Dried Tomato Toast, 159
　Best Brussels Sprouts, 203
　Chickpea Frittata with Tarragon Sauce, 44
　Crunchy Nut Roast with Roasted Carrots, 213
　Desperado Pizza with Dipping Sauce, 161
　Garlic Parsley Bread, 139
　Grilled Zucchini and Leeks with Walnuts, 125
　Hardy Mushroom Soup with Tender and Crispy Croutons, 99
　Red Currant and Mushroom Gravy, 211
　Shepherdless Pie, 172
　Southwestern Salad, 95
　Succulent Bread Dressing, 207
　Sweet and Complete Corn and Pea Salad, 91
　Tempting Toor Dal Tadka with Tangy Tomato Chutney, 199
vitamin A, recipe high
　Badass Black Bean Soup, 109
　Broccoli Fritters, 47
　Carrot-Ginger-Orange Cupcakes, 231
　Infamous Ramen, 113
　Mediterranean Pasta, 151
　Millet and Spinach Patties with Sun-Dried Tomato Pesto, 197
　Pasta Primavera with Rhubarb Tomato Sauce, 149
vitamin A, recipe very high
　Big Bowl, Yummy Style, 178
　Broccoli Bandit Soup with Cashew Creme Fraîche, 101
　Cabbage Roll Casserole, 191
　Creamy Pumpkin Pie, 219
　Crunchy Nut Roast with Roasted Carrots, 213
　Fancy Un-Omelet with Best Bechamel Sauce, 41
　Fasolada Greek-Style Bean Soup, 111
　Fast Teriyaki Stir-Fry, 195
　Fresh Apple and Fennel Salad with Candied Pecans, 87
　Friendly Mac 'n' Cheez, 145
　Grandma's Macaroni, Creamy Style, 147
　Green Bean and Squash Curry with Cucumber Raita, 123
　Krispy Kale Chips, 71
　Lentil and Vegetable Medley Soup, 105
　Let's Flex Tacos, 183
　Mandarin Bliss Salad with Pecans and Slivered Almonds, 81
　Mashed Sweet and Russet Potatoes, 205
　Mexican-Style Rice and Beans with Fresh Tomato Salsa, 51
　Mighty Minestrone, 115
　Nuggets from Heaven: Squash, Lentil, and Chickpea Soup, 107
　Peanutty Tofu Stir-Fry, 193
　Portobello Mushroom Fajitas with Chili-Lime Sauce, 185
　Pumpkin Lentil Risotto, 155
　Quinoa Power Salad with Cilantro-Lime Dressing, 79
　Rainbow Rice Wraps, 167

Roasted Pumpkin Soup, 103
Saloon Gumbo with Cajun Rice and Tofu, 188
Sautéed Greens, 121
Savoury Holiday Tart, 216
Savoury Latke-Style Sweet Potato Cakes with
Savoury Holiday Tart, 216
Savoury Latke-Style Sweet Potato Cakes with Saucy Apple Compote, 49
Scrumptious Spinach Salad with Strawberries, Slivered Almonds, and Mint-Balsamic Dressing, 85
Seriously the Best Chili con Veggies, 175
Vegan Caesar Salad with Tender and Crispy Croutons, 89
Versatile Pot Pie, 169

vitamin C, about, 11

vitamin C, recipe has
Carrot-Ginger-Orange Cupcakes, 231
Cheezy Artichoke-Stuffed Mushroom Caps, 65
Creamy Artichoke Hearts with Spaghetti Squash, 153
Creamy, Dreamy Rice Pudding with Steeped Strawberries and Coconut Whipped Creme, 33
Desperado Pizza with Dipping Sauce, 161
Emerald Dip, 61
Fancy Cranberry Sauce, 209
Fasolada Greek-Style Bean Soup, 111
Lemon and Garlic Oyster Mushrooms with Black-Eyed Peas, 129
Mulled Wine, 221
Nicely Spiced Cran-Apple Cider, 223
Nutty Chocolate Pudding with Raspberry Purée, 229
Orange, Zucchini, Date, Walnut Spice Muffins, 29
Rainbow Rice Wraps, 167
Roasted Pumpkin Soup, 103
Savoury Holiday Tart, 216
Savoury Latke-Style Sweet Potato Cakes with Saucy Apple Compote, 49
Southwestern Salad, 95
Succulent Bread Dressing, 207
Very Berry Almond Cookies, 233

vitamin C, recipe high
Big Daddy Dip (Baba Ghanoush), 59
Cabbage Roll Casserole, 191
Chickpea Frittata with Tarragon Sauce, 44
Fancy Un-Omelet with Best Bechamel Sauce, 41
Fresh Apple and Fennel Salad with Candied Pecans, 87
Grandma's Macaroni, Creamy Style, 147
Green Bean and Squash Curry with Cucumber Raita, 123
Krispy Kale Chips, 71
Mandarin Bliss Salad with Pecans and Slivered Almonds, 81
Marinated Edamame, 127
Mashed Sweet and Russet Potatoes, 205
Mighty Minestrone, 115
Millet and Spinach Patties with Sun-Dried Tomato Pesto, 197
Quinoa Power Salad with Cilantro-Lime Dressing, 79
Rhubarb and Strawberry Treat, 237
Salad with Sliced Cabbage, Apple, Vinegar, and Caraway, 93
Sautéed Greens, 121
Spicy Chili Unfries with Chipotle Aioli, 135
Tasty Pear and Candied Walnut Salad with Cranberry Vinegar Dressing, 83
Tempting Toor Dal Tadka with Tangy Tomato Chutney, 199
Versatile Pot Pie, 169

vitamin C, recipe very high
Badass Black Bean Soup, 109
Best Brussels Sprouts, 203
Big Bowl, Yummy Style, 178
Broccoli Bandit Soup with Cashew Creme Fraîche, 101
Broccoli Fritters, 47

Crunchy Lettuce Wraps, 164
Fast Teriyaki Stir-Fry, 195
Friendly Mac 'n' Cheez, 145
Grilled Zucchini and Leeks with Walnuts, 125
Lentil and Vegetable Medley Soup, 105
Let's Flex Tacos, 183
Mexican-Style Rice and Beans with Fresh Tomato Salsa, 51
Nuggets from Heaven: Squash, Lentil, and Chickpea Soup, 107
On-the-Go Layered Salad with Orange-Tarragon Dressing, 77
Peanutty Tofu Stir-Fry, 193
Portobello Mushroom Fajitas with Chili-Lime Sauce, 185
Saloon Gumbo with Cajun Rice and Tofu, 188
Scrumptious Spinach Salad with Strawberries, Slivered Almonds, and Mint-Balsamic Dressing, 85
Seriously the Best Chili con Veggies, 175
Shepherdless Pie, 172
Strawberries with Chocolate Sauce, 227
Sweet and Complete Corn and Pea Salad, 91

W

walnuts
Big Bowl, 178
bread dressing, 207
candied, 83
crumbled topping, 29
cupcakes, 231
granola, 39
and grilled vegetables, 125
muffins, 27, 29
nut roast, 213
and pasta, 149, 153
and salad, 83
Special Roasted Walnuts, 125
water, about, 23
whole grains, about, 23
With Chocolate, 226
With Rice, 182
Wraps
Crunchy Lettuce Wraps, 164
Rainbow Rice Wraps, 167
Wrap It Up!, 158

Z

za'atar, about, 23
Zesty Chickpeas, 73
zucchini
big bowl, 178
black bean soup, 109
chili con veggies, 175
grilled, 125
latke-style cakes, 49
muffins, 29
stir-fry, 193

Acknowledgements

This cookbook has been in the making for the last eight years. Thankfully I have four hungry males — one husband and three grown sons — to help me with taste testing. They have been there through my many attempts to get the recipes just right. Because of their support and loving feedback, I developed many scrumptious plant-based recipes that satisfy both the body and the soul. It has been a gift to always have my husband, R.J., and my three sons, Eric, Matthew, and Joseph, ready, willing, and hungry.

A few notable folks have stood by my side. They have tasted my recipes, provided me with feedback, and helped me elevate these recipes to the highest level. I am forever grateful for my soul sister, Janet Law, who was there through every bite, always encouraging me to take the next step. A great big thank you to Linda Naiman, Stephanie Koonar, and Paola Murillo, who each, in their own beautiful way, encouraged me and made me feel the love on this journey. I appreciate all my veggie-loving compadres who beta-read my book, beta-tested my recipes, and joined in my cooking parties (where we prepared the recipes together), especially Natalie Finkle, who didn't miss a single party. Finally, an exuberant shout-out to Rosi Hunter, who helped me take the first step in starting this cookbook, bringing her sense of fun and helping me shape the first few recipes.

The talented Venera Smilenova and Zapryanka Vasileva created the outstanding Veggie OUTLAWS illustrations precisely as I envisioned. The amazing Ksusha Harina and Nour Tohmé created additional images as needed and designed the icons. Thank you to Suzanne Doyle-Ingram from Prominence Publishing, who pushed me to complete my first draft. I am incredibly grateful to my editor, Lucy Kenward and my proofreaders, Eric Purcell and Lisa Forbriger. These individuals helped me create a professional and fun cookbook.

Having you all in my life makes me happy as pie.

About the Author

Linda Purcell is the original Veggie Outlaw. She has a Plant-Based Nutrition Certificate, eCornell

and T. Colin Campbell Center for Nutrition Studies. This certificate includes Plant-Based in Practice, Nutrition and Chronic Disease, and Nutrition and Society. Raised on the standard American diet, Linda has been a plant-based enthusiast for more than 14 years and now enjoys healthy vegan foods exclusively. Since 2008, she has been driven by her love of experimenting with food to invent exciting ways to combine different flavours, creating over 1,000 plant-based recipes. She constantly researches how food impacts health, discovering and implementing the latest nutritional findings.

Her goal is to incorporate superfoods in delicious ways to make the Most Wanted Vegan Recipes.

Linda's plant-based journey began when her mother-in-law suffered a heart attack and her husband R.J. asked her to change the family over to a 100% vegan diet. After much research, Linda discovered plant-based foods have repeatedly been shown to provide incredible health benefits. This includes reduced risk of heart disease, cancer, obesity, diabetes, and cognitive decline, all of which she wanted to give to her family.

At the time, there were very few vegan options available in stores, restaurants, or even cookbooks. Linda realized people needed an easier way to make the smart move to plant-based eating — through great-tasting meals.

In a nutshell — and yes, nuts are plants too — Linda developed the concept of Veggie OUTLAWS to shoot down the negative belief that vegan food can't be over-the-top delicious. And she has done it by rounding up the Most Wanted Vegan Recipes and putting them in one easy-to-use book. These recipes are for anyone, anywhere on their plant-based eating journey, who wants to enjoy healthy foods without compromising on taste.

A Note to Parents and Families

At the outset of their journey — and prior to this cookbook — Linda and R.J.'s decision to go plant-based was not initially greeted with squeals of delight from the kids. Crazy, right? At that time, the school-age boys were used to lots of fatty and sugary foods, and they were not at all shy about expressing their horror at seeing these essential nutrients cut back. Still convinced she was doing the right thing, Linda began the process of recreating her family's favourite meals.

One of the first recipes she converted was a traditional Shepherd's Pie and thus was born the first incarnation of Shepherdless Pie. It was created without any fat, beef, or butter, and... literally everyone, including Linda, felt it was lacking. But she didn't give up; instead, she stepped up — and after several more attempts with various ingredient combinations — she created a recipe that pleased everyone. Shepardless Pie was a winner — savoury, satisfying, and yummy.

Like all kids, Linda's boys love comfort food, including mac 'n' cheese. So next, Linda created a savoury dish that became a weekly family favourite. However, the first time she served Veggie OUTLAWS Mac 'n' Cheez (made with cashews and butternut squash instead of cheese) to her son Matthew he was skeptical. But after the first bite, he blurted out, "That's amazing!" And once his bowl was empty, he held it out smiling, asking for more.

While the boys all still eat a variety of foods like pizza and ice cream outside the house, they have now come to appreciate and love plant-based eating.

It's Linda's intention that with just a little taste testing of your own, you will have your family asking for seconds too.

Website: https://veggieoutlaws.com/ or click on the QR Code

www.ingramcontent.com/pod-product-compliance
Lightning Source LLC
Chambersburg PA
CBHW042024100526
44587CB00029B/4285